HUBRIS

HUBRIS

How HBOS wrecked the best bank in Britain

Ray Perman

BIRLINN

First published in 2012 by
Birlinn Limited
West Newington House
10 Newington Road
Edinburgh
EH9 1QS

www.birlinn.co.uk

ISBN: 978 1 78027 051 7

British Library Cataloguing-in-Publication Data
A catalogue record for this book is available from the British Library

Typeset by Iolaire Typesetting, Newtonmore
Printed and bound by MPG Books Ltd, Bodmin

'In the eye of the storm, Nemesis followed Hubris'

Lord Stevenson of Coddingham,
chairman, HBOS, annual report 2007

Contents

List of Illustrations

Sir Walter Scott broods before the former Bank of Scotland head-quarters in Edinburgh.

Covenant Close, off Edinburgh's Royal Mile, once housed the Cross Keys Tavern, where in 1695 shareholders first subscribed for Bank of Scotland shares.

An early Bank of Scotland note.

The Bank of Scotland board in 1995.

The Bank of Scotland crest outside The Mound.

Peter Burt and Halifax's James Crosby announce the merger which formed HBOS in 2001.

Gordon McQueen, Peter Burt and George Mitchell.

George Mitchell.

The HBOS board in 2006 in the old Bank headquarters.

Peter Cummings.

The former Bank of Scotland headquarters on the Mound.

Sir Philip Green.

Vincent Tchenguiz, one of the high-rolling 'FOPs' (friends of Philip Green).

Former Rangers Football Club owner Sir David Murray.

Tom Hunter.

Graeme Shankland, one of Peter Cummings' key lieutenants.

Foreword

My years in the Treasury during the financial collapse of 2007–8 gave me more hands-on practice dealing with banks than any Chancellor of the Exchequer in living memory. During frequent increasingly tense meetings I also came face to face with the men running those institutions. It is not an experience I would recommend. Northern Rock was the first British casualty of a storm which was to engulf dozens of banks in the US and Europe, but in August 2007, when I asked for a list from my officials of other banks that might be exposed to the US market, HBOS was there.

This is a story about the downfall of one bank, but it is more than that. The consequences of the 2008 banking collapse in Scotland, the UK and in Europe have proved catastrophic. The economic crisis that resulted threatens years of stagnation, with little growth, high unemployment and lost opportunities. How could it happen? We need to understand that to know what lessons to draw from it.

The headquarters of the Bank of Scotland on the Mound dominated the Edinburgh skyline for centuries. It was a symbol of strength. The Bank of Scotland, founded in 1695, had come to represent all that was best in Scottish financial acumen. It began lending money to the Scottish nobility with loans secured on good quality land. It understood the risks it undertook and it prospered. By the late 20th century it was seen as a solidly sound if unexciting bank. Then, in the late 1990s, the bank made the decision to merge with the Halifax Building Society to form HBOS. The Halifax was Britain's biggest building society. It too had prospered. But this was a marriage made on the rebound.

The Bank of Scotland had decided to pursue the takeover of the National Westminster Bank, one of the UK's biggest banks which was viewed as under-performing No sooner had it done so than its old rival, the Royal Bank of Scotland, entered the fray. The Royal Bank pursued an aggressive campaign to win Nat West, judging that whichever bank seized the prize would establish itself as a dominant UK presence. The Royal Bank won. Shortly afterwards, the Bank of Scotland felt exposed. Having lost the bid it could not afford to stand still – hence the merger with the Halifax.

The new bank was now under a different management style. It began to pursue an aggressive lending policy to personal and business customers. In particular it pursued a policy of expanding its market share in the domestic mortgage market and also started lending billions of pounds for commercial property. It was taking on risks that it did not understand. By 2008, as the global banking crisis took hold, HBOS found itself hopelessly over-exposed and facing collapse. It had no option but to agree to a takeover by Lloyds Bank in September of that year.

HBOS was not alone in lending billions of pounds on the back of rapidly rising house prices and a property market which seemed to promise limitless returns. In Ireland, the banks were similarly exposed. So too was HBOS and RBS, through its subsidiary Ulster Bank. The sheer scale of the losses incurred by the Irish banks were to bring down the Irish government which was forced to go to the International Monetary Fund and to fellow eurozone members for a bail out. A similar property bubble left many Spanish banks in a similar state, forcing the Spanish government to seek almost 100 billion euros from eurozone members in the summer of 2012. Other banks too, particularly in continental Europe, remained fearful that the continuing economic downturn would result in many of their loans turning bad, leaving them with losses.

Although it is easy now to identify what went wrong, no regulator anywhere in the world picked up on the growing risks the banking system faced in the mid part of the last decade. But the warning signs were there. Indeed many of the symptoms were spotted, but nowhere did anyone bring together all the warning signs before disaster struck. In particular, the trade in sophisticated financial products which brought down many US banks and RBS here in the UK were not fully understood by the banks themselves. There seemed to be an assumption that if everyone was making money from these trades that they must be all right. Very few were prepared to ask themselves what exactly these products were worth. The answer was very little.

Primary responsibility must rest with the boards of these banks.

The board of a company has a legal responsibility to its shareholders. Board members should have asked themselves whether they understood the risks to which the bank had become exposed. In lending such huge sums they should have asked themselves what would happen if the borrowers got into trouble and could not repay the debt. This is not rocket science, it is basic banking and as this book shows, it used to be second nature to bankers and to bank boards.

The regulators for their part failed to understand just how exposed some of these banks had become. Worse, they did not appreciate how interconnected the world's banking system had become. They looked at each bank on its own. They did not ask what would happen if a bank got into trouble, perhaps on the other side of the world and how its problems would spread rapidly through the global banking system. Northern Rock was a well-established provincial building society with deep roots in the north east of England. It had, along with a number of other building societies, demutualised in the 1980s to become banks. During the course of the crisis every single building society that demutualised either failed or had to be taken over. It is instructive to see what happened in the case of Northern Rock.

When building societies were first set up they had a simple model. They took in money from hard-working artisans who in turn borrowed money when they wanted to buy a house. But in the 1990s and in the decade that followed a new model emerged. Banks discovered they could borrow money from other financial institutions across the globe and in particular in the US. The money there was to a large extent generated by the trade of sophisticated financial products, many based on what is now known as the 'sub-prime mortgage market', involving home loans to people on low incomes, secured on property of little or no value. It was inevitable borrowers would eventually default, and so they did, on an industrial scale. When the crash happened, the money that Northern Rock relied on from this wholesale market dried up and the bank rapidly became insolvent.

It was not just the former building societies that got into trouble. HBOS too had followed a policy of expansion based on lending substantial sums of money to as many people as possible. It was a classic case of pile 'em high, sell 'em cheap. For a bank this was disastrous.

That was bad enough in itself, but what the regulators failed to foresee were the consequences of banks being so dependent on each other for cash. They routinely lend billions of pounds to each other overnight and over long periods – perhaps six months or even two years. What happened at the end of 2007 was that as banks realised how exposed they were to other banks which had done exactly the same thing, they took fright and refused to lend to each other. The consequences were catastrophic.

So another big lesson for the future is that it is not good enough to judge the health of a bank by simply looking at its own position. Rather, regulators have to ask: what are the consequences of another bank failure, perhaps in another part of the world.

The economic, social and political consequences of a banking collapse mean there is a real public interest in what goes on in a bank. A noticeable feature of my tours of the country to speak about my own book (*Back from the Brink*, published by Atlantic Books in 2011), was the understandable concern and knowledge expressed by my questioners. Regulators cannot stand in the shoes of each bank manager and impose their judgement every time a loan is made, but they can insist that banks carry more capital in reserve as a safety cushion, and that the business is organised in such a way that in the event of a crisis it can be broken up or at least managed through it.

There is an argument that some banks are too big to be allowed to fail, so they should not be allowed to exceed a certain size. The problem with this is that in the event of a crisis no bank, no matter how small, can be allowed to fail. The risk is that if one bank goes, people will immediately ask: who is next? That is why we had to step in to deal with the Dunfermline Building Society when it collapsed in 2009. Under new legislation we were able to transfer it to the Nationwide Building Society.

In more tranquil economic times of course a bank, like any other business, can be allowed to fail. It happened with Barings and BCCI in the 1990s. And we must get to a situation where those who gain from a profitable bank share the losses when it goes wrong. But this will take time. So regulation needs to be tightened up, it must be more intrusive and there has to be far greater international co-operation between regulators.

As I write this, in the summer of 2012, the banking crisis is far from over. In the US and in the UK we cleaned out the banking system in 2008 when the crisis struck. Different mechanisms were used, but the bad debts and the toxic assets were identified and dealt with. More capital was put into the banks, and in the case of the UK, the government acquired major shareholdings in RBS and the Lloyds group.

In Ireland too, the government removed these bad assets from their banks. But there was a terrible cost as the banks were far bigger than the Irish state. When the bank debts became Ireland's debts, the country was brought to its knees. There is an important point here. In the future, people will look very closely at who stands behind financial institutions. To put it bluntly, does that country have enough money to bail out any bank that needs it? Banks that grow too big for the country they are based in pose a serious threat. In the last decade the Scottish National Party used to boast of an 'arc of prosperity', including Iceland and Ireland. They wanted Scotland to be part of it. We don't hear much talk of that now.

Unless and until the eurozone ensures its banks are cleaned up we will not get economic recovery. Spanish banks are exposed hugely to a collapsed property market. In turn the problems in Greece and Italy run the risk of defaults that could hit larger French and German banks. The inter-connections are still there and could still prove fatal.

The story of HBOS is salutary. Surely it is a classic case of trying to fly too close to the sun. The bank took on risks it did not understand and failed to make provision for. The result is that the name may exist but it is not the bank it was. A walk around the former headquarters on the Mound is a depressing experience. The building is more museum than the beating heart of the self-confident and prosperous bank it once was.

Alistair Darling
25 June 2012

Preface

In the autumn of 2008 I attended a black tie business dinner. I forget the occasion or the organisation responsible, they are all very similar and after a while the memories of each merge into one. Next to me at the table was a man with whom I had little in common. He managed a commercial real estate company and, although he took a keen interest in the collapse of the property market then in free fall, it did not directly affect him. His portfolio was mature with established tenants paying good rents. I only half listened to his conversation, nodding and smiling occasionally so as not to appear too rude. Then he said something which seized my attention: 'I withdrew £20 million today from Bank of Scotland to put it in a safe place.'

There had been rumours for days swirling around HBOS, the unlovely conglomerate which now owned the Bank. ('The Bank', with an initial capital letter, might mean the Bank of England south of the border, but north of Berwick and Carlisle it had always meant Bank of Scotland). It was clearly in trouble, but the thought that it might go down, taking its depositors' money with it had never occurred to me and came as a real shock. The Bank had been part of the Scottish landscape for more than 300 years, as solid and as tangible as the rock on which Edinburgh Castle stood. My wife and I had entrusted our savings to it. My sons had been Bank of Scotland customers since we opened Super Squirrel saver accounts for them as toddlers. The Bank had supported my own company – and countless other new start businesses – through thick and thin and when I sold it, that's where I deposited the proceeds.

Now it was also banker to another small business I chaired. We had not been in business as long as my dinner companion and we did not have £20 million, but we had a substantial sum on deposit, hard-earned money which was keeping us safe through the recession. Britain had already seen the first run on a bank for 70 years.

Unsettling television pictures of queues of savers waiting to withdraw their cash had spooked ministers and helped to hasten the end of Northern Rock. I had no wish to do even a small part in pushing Bank of Scotland down the same path, but our company could not afford to lose that money, nor see it tied up in administration or liquidation proceedings for months or even years. I called my company's chief executive the following morning and told him to open an account in a safer bank and transfer the money immediately. When I called him later in the day his news was not encouraging. It had taken him hours to get through on the telephone and when he did it was to be told that because of the volume of new accounts being opened, it could be days or even a week before our application was considered. The rush away from the Bank was headlong.

What happened to HBOS in the weeks following is part of this story, but only part. The excesses of bankers during the first decade of the twenty-first century are lurid enough to grip the interest of readers, but to dwell too long on them would be to lose sight of what we have lost. The Bank of Scotland which all but disappeared with the collapse of HBOS was not the same Bank that I and many of its customers knew in the last few decades of the last century – and bears no resemblance to the institution behind the Bank of Scotland name which is still over the frontage of hundreds of bank branches – merely another brand of the massive Lloyds Banking Group.

The Bank whose story I want to tell was quantitatively different to banks operating now. It was not insubstantial, it was after all a FTSE 100 company – one of the biggest companies on the stock market. But it was a fraction of the size of banks today and operated on a human scale. Customers could telephone branches and speak to people whose names they knew and faces they recognised. If you called back, you could speak to the same person. For Bank of Scotland managers 'know your customer' did not mean look at a computer screen, but recognise their names, remember their banking history, their businesses and perhaps their families too. A human scale meant that the chief executive could review all large lending propositions and all customer complaints, replying to them personally if he felt they had not been adequately answered.

This was a bank which never called you at dinner time to try to sell you 'products'. Thirty years ago when I began my relationship with it, the Bank took the view that if you needed its services you would ask.

Later its managers were encouraged to try to sell to customers, but it was never pushy and sometimes they looked rather embarrassed in doing so. It seems incredible to me to write this now, but it was a bank which was trusted by its customers. When it adopted the advertising slogan 'A Friend for Life' it was not greeted with cynicism. People believed it meant it, and more importantly, it did.

To say the Bank was rooted in the community is an understatement. It had been part of Scottish history since before the Act of Union and there was no major historical event since in which it had not played a part. It acted as banker to a large proportion of the country's employers and their employees. It banked charities and community groups, golf clubs and trade unions. It looked after the millions of some of Scotland's richest men and women, but was also one of the first banks in the UK to offer bank accounts for all in disadvantaged communities. When *The Big Issue* wanted to open accounts for its homeless magazine sellers to deposit the cash they collected, the Bank's Treasurer defied the money-laundering regulation which said that a bank had to verify the home address of all its customers and opened them all with the address of the Bank's head office.

Don't get the impression that this was some hick bank. It was one of the most innovative in the world, the first to bring electronic banking to Britain, a leader in leveraged finance back in the days when those were not dirty words, the first clearing bank to get its cost/income ratio below 50 per cent and a pioneer in getting others to sell its services so that it could extend its reach further than bricks and mortar would allow. It was at the same time a risk taker, known for backing entrepreneurs, and a prudent institution, maintaining high capital ratios. And it became the best-performing bank in Britain in terms of its return on equity. Its share price quadrupled in ten years.

Bank of Scotland was not unique. Many of its characteristics were shared by the other Scottish banks, The Royal Bank of Scotland and Clydesdale Bank, and they had once been replicated across the UK. But with the exception of Yorkshire, which kept its bank longer than most, other regions lost their financial institutions to a relentless process of consolidation during the twentieth century, which shrank competition and extinguished local responsiveness.

Bank managers used to be among the most respected in their communities – and they were in the community because managers managed branches and branches were part of the fabric of small towns or city neighbourhoods. With the local clergyman and the school teacher, the bank manager was trusted to sign the back of your passport photograph or give you a character reference when you went for your first job. A retired manager writing in the Bank of Scotland staff magazine noted how 'Bank men' usually ended up as the treasurer of the golf club, the church committee or the parent-teacher association. I suspect that was once true of all bank managers anywhere in the UK – people knew the cash was safe with them. Part of the branch manager's standing came because he (almost invariably 'he') could make real decisions. He could agree a personal loan or business overdraft and he made his decision not only on the basis of working out the figures, but also on his assessment of character based on years of local knowledge. Only in the case of large amounts would he need to get sanction from Head Office, which took into account his recommendation and the fact that since he was likely to be in post for years at a time, he would have to live with the consequences if the decision turned out to be the wrong one.

Now many thousands of branches across Britain have been closed and those that are left are manned by 'relationship managers', who probably do not live locally, do not have time after the stress of work to be treasurer of anything and will not be in post long enough to build a relationship with anyone or any business. Face-to-face meetings have given way to call centres, risk assessment to credit scoring. Personal recommendation has been replaced by 'customer acquisition', services replaced by 'products' sold to reach targets, rather than to answer the needs of customers. As recent fines imposed on the big banks by the regulator have shown, some products were 'toxic' – they did the customers who bought them more harm than good – and in some cases the banks knew this before they sold them. To meet constantly rising profit expectations, big banks have continually to drive down cost – mostly at the expense of customer service and satisfaction – and expand their sales, often by swallowing other companies to gain their customers. At each stage banks became more remote from their customers, geographically and by hiding behind automated telephone systems. What has been lost in this process is trust.

This is the story of how one bank went from being one of the most trusted, to one from which customers could not wait to remove their money.

I am grateful to all those current and past executives of Bank of Scotland and HBOS who have spoken to me. Many asked for anonimity, so I feel it indivious to name those who did not. Where I have attributed quotes to individuals, their words were already on the record, either in newspapers and magazines or company or Government reports. There were also many who would not speak to me. As I say later in this story, I do not criticise them for that; I have no right to demand their response, but it does mean that I have not been able to check facts with them. I am grateful to those who considered my request for an interview and then wrote to decline. Several did not give me the courtesy of a response.

I have tried to report only actions and not to attribute motives without evidence. I have also tried not to apportion blame. Readers should make up their own minds.

Banker to the Stars

The family of retail billionaire Philip Green knows how to throw a party. For his 50th birthday the tycoon's wife Tina organised a three-day bash in Cyprus which reportedly cost £5 million. Rod Stewart and Tom Jones provided the music, the guests were expected to wear togas and the birthday boy himself dressed as the Emperor Nero. The tycoon's 55th was even more exotic, with the Greens flying 100 guests 8,500 miles in two private jets to an eco-spa on a private island in the Maldives, where singers Ricky Martin and George Michael performed.

There were no togas for son Brandon's bar mitzvah in 2005, but no expense was spared nonetheless. The Greens took over all 44 rooms and nine suites of the Grand Hotel on Cap Ferrat, one of the most luxurious and expensive hotels in the South of France. Rooms can cost up to £1,000 a night, but *The Sunday Telegraph* speculated that the Greens would have paid much more to ensure exclusivity at a time when the hotel could expect to be busy with stars attending the Cannes film festival[1]. In addition to its Michelin-starred food and extensive cellar, including rare vintages of Château d'Yquem from 1854 and Château Lafite Rothschild from 1799, the hotel boasts an auditorium with outstanding acoustics designed by Gustave Eiffel, of tower fame. It was not big enough for the Greens' party of 200 so they built their own. A synagogue is also an essential part of a Jewish boy's coming of age and the hotel did not have one, so that was constructed too. These weren't flimsy structures. So much wood and stone was used that guests marvelled that the buildings were only temporary.

Some guests arrived in the charter flight from London laid on by the Greens, others came from nearby Monaco in a fleet of luxury cars and a few in their own speedboats. It was a private party and locals moaned that public footpaths around the hotel had been closed for the event, but paparazzi lurked under the Aleppo pines in the grounds, or behind rocks on the Mediterranean shore to snap

celebrities such as television impresario Simon Cowell, pop star
Beyoncé, who was providing part of the entertainment, racing driver
Eddie Jordan and film director Michael Winner. From the world of
business came Tom Hunter, the Scottish entrepreneur, Royal Mail
chairman Allan Leighton and the property-developer brothers
Robert and Vincent Tchenguiz. There were also the high-powered
international investment bankers who had part-financed Philip
Green's string of acquisitions of high street fashion chains – Mike
'Woody' Sherwood, top banker in the UK for the mighty Goldman
Sachs and worth a reputed \$48 million[2], and Bob Wigley, Chairman
of Merrill Lynch in Europe.

And there was Peter Cummings.

Short, balding and smartly dressed in black tie, Cummings looked
no different to many of the business people present, but he was not
like them. He had been educated at St Patrick's High School,
Dumbarton, not expensive private schools like Sherwood and Wigley.
He did not own his own yacht like Green and Hunter, although he
counted scuba-diving as one of his hobbies. He did not have an
apartment in Monaco – in fact he still lived in the modest semi-
detached home he had bought with his teacher wife Margaret in the
town in which he was born and went to school. He had a reputation
among those who knew him well for being quiet, thoughtful and
meticulous. He gave to charities – the Maggie cancer support centres
and a school in Malawi, which he was quietly co-funding with his wife
– but not in the ostentatious way of some of the millionaire philan-
thropists at the Riviera party. He was a banker, but not for one of the
glamorous Wall Street investment houses like Goldman or Merrill
and his had not been a quick rise to the top.

After school Cummings had taken the path many bright kids had
chosen in an age when university entrance was only considered for
the fortunate few. He had joined Bank of Scotland as a trainee and
studied at night for his banking diploma. The Bank moved him
around – unspectacular jobs, but he broadened his experience and
steadily climbed the hierarchy: regional manager in Carlisle, manager of the Glasgow Chief Office, head of corporate recovery,
director of corporate banking. His experience had also given him
something many of his younger competitors lacked. He had worked
through three recessions as well as the prolonged boom of the first
decade of the twenty-first century.

Among other bankers he was envied, despite his unglamorous early career. No one had a closer relationship or had been able to pull off such big deals with Philip Green. Bank of Scotland had backed Green through a succession of larger and larger buys, culminating in the purchase of the Arcadia group in 2002 which had brought him household names such as Burton, Dorothy Perkins, Evans, Wallis, Miss Selfridge and Top Shop. Green borrowed more than £800 million to secure the deal, but paid it all back in two years. The Bank earned handsome fees and huge kudos, but there was more. Green allowed Cummings to buy a small shareholding in the business for the Bank, a privilege given to no one else. When Green paid his wife the biggest personal dividend in UK corporate history a year later, the Bank made £100 million profit – one hundred times what its stake had cost.

On the strength of his relationship with Green, Cummings had been able to meet and work with entrepreneurs like Tom Hunter, the Tchenguiz brothers, hotelier Rocco Forte and property magnate Nick Leslau. These were the high rollers, the guys who did the big deals and were fêted by the press. Newspapers began to call him 'Banker to the Stars' and within HBOS, the conglomerate which Bank of Scotland had joined in 2001, he was seen as a star in his own right, responsible for a growing proportion of the group profits. The Bank commanded respect and admiration far beyond its size and modest roots and rivals wanted some of the action. Cummings had turned down several lucrative job offers from international investment banks, but when he 'sold down' his deals – reducing risk by offering part of the loan to other banks – there was no shortage of takers.

The bank Peter Cummings joined had been very different to the one of which he became a director 35 years later. Then it had been an institution with modest ambitions with, some would have said, a lot to be modest about. It was not even the biggest bank in Scotland let alone being taken seriously as a challenger on a UK scale. It was conscious of the weight of history on its shoulders, conservative in its outlook and particular about the people with whom it did business. There was an instinctive distrust in the Bank for anyone regarded as 'flashy'.

The thought that one of its senior managers might be seen in the same company as men and women who appeared regularly in the gossip columns of the cheaper newspapers and magazines would have filled the directors of 30 years ago with horror. When he had been making the tea in the Dumbarton branch, Cummings cannot have dreamed that years later he would be sipping Louis Roederer Cristal Vintage Champagne in such exalted company on the Côte d'Azur. Nor that his bosses would have thanked him for it and assured him it was part of the job.

Nor can he have foreseen that a few years later his star would have fallen so precipitately. His bank would be scorned for its overweening ambition and short-sighted risk-taking. Newspapers would accuse him of bringing down his bank almost single-handedly and call him 'the banker of last resort' – the man who lent money when everyone else was too sensible to do so. Associates who previously wanted to get close to him would now give anonymous quotes to journalists saying that all along they had thought he had been too aggressive and taken too many chances. The financial regulator, which had given his bank a clean bill of health, would pursue him to admit to things he had never believed he had done.

How had it happened?

2

Base metal into gold

To understand why the Bank met the end that it did, I went back to its beginning. We live in turbulent times but they are not unique. The era into which Bank of Scotland was born at the end of the seventeenth century shared a remarkable number of characteristics with the first years of the twenty-first. A long-standing political dynasty had recently come to an end. One head of government (in this case the monarch, Charles II – not universally liked, but with a deft enough touch to ensure his survival) was replaced by his unpopular brother, James II, who lost his throne in short order. The new leader who deposed him, young and fresh-faced William III, announced a power-sharing agreement, although a co-regency with his wife Mary rather than a coalition. The first years of their reign were marked by unrest at home and expensive wars abroad. To pay for them, the Government borrowed heavily, depressing the economy. Does it sound familiar?

The end of the seventeenth and start of the eighteenth centuries was an Age of Reason and an age of science. The philosopher René Descartes was not long dead and John Locke was laying the ground for modern political thought. Isaac Newton, one of the greatest scientists and mathematicians of all time, was at the height of his powers and Robert Boyle had published the treatise which was to lay the foundations of modern chemistry. New discoveries were being made in every field and examined in literature and debate. Alongside science and mathematics there was a new interest in economics and the disciplines of banking, finance and accounting as mechanisms for expanding trade and economic well-being. Yet despite the spread of rational thought, belief in magic was still strong. In Salem, Massachusetts, they were hanging witches. In Europe the study of the occult was a respectable intellectual pursuit. Newton himself was deeply interested in alchemy and the quest for the mythical Philosopher's

Stone, which was said to be able to turn base metal into gold. Among the financial rationalists there were also alchemists – men who saw banking as a way of creating profit from nothing – another parallel with our own era.

Scotland in the 1690s was still nominally an independent country with its own parliament and institutions, although it had shared a monarch with England since James VI of Scotland had succeeded Elizabeth I in 1603. The relationship between the two countries was ambivalent. Many Scots had followed the king to London and played important parts in the city's life and commerce, but Scottish goods still faced high tariffs when imported into England. Scotland was decidedly the smaller and the poorer partner. Its population, at about a million, was a fifth of the size of its southern neighbour and its economy was much less developed, relying heavily on agriculture and natural resources like coal.[1] This became apparent when a series of bad harvests brought famine and hardship at home and reduced the surpluses available for export. Importantly, Scotland also had a much weaker and more fragmented financial system, which restricted credit and cramped growth.

The renaissance states of northern Italy had developed banking in the fourteenth and fifteenth centuries, and the Netherlands, the leading financial power of the seventeenth century, had established the Bank of Amsterdam in 1609, but before 1694 neither Scotland nor England had banks. There were bankers, wealthy landowners or merchants who lent money at interest, but they acted as individuals rather than in organised companies. Goldsmiths were especially prominent and had their booths around the cathedral of St Giles in Edinburgh.[2] The most famous was George Heriot, known as 'Jingling Geordie', a prosperous smith who became both jeweller and banker to the court of James VI and followed his best customer to London in 1603. Churches sometimes also lent money: the elders of Alyth Church, Strathmore, Perthshire, a prosperous village at the meeting point of several drovers' roads, charged 4–6 per cent on their loans and members of the congregation who were late in meeting their repayments could expect to be denounced from the pulpit.[3] But those able to lend money and those able to borrow it, were the exception rather than the rule. Credit was hard to come by.

To make matters worse, Scotland and England were short of coin; there simply was not enough gold and silver to go round. William III took much of what was available to pay his armies fighting Continental wars, leaving a less than adequate supply for merchants and entrepreneurs who needed ready money to expand their trades. As an alternative, barter and payment in kind were often used to settle domestic debts – tenants paying their rents for example – and Scots merchants paying for purchases from England or abroad or receiving payment for goods sold, used bills of exchange, essentially IOUs. The weakness of the Scottish economy, however, meant that Scottish bills were often discounted in London – by as much as 10–15 per cent in bad times.[4] Clearly there was a need for banks.

It is an irony that has often been remarked that a Scotsman was a prime mover in the establishment of the Bank of England in 1694 and an Englishman was the first Governor of the Bank of Scotland a year later. But their nationality was not the most important distinction; they had very different backgrounds, very different temperaments and left very different legacies to history.

The Scot was William Paterson, who was born in rural Dumfriesshire in 1658 to parents who were small tenant farmers. Not much is certain about his early life; by some accounts he moved to England at a young age, but others have him living with his parents until the age of 17, then moving to Bristol and later to the West Indies. One of his most recent biographers places him as a young man in Port Royal, a British colony in Jamaica rivalling Boston in size and importance as the largest city in the Americas, but also a nest of pirates ruled over by the notorious Captain Morgan. There Paterson is said to have first dreamed of the riches of Central America.[5] However colourful this part of his life may have been, we do know that by his mid-twenties he was in London making his way in business.

He bought his way into the Merchant Taylors' Company, one of the 12 medieval guilds of the City of London and in 1689, at the age of 31, was 'admitted to its livery', giving him a position of respectability, contacts and influence. He had already buried a first wife, but by now had married again and had a child. We cannot be sure what he looked like; an etching in the National Portrait Gallery, London, shows a rather sharp-nosed, haughty face beneath a full periwig. But other contemporary pictures show him in profile with a softer, more thoughtful look. He was God-fearing, a lifelong teetotaller, of modest habits, although not a Puritan.

Paterson was clearly clever and he was a thinker who published

numerous essays and articles on economic and financial matters. He
would later be hailed as a visionary with ideas well before his time, but
he had a more sinister side too. His entry in the *Dictionary of National
Biography* describes him as gaining 'a reputation for double-dealing
and insincerity, as well earned as that for imagination and persua-
siveness'.[6] One contemporary was blunter, describing him as 'one
who converses in darkness and loves not to bring his deeds into the
light'.[7] Others were more kind in their assessment: 'He trusted people
he should not have trusted and lacked any sense of humour.'[8] He was
a serious man, who never told a joke or a funny story.

Wartime shortages always provide opportunities for spivs and
speculators and Paterson, although there is no evidence that he ever
acted illegally, seemed to have some of the characteristics of both.
The main shortage that King William's foreign wars created was
money. The monarch needed cash to pay his troops and supply his
armies and Paterson saw an opportunity to supply it and make a
profit.

He realised that there was money to be made by setting up a bank
specifically to lend to the king and his government and, by persuading
Parliament, to guarantee the interest payments from taxes. He was
also quicker than most to understand that by issuing notes – promises
to pay in coin if the note was presented – the bank could expand the
money supply beyond the amount of cash it actually held. Provided
the bank could inspire enough confidence to prevent all holders of its
notes from demanding payment at the same time, it could go on
creating credit indefinitely. This was not an original thought, it is one
of the basic principles of banking and a number of English pamph-
leteers had been proposing schemes for banks for years. But previous
theorists had concentrated on the effect bank credit would have on
commerce and general economic growth. Paterson was much more
interested in the profit it could bring to the bank and its owners. By
lending the credit it created it could earn interest. He wrote: 'The
bank hath benefit of interest on all moneys which it creates out of
nothing.'

Other schemes had been tried and failed. Paterson's masterstroke
was seeing how it could be applied in the conditions of the time and
making it work.

In 1691 he got together a group of prominent merchants, proposing
to found a bank on the Dutch model specifically to lend money to the

king and government to finance the war with France. He also took the lead in persuading the Treasury to let it happen and recruiting the investors.[9] Initially rejected by Parliament, a refined plan, largely written by Paterson and pushed by him with dogged persistence, won approval three years later and the Bank of England was born. It had a Royal Charter and its sponsors, including Paterson, who was also a director, undertook to raise £1,200,000 and lend it to the Government in perpetuity at an annual interest rate of 8 per cent. In fact most of this money was not raised in coin, or gold or silver, but in bills of exchange – promises to pay – which were passed to the Government which then used them to pay its bills.[10] Interest was thus being earned on money which physically did not exist. The alchemy had begun.

Paterson may have been the genius behind the Bank, but it did not bring him either the recognition or the wealth that he had hoped. His claim to be paid for all the work he had done in devising and promoting the Bank was rejected by his fellow directors. His less attractive characteristics were not long in asserting themselves and the following year he fell out with the board over a rival scheme he was also promoting. He sold his stock and left London.

If this was a setback, it did not last long. Paterson had another scheme and he set about pursuing it with vigour. Scotland had long envied the success of the East India Company, which had acquired from the English Parliament lucrative monopolies on trade with England's colonies. Paterson proposed a similar concern north of the border, a 'Company of Scotland' and in June 1695 used his considerable powers of persuasion to convince the Scottish Parliament to pass the legislation allowing him to set one up. Since Scotland, unlike England, did not possess colonies, Paterson proposed to found one at Darien on the isthmus of Panama where, by means of an overland route, it would be able to link the trades of the Atlantic and Pacific.

Meanwhile Paterson's success with the Bank of England had not gone unremarked among Scots merchants in London and Scotland. A group of them got together to propose a Bank of Scotland and the man to whom they turned to make it happen was an Englishman, John Holland.

Holland was very different from Paterson in both upbringing and temperament. Where Paterson was a visionary, impulsive and devious, Holland appears to have been the opposite, diligent, meticulous and straightforward. He had been born in London, the son of a sea captain who had served in both the English and the Dutch navies and was a sometime friend of Samuel Pepys. As a young man, John had spent time in the Netherlands learning bookkeeping and accounting, before returning to London as assistant to the Dutchman Francis Beyer, auditor general of the East India Company. He also made his fortune by investing in some of the company's voyages.[11] Beyer supported the plan for a Bank of Scotland and was one of the original subscribers. It is likely that he recommended John Holland, who drew up the plan for the new bank, taking the Royal Charter of the Bank of England as his model.

Paterson was furious. Although his public plan for the Darien Company (as his new venture became known) was to establish a colony and engage in trade, he also secretly intended it to be a bank and he urged his supporters in Scotland to lobby against the potential new rival. They failed and on 17 July – less than three weeks after Paterson got his Act establishing the Company of Scotland – the Scottish Parliament passed an 'Act for Erecting a Public Bank'. Paterson cursed that the Act had been 'surreptitiously gained and which may be of great prejudice, but is never like to be of any matter of good neither to us, nor those that have it'.[12] Nevertheless, Bank of Scotland was born, with John Holland as its first Governor.

Although the new institution had been inspired by the Bank of England, it was to be a very different business. Whereas the London bank lent only to the government, the Edinburgh bank was to lend only to the private sector – landowners, merchants, traders and manufacturers – in fact its charter prevented it from lending to the state. It was thus Britain's first commercial bank. The Scottish Parliament had granted it some very special and valuable privileges. It was to be incorporated with limited liability, meaning that its shareholders could not be held responsible for its debts, and for its first 21 years its dividends were to be tax-free and it was to enjoy a monopoly over banking in Scotland.

The Bank had first to raise its capital, £1,200,000 like the Bank of England, but since Bank of Scotland's capital was to be in Scots pounds and the exchange rate was £1 sterling to £12 Scots, it would be a much smaller enterprise than its older sister. A subscription book was opened in the Cross Keys Tavern, in a close off Edinburgh's High

Street, and another in London. The Bank's shareholders, quaintly called 'Adventurers', were only asked to put up an initial tenth of the capital, although in the ensuing turbulent years they would be asked to put their hands in their pockets again. Of the 172 people – including seven women – who were the Bank's subscribers, three-quarters lived in Scotland and comprised the great and the good – landowners, lawyers and judges, merchants, nobles and government ministers and officials. The Act of Parliament also specified that any non-Scottish subscriber was to be given automatic Scottish citizenship. The Bank opened for business on New Year's Day 1696.[13]

Since there were no precedents for a bank of this type, the directors and proprietors of the Bank had to make up the rules as they went along. From the start their Presbyterian rectitude asserted itself. Although John Holland was Governor and manager, he was not to be allowed to decide loan applications on his own. A committee was set up – and there were to be similar committees in branches when they were opened – consisting of men of 'Credit and Substance' who would decide each application by ballot – the first-ever credit committee. A cashier would look after the money, but there was also to be an 'Overseer' to watch over him, effectively an auditor. The directors intended to keep a very close eye on the day-to-day running of the company and their sanction was needed to increase salaries or to sack staff, a restriction which remained in force for 200 years.[14]

Holland invented some very prudent rules. The Bank would make money by lending, but its advances were to be made on a very cautious basis. Loans were for a maximum of one year and could be recalled by the Bank at 30 days' notice. They all had to be backed by collateral, in the form of land, a personal security or pledges of 'non-perishable commodities'. In the case of personal security, the Bank not only demanded the ability to seize the borrower's 'moveables' in the event of a default, but also insisted on having two 'cautioners' to act as guarantors. It would also take deposits and, crucially, would issue its own banknotes – promises to pay the bearer on demand the face value of the note in coin.

The Bank rented a head office in Edinburgh's High Street and branches were quickly established in other major Scottish commercial centres. In June Holland returned to London with the thanks of the directors for getting the Bank up and running. He had been paying his own expenses while living in Edinburgh and drawing no salary, his remuneration being set at ten per cent of the Bank's profit after the Adventurers had taken a 12 per cent dividend. Since the bank was in no position to pay a dividend in 1696, he must have received nothing.

No sooner had he gone than Paterson struck. Using his considerable powers of persuasion and unrivalled contacts, he had been phenomenally successful in raising capital for his Darien Company, amassing pledges of £400,000 sterling, a sum which dwarfed the nominal capital of the Bank, which at that time stood at a quarter of that figure, and of which only a puny £10,000 sterling had been subscribed in cash.[15] Organising and equipping an expedition to Panama would take time, but in the meantime Paterson intended to put his funds to profitable use.

From offices on the opposite side of Edinburgh's High Street from the Bank, he began making loans and issuing notes, ignoring the monopoly given by Parliament to Bank of Scotland. There was concern as the Darien Company began lending to many of the people the Bank had regarded as its natural customers. Rumours began to circulate about the Bank's stability and its notes were being presented for payment in cash in large quantities, straining the Bank's reserves. The directors were in no doubt who was behind these moves and wrote in alarm to Holland: 'We understand that there are formed designs to break us.'[16] Holland tried to broker a peace and met Paterson, who rejected any compromise.

For a while it looked as though the Bank might go under before it had really got started. The Darien Company itself had acquired large amounts of Bank of Scotland notes and might at any time present them for payment, precipitating a collapse. Holland initiated emergency action. Branches were ordered to return as much cash as possible to Edinburgh, the Bank began to call in its loans and demanded that its subscribers stump up a further 20 per cent of the authorised capital, precipitating a dispute between the Scots shareholders, who paid up promptly, and the Londoners, who were more reluctant. Even so the Bank came perilously close to running out of cash and was itself forced to borrow.[17]

This was effectively the first run on a bank in British history and the directors of Bank of Scotland learned one of the fundamental lessons of banking: always ensure you do not run out of cash.

But before the crisis came to a head Paterson dropped his

campaign. His shareholders had put their money behind an ambitious and romantic vision to propel Scotland from parochialism into the first rank of global powers. Paterson himself had sold it to them with poetic descriptions of Scotland one day controlling 'the keys of the Indies and the doors of the world'. Lending money to each other was not part of the dream and, it transpired, a lot of the lending done by the Darien Company was to its own shareholders. Worse than that, the running of the company was inefficient, there had been embezzlement of some of the funds and the lending decisions it had made were poor. The company had trouble in getting its loans repaid on time and bad debts began to mount.

Paterson had learned another fundamental lesson: make sure the people to whom you lend have the means to repay you.

By this time he had unveiled his vision of a colony at Darien to the directors of the Company of Scotland and put all his energies into making it a reality. The banking business was soon forgotten.

The reverse for Paterson was nothing compared to the tragedies to come. Darien was a catastrophe on a national scale for Scotland, which lost a substantial proportion of its national wealth in the ill-conceived venture. Disease, an appallingly difficult terrain and hostile attacks made the colony untenable. The trauma and financial loss was one of the factors which led in 1707 to the Scottish Parliament voting to give up its independence and merge with the English Parliament at Westminster. Individuals suffered much more: many of the original settlers died or were killed. Others lost their wealth and/or their health. Paterson's wife and child both died in Panama and he became so ill that he lost his reason for a while. He recovered enough to become an MP in the newly merged parliament at Westminster, sitting for a rural constituency in the county in which he was born. He also continued to write pamphlets and essays projecting his views on money or state finance, but he was never again as visionary, persuasive or effective.

Bank of Scotland had survived for the time being, but its future was by no means secure. Under the Treaty of Union, which combined the two parliaments, Scotland was to receive considerable sums of money 'equivalent' to the loss of Scottish taxes, which would now go to the joint exchequer in London. Those who had lost their fortunes in the Darien fiasco were also to be compensated and there was money to redeem public debts, to pay for a re-minting of Scottish coins and to pay the expenses of the Scottish commissioners, who had brought about the union.[18] Importantly, there was also an end to discrimination against Scottish goods and traders and access for Scots to the English empire in India, the Americas and beyond.

The years following the Act of Union saw an improvement in Scotland's economic fortunes and the Bank, which also profited from a commission on the re-minting of the coinage, did exceptionally well, paying a tax-free 20 per cent dividend every year from 1707 to 1714.[19] But the good fortune could not last.

William III had died in 1702. Mary, his co-regent and Queen, had succumbed to smallpox eight years earlier and they had no children. He was succeeded by Mary's sister Anne, who reigned until her death in 1714. She was also childless, although it was not for the want of trying. Anne had been pregnant at least 17 times; she miscarried or gave birth to stillborn children at least twelve times. Of the five children born alive, four died before reaching the age of two years. Her final pregnancy ended with a stillborn son.[20] Parliament again looked for a member of the Stuart family who was Protestant – a condition now enshrined in law – and invited George, the Elector of Hanover, a great-grandson of James I & VI, to become monarch of the United Kingdoms of England and Scotland. He ruled as George I, first of the Hanoverians.

The move provoked a renewed upsurge in Jacobite unrest. James II, who had been deposed in 1688 by William (his nephew and son-in-law) and Mary (his daughter) had died in exile in France. In 1715 an insurrection in Scotland and parts of England aimed to displace George and put James II's son James Francis Stuart, known as the Old Pretender, on the throne. An army was raised in the north and many members of the Scots nobility rallied to the cause, including two directors of Bank of Scotland, the Earl of Panmure and Lord Basil Hamilton. Hamilton was captured at the battle of Preston (and subsequently pardoned) and Panmure at the battle of Sheriffmuir, although he escaped to live in exile.

The rising was crushed, but not before there had been another run on the Bank which forced it to stop trading for eight months, with loss of business and profit. The participation of the two directors in the insurrection and the fact that the Bank's Treasurer raised funds for Jacobite prisoners, were enough to brand the Bank as sympathetic to the rebels, with substantial political and commercial consequences.

When its 21-year monopoly on Scottish banking came up for renewal the following year, parliament had no hesitation in ending it. The Bank had been weakened and its enemies saw their opportunity to strike. Those men fortunate enough to receive government money under the 'equivalent' provision of the Act of Union had formed a company which traded bills secured against the funds. For several years they had been trying to formalise the arrangement into a bank. In 1727 they succeeded and the Royal Bank of Scotland gained parliamentary approval. Bank of Scotland (henceforth known as the 'Old Bank') made a last ditch attempt to stop the birth of a rival, but the political mood was against it.

From the start the Royal (the 'New Bank') was a formidable competitor. It was better capitalised than Bank of Scotland and its charter and its political connections gave it access to government funds and lucrative business. From the start it used its position and its muscle to try to drive the Old Bank out of business, collecting large quantities of Bank of Scotland notes by offering its own in exchange and presenting them for payment without warning.[21] The Bank was again forced to call in loans, delay payment and eventually shut its doors. Yet despite a campaign of harassment which lasted two years, the Old Bank survived, rejected the New Bank's takeover offer, and – inspired by the competition – revitalised itself, again opening branches and expanding its business.

Scotland now had a two-bank system (unlike England which still only had one). The Royal and the Bank learned to get along, sometimes co-operating, sometimes in fierce rivalry and both seeing off many other competitors, or absorbing them along the way. They were tempered by periodic financial crises and boosted by times of economic boom. Adam Smith credited Scotland's banking system, of which these two were the pillars, with being responsible for the dramatic change in the Scottish economy during the eighteenth century from a poor agricultural base to one of the leading industrial powers. A twenty-first century banker has described the relationship between the two banks as like that of two brothers – intensely competitive between themselves, but standing united against any outside threat. It was a sibling relationship which was to culminate in a bitter bid battle in the last years of the twentieth century and a simultaneous collapse in the first decade of the twenty-first.

3

A cosy world

It is not the intention of this book to be a detailed history of the Bank,[1] so we'll fast forward 250 years. By the 1970s there were three banks in Scotland rather than two: the Bank and the Royal had survived booms, busts, banking crashes and world wars and were still head-quartered in Edinburgh. Glasgow was home to their younger and smaller rival, the Clydesdale, although it was owned by an English bank, the Midland. Since 1720, however, dozens of banks had come and gone, some lasting centuries, others just a few years.

A walk through Edinburgh's Georgian New Town from St Andrew Square, along George Street to Charlotte Square, or along Glasgow's George or St Vincent Streets, takes you through much of the country's banking history. The first action of new banks in the nineteenth century had been to build headquarters in the Greek or Roman style, with columns, porticos and pilasters to give the impression of solidity and longevity. It was not enough. Their buildings may have had foundations of rock, but their finances were built on sand; most succumbed sooner or later to bankruptcy or predators. The institutions may have been ephemeral, but their head offices live on, imposing stone facades now often housing bars and restaurants rather than banking halls and teller counters.

By the 1970s Bank of Scotland, as befits the 'Old Bank', was headquartered in a grand Victorian pile on The Mound, a man-made causeway which leads up to the Castle rock and a short walk from its modest first premises on the High Street, heart of the Old Town of Edinburgh. A substantial head office had been completed in 1806 at the then enormous sum of £43,000, but half a century later it was doubled in size; new wings surmounted by domes were added on either side and the central dome was replaced with an enlarged version. From its three flagpoles flew the Union Jack, flanked by the St Andrew's cross of Scotland and the Bank's own standard, a saltire with four gold discs to represent piles of coins. The building spoke of confidence and complacency. From the boardroom windows its directors could look down on the city spread below them. The Royal, the 'New Bank', appropriately had its head office in the New Town (still called 'new' although it was largely completed 200 years ago) – an upstart junior lower down the hill, beneath the eyes of its elders and betters.

In the preceding two and a half centuries the Bank had absorbed many of its rivals, including the Central, the Caledonian, the Thistle, the Ship, the Glasgow Union, the Paisley Union, Perth United, the Kilmarnock, Hunter's Bank, Sir William Forbes Bank and more recently the Union Bank in 1955 and the British Linen Bank in 1971, the last nearly as old as the Bank itself. The Royal had gone through a similar Darwinian process, picking up smaller and weaker institutions over the centuries.

Natural selection had allowed Scottish banking to evolve into a closed and comfortable world. Banks competed with each other, but not too fiercely. One manager, newly promoted to be in charge of his own branch in a small rural town, suggested he might write to every business customer of his rivals in the area inviting them to meet him to discuss moving their accounts. He was soon slapped down by his superior: 'This is banking, it is not total war.' Senior bankers from the three Scottish banks met together in the Committee of Scottish Clearing Bankers, ostensibly to discuss items of mutual concern, but in effect to collude on interest rates, fees and charges. No one wanted to get too far out of line and the law took a more relaxed view in those days. The lack of competition even extended across the border. A 'Gentlemen's Agreement' made in 1876 prevented English banks from opening branches in Scotland and Scottish banks from expanding in England, apart from small offices in London.

Similarly banks did not poach each other's staff. Typically a boy (they were still mostly boys) would join the Bank straight from school and stay with the same employer until retirement. If passed over for advancement, leaving to go to a rival Scottish bank was not an option; they simply would not consider employing you. Even moving to England was not a guarantee of a job, so in the post-war period many left Britain for British banks in the old empire, the Far or Middle East or Southern Africa. The Hongkong & Shanghai Banking Corporation was especially keen to recruit bright, well-trained young men from the old country, so much so that it was sometimes joked that the initials HSBC really stood for Home for Scottish Bank Clerks.

And they were well-trained. A typical bank recruit would be a boy who had done well in his Higher certificate exams at school. Where today he would probably go on to university, then he would try for an apprenticeship with an industrial firm or enter a bank or insurance company. He might not earn much at first, but he would be paid something, would gain working experience and get an education which would equate to degree level. On his first day in a branch a new recruit would be shown where to sit and then given the time and place of the enrolment for night classes for the 'Institute' exams. The Institute of Bankers in Scotland,[2] established in 1875, was the first banking institute in the world and its professional qualification, taken after years of study in night classes or by correspondence, gave a thorough theoretical grounding in all aspects of the business. On top of this the Bank imposed its own practical training by moving recruits of promise around branches and head office departments so that by the time they had been in the Bank for a decade or so they had experienced most things that day-to-day operations were likely to throw at them.

Unlike English commercial banks, Scottish banks (and those in Northern Ireland) had retained the right to issue their own bank notes. Each bank liked to dispense only its own notes, but in the normal course of business they would accumulate piles of their rivals' notes as well as Bank of England notes. This meant that they had to co-operate closely. In towns and cities a regular ritual would be enacted where clerks from different banks would meet to exchange notes, giving up those of their competitors and taking back their own. One apprentice banker remembers walking through the mining town of Cowdenbeath, Fife, in the late 1960s lugging a suitcase containing £500,000 in used notes to be exchanged in the branch of another bank – a grown-up version of exchanging cigarette cards or playing happy families.

Very few people were recruited from other professions and if they were it was generally acknowledged that their careers would be limited. Unless you had 'passed money over the counter' you could not reach the top. Time-served bankers filled every post, in personnel (not yet called HR), in the management of computer departments (not yet called IT) and in marketing. This led to an in-bred, conservative culture, but also to an immensely strong sense of shared values. Talent and hard work were no guarantee that you would rise. After the merger of Bank of Scotland and British Linen Bank it was agreed that promotions would be in turns, one from each bank, rather than on merit.[3]

It was a paternalistic world. Margaret Taylor[4] remembers the Bank as being 'a very sleepy sector and was seen as full of dusty old men and dusty old offices, and actually was. The sector was entirely different to what it is now, banks didn't really have to go out looking for custom at that time, people came to them, and there wasn't the same competitiveness. The old idea that if you work in a bank you're well looked after and you've got a job for life and a cheap mortgage still prevailed.'

Staff were expected to open accounts with the Bank and use them to conduct all their financial affairs. David Jenkins, who joined from academic life as the Bank's Economist in 1976, was shocked to be told that not only must he move his own account to Bank of Scotland, but his wife must do so too. This was partly so that the Bank could keep an eye on its staff and know if any of them were getting into financial difficulties which might affect their work, but it was also a big source of business. 'Staff Branch' was very profitable.

Systems within the banks were still mostly paper-based at the start of the 1970s. Bank of Scotland had bought its first IBM computer in the 1950s, but it performed only very basic accounting tasks and 'cashing up' at the end of each day was still the method by which branch managers knew how much business they had done.

They had no idea whether their branch was profitable or not, because they were not told its costs and it is doubtful whether Head Office knew which branches made surpluses and which did not, let alone which products made money and which lost it (not that banks spoke of 'products' in those days). The Chief Accountant (not actually a qualified accountant, but a banker who had done his Institute exams and come up through the ranks) was the guardian of the balance sheet. His was the responsibility for making sure that the Bank was always solvent. The profitability of the Bank was a secondary consideration: as long as it earned a profit and could pay a dividend that was enough. No one in the management thought much about the share price and shareholders ('proprietors' in the Bank's seventeenth-century terminology) seldom complained. Banks were expected to be solid, not to grow.

In England newly affluent workers were opening chequebook current accounts, which paid no interest and incurred charges. But canny Scots clung to their deposit accounts and the Scottish banks were slow to move them. Frequent bank mergers had left branches dotted along High Streets, often within a few hundred yards of each other, so it was no hardship for a Scottish bank customer to pop into a branch every time he needed to withdraw cash to pay a bill, rather than use a cheque. In the meantime his balance earned interest and he paid no bank charges. No wonder the profitability of the Scottish banks lagged behind their southern neighbours.

Scottish banks were austere institutions. The Institute of Bankers did not teach ethics (it does now), but a strict ethical code was implicit in the Presbyterian character of each of the banks. Lines were imaginary, but everyone knew where they were and once crossed there was no way back. If you were asked to leave the bank, your career in banking was over. Discipline was maintained by the bank inspection department, which scrutinised lending applications down to very small amounts and made unannounced visits to branches. Gavin Masterton, who later became the Bank's Treasurer, remembered his time in the department: 'Bowler hats were mandatory and you had six white collars delivered every Saturday. Not too many people in Dunfermline wore bowler hats, so I had to smuggle mine across the River [Forth] to Edinburgh every day.'[5]

The relationship was not quite that of the KGB to the Soviet Union, but the sudden arrival of the bank inspectors, typically wearing black overcoats and bowlers, could induce anxiety in a branch manager. The story is told of the inspectors arriving in a northern town, checking into the station hotel during the evening and having dinner and a few drinks before retiring, so that they were less than fully alert on the doorstep of the branch the following morning when the manager arrived to open up. After spending the day in the vault, counting money and matching totals against the ledgers, they summoned the manager to his own office for the verdict. All the sums were correct, everything balanced, but the inspectors never liked to leave without finding at least one fault: 'You have a large amount of Royal Bank notes in your safe,' they challenged. 'Well of course,' replied the puzzled manager, 'this is the Royal Bank. The Bank of Scotland branch is on the opposite corner.' Despite this momentary lapse, the inspection department grew very powerful in the Bank, exercising sway over promotions as well as over lending. If the inspectors remembered a bad debt they thought could have been avoided, it might hold back your career.

Bankers lent on the basis of a few simple rules, mostly based on the experience learned from crises past. For example, there was the liquidity rule:

'Lend short and borrow long',

a lesson which might have gone back all the way to the Bank's early struggles against the Darien Company and the Royal Bank. A run on the bank was every senior banker's ultimate nightmare, so this rule was designed to make sure you could get your money back from those you lent to before you had to repay those from whom you borrowed it. This rule propelled banks to look for personal deposits (now known as retail deposits) because individuals were likely to be saving for long-term aims – to pay the deposit on a house, to buy a car, to pay for a daughter's wedding or a son's education, or just against a 'rainy day'. Having thousands of small depositors also had the advantage that it was very unlikely they would all want their money back at the same time. It was this rule which also deterred banks from offering mortgages. They did not like having their funds tied up for 25 years and preferred to leave this market to the building societies.

Then there was the lending rule:

'Look at the borrower, not the asset'.

The test a manager applied was whether the borrower had sufficient income to repay the loan, even if things went wrong. The value of the asset being purchased which might provide security, was secondary because a factory, or a company, or a machine tool was worth much less to a bank which had to repossess it and try to sell it again, than to the businessman who had originally bought it. This test equally applied to individual borrowers when car loans and hire purchase began to be introduced. It meant, in the words of one senior banker, that a Scottish bank manager looked deep into your soul and only when he was convinced that you did not need the money would he agree to lend it to you. A supplicant could quite often be sent away empty-handed with the manager telling him it was for his own good, but it also meant that the bad debts of Scottish banks were low.

This was not only the result of careful appraisal before an advance was granted. If things did go wrong, Scottish banks were reluctant to call in a loan and write off a debt, particularly if that meant plunging a borrower into bankruptcy. They were prepared to accept reduced or deferred payments until such times as the borrower was in better financial shape. In this they were helped by an accounting regime which was much more lax than it is today. Loans did not have to be publicly branded as 'non-performing' or marked down if interest payments were not being met and they could be hidden away in a suspense account until such time as the loan was repaid or the bank finally had to admit that the money had to be written off.

Supervision of the banking system was the responsibility of the Governor of the Bank of England, a figure held in such awe that it was said that the raising of his eyebrows was enough to deter behaviour of which he did not approve. Mergers of banks had to be agreed by the Governor, who would not sanction hostile takeovers or a bank being acquired by a non-bank company or a foreign bank not under British jurisdiction. Scrutiny of the solvency of individual banks was delegated to deputy governors and other senior officials, but their authority was also absolute. One Scottish executive complained to a Bank of England Deputy Governor that one of his rival banks was almost certainly bust. 'It is bust when I say it is, laddie, and not before,' was the reply.

The primary concern of the Bank of England was to preserve the integrity of the banking system, which ultimately meant protecting depositors from loss, should a bank get into difficulties. Its authority and competence were severely tested early in the 1970s when a sudden drop in property prices following a long, unsustainable boom precipitated around 30 small banking companies into bankruptcy. These 'secondary banks', as they were known, had broken both fundamental rules of banking. They had borrowed short to grant long-term mortgages on homes and commercial properties and when the market plunged they were unable to get their money back. They had also been fooled by a period during which property prices had risen dramatically into believing that the value of the assets against which they had lent could not go down. When interest rates were suddenly increased to 13 per cent, borrowers could not afford their massively increased interest charges and property prices plunged.

What concerned the Bank of England was that not only were the individuals and companies which had deposited money with the secondary banks at risk, but so were large banks, including National Westminster, which had lent to them. It stepped in to support the large banks and oversee an orderly wind-up of the secondary companies. Depositors were safeguarded and the system survived, but at a cost – and not only to the Bank of England. To ensure that the lesson was well-learned by the rest of the banking system, commercial banks were compelled to meet part of the cost. The Scottish banks felt aggrieved since the problem was mostly confined to London and the South-east, but nevertheless had to pay up. Bank of Scotland's share amounted to £31 million.[6] They had also had to meet the cost of mopping up after a more domestic failure a short time before, when the Scottish Co-operative Bank collapsed.

Regulation and supervision was largely voluntary and relied on all the players understanding the unwritten rules and respecting the authority of the Bank of England. It worked when the participants were confined to the narrow old boys' clubs of London and Edinburgh but became stretched when the game began to be played over a wider field. The effectiveness of the Governors' eyebrows was tested at the end of the decade when in response to an agreed bid for the Royal Bank of Scotland by Standard Chartered, a British bank headquartered in London, but with its main activities in the Far East and in Africa, a rival counter bid was made. This came from the Hongkong & Shanghai Banking Corporation (HSBC), which although technically a British bank, was headquartered in Hong Kong, then a British colony. It did not have the support of the Royal Bank board and the Bank of England Governor made clear his displeasure – and was ignored. HSBC went ahead with its bid and looked likely to win until the Government referred both bids to the Monopolies Commission. Both were eventually blocked on the grounds that a bid would damage the 'regional interest' of Scotland, but it was widely believed that the real reason was to preserve the authority of the Bank of England.

The 1970s were not an easy time to make money in banking. The British economy lurched from boom to bust under the Conservative government of Edward Heath, the Labour governments of Harold Wilson and James Callaghan and Mrs Margaret Thatcher's first Conservative administration. Inflation rocketed reaching 22 per cent in 1975, interest rates were high and the Labour Chancellor was forced to seek a loan from the International Monetary Fund (IMF). Ministers changed policies often. Heath placed restraints on lending, then removed them. Thatcher taxed deposits and abolished exchange controls. Economic growth was sluggish and companies found it hard to move forward.

The high rate of inflation took its toll on bank costs, which were predominantly wages and salaries. High interest rates gave the banks the opportunity to widen their margins, but high costs and a poor economic outlook did not encourage customers to borrow. In 1978 Bank of Scotland reported a pre-tax profit of £16.7 million, the same in money terms as it had achieved five years earlier. When inflation was taken into account the Bank was going backwards rather than forwards, a conclusion confirmed by the fact that its rivals, the Royal Bank and Clydesdale Bank were achieving much higher returns on their equity.[7]

The 1970s was a decade dominated by oil. In 1973 came the first 'Oil Shock' when Arab oil-producing countries imposed an embargo on supplies in protest at US support for Israel in the Yom Kippur War. When supplies were resumed, prices were increased dramatically, sending growth rates in Western countries plunging. Further effects took a while to materialise, but in the meantime Burmah Oil, a Scottish-based international oil company, got into trouble and had to be rescued and restructured. Bank of Scotland lost the account, which had been one of its biggest.

Not all the news was negative. In the early part of the decade oil was discovered in the North Sea, bringing dozens of oil companies to Scotland, and in their wake more than 30 international banks looking to finance new developments. The London banks, seeing their international competitors getting near to the action, tore up the century-old 'Gentlemen's Agreement' and opened offices in Edinburgh and Aberdeen. This was initially treated with dismay by those in the headquarters on The Mound who saw only the downside.

Oil field financing was far outside the Bank's experience, but it began to get calls asking if it was participating in this or that and younger executives began to press the senior management to take action. In 1972 the Bank recruited its first expert from the oil industry and in the same year, Bruce Pattullo, a 34-year-old manager, persuaded the Treasurer (as the Chief Executive was still called) to allow him to organise an oil conference in London. The event,

'Scottish North Sea Oil', held at the Savoy, branded Bank of Scotland as the 'oil bank' and led to it being invited to participate in the financing of BP's Forties oil field.

By the standards of the time, the total sum to be raised was massive at £360 million, to be split between a consortium of banks. The deal tested the Bank in a number of ways: the structure was complicated, the margin was finer than the Bank had been used to on industrial lending, but also it challenged one of the fundamental lending principles. The lenders would have no recourse to BP, despite its huge assets and strong cash flows from elsewhere in the world. They were to be repaid from the profits of the field and so had to make their own assessment of how much oil it held, how much of it was recoverable and at what price it could be sold. They were being asked to lend against the asset, not the ability of the borrower to repay. Despite its inexperience and misgivings, the Bank was the first to sign up, a move which cemented its reputation in the industry. Forties turned out to be one of the largest, longest-lasting and most profitable of the North Sea fields.

The Bank went on to part-fund a number of other oil developments, to open an office in Houston, Texas, the US oil capital, and to look at financing elsewhere in the world. At home North Sea business was also boosting its industrial customers in engineering, shipping and construction and providing opportunities for its clients in the investment sector. But in taking up the chances offered, the Bank also crossed another line – it took equity stakes (that is, it owned shares) in some ventures as well as providing loans. The Bank had previously maintained that providing both debt and equity opened it to the risk of conflict of interest. As a pure lender a bank had only one concern – to get its money back – but when it also became a part-owner its loyalties could become divided. It comforted itself by saying that these were exceptional circumstances, that its participation was small and that none of its customers objected; it overturned centuries of practice, but the Bank took the risk nevertheless and mostly did very well out of it.

The Oil Shock had other repercussions for the banks years later. Higher oil prices meant that the governments of oil-producing countries, companies and individuals, particularly in the Middle East, accumulated huge financial surpluses and began to deposit them with banks in the US and Europe. The question for the banks was where to lend this money profitably. The economies of the developed world were still suffering the effects of the oil price rises and the demand for borrowing was weak, so they turned instead to the developing world, and especially Latin America. Governments there were desperate to borrow and willing to pay high rates of interest. These were not the sort of customers Western banks would normally consider taking on. Their governments tended to be unstable and short-lived, their economies were erratic and corruption and inflation were endemic. But the banks' executives clung to a belief that countries, unlike companies, could not go bust – the IMF would step in to prevent a default. Third World lending therefore looked like a one-way bet; your money was guaranteed and margins were much higher than you could get anywhere else. Loan officers from US and European banks began touring Central and South America pressing cash on willing borrowers.

This proposed a dilemma for Bank of Scotland. Lending on the large scale required by governments was done by consortia of banks. The Bank was too small to be part of the leadership of any of these groups, it had no international network of branches and offices and its experience of currency lending was confined to meeting the export needs of its domestic customers. Nevertheless some of the Bank's executives in the newly formed international division wanted to be part of the action – the margins on offer, even for those lower down the food chain as the Bank would be, were too fat to ignore. Barclays, which had a big shareholding in Bank of Scotland, was also pressing the Bank to take part in consortia which it was leading. The board was cautious about 'taking crumbs from other men's tables', as one board paper put it,[8] but nevertheless, the Bank did lend.

The total debt of Latin American governments quadrupled over eight years while at the same time economic recovery meant that interest rates rose. Inevitably some countries could not meet their interest charges and repayments and panic ensued when first Mexico, then Argentina and Brazil teetered on the edge of default. The consequences for the banks were dire. The total capital of some US and London banks would have been wiped out had they been forced to write off all their lending to the region. The IMF did have to step in, but the sums were so large that all it could do was extend debt terms to allow banks time to write off their loans. Bank of Scotland had the least exposure of any UK clearing bank, but had it had to write off the lot in one go, it would have lost more than a quarter of its capital.

The international rescue bought time and although the Bank wrote off some debts, it adopted an innovative solution to others. David Jenkins, the Bank's Economist, was pressed into a new role, travelling South America to negotiate debt-for-equity swaps which saw the Bank acquire, among other things, a hotel on Copacabana Beach in Rio de Janeiro, a tomato-paste factory in north-east Brazil, and a stake in the country's third-largest paper producer.[9] Jenkins, short, bald, dapper, with a wry wit and ready smile, must have cut an unlikely figure touring some of the more remote areas of Brazil and Chile. He turned his adventures into a series of humorous articles for *The Scottish Banker* magazine.

4

Cometh the hour, cometh the man

At the end of the 1970s a quiet revolution occurred at the top of Bank of Scotland. The appropriately named Tom Risk was appointed one of two deputy Governors.*

Risk was a corporate lawyer who had been a director of the Bank for some time. Importantly, he had chaired its corporate banking subsidiary, initially named Bank of Scotland Finance Company, but later relaunched with the old British Linen Bank name. His chief executive there had been Bruce Pattullo, the manager who had led the Bank to raise its profile in the oil industry. Risk was a strategist and a shrewd judge of character. Along with some of the other board members he was concerned that the Bank's lacklustre performance over the previous decade made it vulnerable to a takeover. With the retirement of the Treasurer (Chief Executive) looming, he persuaded his fellow directors to leap a generation, ignore the potential candidates among the general managers and promote Pattullo, who was made Deputy Treasurer and Chief General Manager in 1979 and promoted to the top post the following year at the age of 41.

It was not only Pattullo's youth which was unusual. His background made him a very strange animal in clearing banking on either side of the border. Whereas most recruits had joined the Bank from state schools, Pattullo had been educated at prep school, Rugby and Hertford College, Oxford. There he had developed an interest in economics and fancied a career in finance, but while his university contemporaries might have gone into stockbroking or one of the blue-blooded London merchant banks, he opted to join Bank of Scotland as one of the first of a handful of candidates on its new graduate programme. Recruiting from university was a radical departure for

---

* By now the Governor was no longer a full-time appointment, but was non-executive chairman of the board of directors.

the Bank, but any difference to its usual method of training stopped there. Pattullo was still required to work in a branch 'passing money over the counter' and to study for the Institute exams, although having acquired the habit of studying on his own at Oxford, he opted for correspondence, rather than night classes. He won the Institute's first prize in his exam year. As with other recruits, the Bank moved him around, so that by the time he reached the top nearly 20 years later he had acquired a broad experience of practical banking.

Pattullo was intelligent, rather than clever, thoughtful rather than impulsive. By temperament he was a quiet, cautious man, not given to overstatement. I had known him for a couple of years by the time he was appointed to the Treasurer's position and I interviewed him for the *Financial Times*. I asked him his ambition and was surprised by the answer:

'To make this the best-performing bank.'

'The best-performing bank in Scotland?' I asked.

'The best-performing bank anywhere,' he said.

His leadership marked a radical change in character and culture. Previously the Bank had been constrained by its hierarchy. Information had a long way to climb to get from the customer to top management and decisions wound their way down through many layers before being implemented. Pattullo was open and approachable and, in some ways despite his middle-class upbringing, unconventional, prepared to consider new ways of doing things and to listen to his subordinates as well as to his peers. For the senior executives who wanted to get the new chief's ear there was another marked change. Unlike previous generations of top Scottish bankers, Pattullo was not a golfer. He played tennis and had a court built in the garden of his Edinburgh home. Several of his senior lieutenants started to work on their serves.

By the time he became Treasurer, he had had two decades to observe how the Bank's management structure inhibited innovation and made decision-making cumbersome. He introduced a Management Board[1], consisting of the top half-dozen or so senior executives who met regularly to discuss the progress of the Bank in their various fields. Everyone, whether they were in International, Treasury, managing the East of Scotland business, the West or London, got an overview of what was happening, where problems might occur and where opportunities were being presented. This group became the engine of change within the Bank, reinforced by the fact that most of its members had offices on the first floor of the headquarters building on The Mound. If they were in the office they took coffee together and often lunched together.

Risk and Pattullo redesigned the governance of the Bank. They created a clear separation of the functions of the main board – now focused on strategy and a role as trustees of the proprietors' (share-holders') funds – and the Management Board, which ran the Bank day to day. To link the two, the Treasurer sat on the main board as a full member, and the Governor attended the Management Board. The minutes of Management Board meetings were made available to directors, and executives attended the main board meetings, sitting at the back and silent unless asked to speak.

Pattullo also ended the stranglehold the Inspectors' Department had over innovation and promotions and focused it on internal audit. He promoted younger, able managers and he changed the culture, abolishing the Business Development Unit, a head office team supposedly responsible for finding new opportunities, and sent a circular to all managers telling them they were all responsible for growing the business. No more would initiative be slapped down: 'The Treasurer has let it be known that he is open to ideas from anywhere,' one young manager told me with enthusiasm at the time.

Tom Risk was appointed Governor in 1981 and the two men formed a formidable partnership at the top of the Bank, each passionately committed to its independence and to making it a force to be reckoned with. When the chairman of the Distillers' Company, Scotland's biggest whisky producer and by common consent a poorly managed dozy giant, came to suggest that it might buy Bank of Scotland, Risk politely but promptly walked him to the door and closed it behind him. A more credible threat was posed when Barclays, which had owned 36 per cent of Bank of Scotland since its acquisition of British Linen Bank, decided it wanted either to acquire the remainder of the Bank or to sell its stock. There was no appetite on The Mound for becoming a subsidiary of Barclays, which had its own problems and was still in the grip of the founding families. Instead Risk arranged to have Standard Life, Scotland's largest life assurance company, buy the holding, rather than have it acquired by a possible predator. 'It was a squalid Scottish stitch-up,' remarked one Bank executive. Standard Life was criticised for the deal on the grounds that such a big stake, representing over 7 per cent of its equity holdings, would unbalance its portfolio, but it held the shares for ten years and sold them for four times what it had initially paid.

Pattullo turned conventional thinking in the Bank on its head. Whereas the previous generation of managers had seen the ending of the Gentleman's Agreement as a threat that the English banks would come into Scotland, he saw it as an opportunity. With an English market ten times the size of Scotland to go after, Pattullo saw that he had the best of the deal. Whereas others saw Bank of Scotland's tiny percentage of the UK banking market as a weakness, he regarded it as a strength. He could realistically aim to double his share, whereas any of the 'Big Four' English banks, each with about a fifth or more of the market would struggle to gain any increase.

His strategy was to move into England with a series of carefully positioned branches in fast-growing English regions. Birmingham was the first, quickly followed by other major cities. He recognised that in a new market it would be impossible to make enough profit from retail business to justify the property and manpower costs of opening a large branch network, so the new offices were to concentrate on corporate business, lending and, crucially, taking deposits. That would mean a fewer number of bigger and more profitable deals.

He intended to tackle the English retail market by a twin-approach of getting other people to sell Bank of Scotland products, and pioneering direct sales channels which did not need bricks and mortar. Before long the Bank was providing credit to customers of Marks & Spencer, the clothing retailer C&A, Renault cars, the Henley Group car dealership, British Rail and the motoring organisation the AA. Banks had got over their fear of mortgages, realising that although the loans were granted for 25 years, many people moved house and redeemed their debts long before that. The average life of a mortgage was less than a third of the nominal length. Bank of Scotland processed home loans centrally, but marketed them in this pre-internet age through newspaper ads all over the country. It also launched a Money Market Cheque Account, aimed at people with above-average incomes or wealth – the first account in the UK to offer near-market rates on credit balances above a minimum level. The address of the Bank's Threadneedle Street branch in the City of London was on each cheque, but the account was run from a computer centre in the Edinburgh council estate of Wester Hailes.

Innovation was now the Bank's guiding principle and this was dramatically illustrated by the introduction in 1985 of HOBS – the Home & Office Banking System, the first electronic banking system in the UK. It was initially run on Prestel, an early electronic network. For the first time customers could see their account balances and move money between deposit and current accounts from a screen on their desks or on their home televisions. We now take this for granted with internet banking, but at the time it was revolutionary. The Bank was freed from its dependence on a branch network largely confined to the most northerly quarter of the country and customers did not have to telephone their branches or visit them to find out what their balance was. HOBS brought Bank of Scotland tens of thousands of new accounts, but it failed to make the most of it. 'We still had a Presbyterian culture,' Pattullo remembered later. 'We didn't believe that we were that much ahead of any other bank. It was a great success, but we could have expanded the account base twice as fast if we had thrown everything at it.'

Other electronic developments followed: an internal network which allowed any manager to access the account details of any customer – another ground-breaking system – and an international payments system which was used by the Government to pay pensions and other benefits to British citizens living abroad.

There was financial innovation too. In the early days of North Sea exploration, when the Bank began participating in oil field financings, it had learned new skills by being able to forecast cash flows and structure lending deals. Archie Gibson, one of Pattullo's closest allies, and Gavin Masterton, Gibson's young protégé, began to apply these techniques to a new corporate phenomenon – the management buy-out.

In boom times big corporations had often acquired companies without obvious logic and diversified conglomerates became fashion-able. As the economy tightened in the early 1980s, these same big groups began to sell off unwanted subsidiaries, often to their manage-ments, who understood the business and recognised its potential to grow if freed from the burdens and restrictions imposed by the parent group. Unlike later leveraged deals, these were usually companies in basic industries, with long track records and predictable cash flows. The Bank realised that the companies could afford to borrow a large proportion of the purchase price, with the loans being repaid a few years later when the firm was either bought by another trade buyer or floated on the stock market. It set up a unit to specialise in management buyouts (MBOs) and quickly became the leader in the field, topping the league table of lenders ahead of banks many times its size. Crucially, it began to gain a UK rather than just a Scottish reputation as a shrewd corporate lender and its younger managers got to work on bigger and more complex deals than they would have done had they worked for one of the big London banks.

The core retail market in Scotland was not neglected. In 1984 Pattullo launched the 'Friend for Life' campaign, an attempt to shake off the Bank's 'stuffy and dour' image and replace it with an attempt to provide 'the most friendly, efficient and constructive service of all the banks'. The advertising was backed up with staff 'training and retraining', to ensure that the actual service experienced by customers lived up to the hype.[2] The Bank also supported the Institute of Bankers, and put any of its managers it believed had potential through the Institute courses and exams. Exceptionally talented people were sent to Harvard to take the Advanced Management Programme.

In 1985 Pattullo presented figures to his senior managers at an internal conference. Over the past year the Bank had increased its pre-tax profit by 35 per cent, marginally behind its old rival the Royal Bank, but well ahead of any of the English clearers. Over five years the record was more impressive: the Bank was well ahead of the pack with an almost doubling of profit. Over ten years it had achieved an increase of 474 per cent, beaten only by Lloyds. Its return on equity – a measure increasingly looked at by professional investors – was running at 23–25 per cent in the late 1980s, a very high rate of return for a bank which was still regarded as well capitalised and not unduly risky. In 1989 *The Economist* magazine's survey of the financial sector resulted in the Bank being voted by its peers as 'the most admired bank' for its technical innovation, and the Institution of Electrical Engineers asked the Bank to deliver the annual Faraday Lectures, under the title 'Electric Currency'.

For all his willingness to try new things, Pattullo remained innately a cautious man. While trumpeting to a management conference that the Bank was now 'advances led' – that is its growth was being propelled by its success at lending – he exhorted them to match this by bringing in more deposits. Although he sanctioned large corporate

loans, he wanted to be sure that there was a near-certain chance of
the money being repaid and he often expressed his belief that banks
'should not be in the risk business'.

The philosophy that the Bank was a custodian of its depositors'
funds lay behind its governance structure. In addition to the main
board, there were area boards in the East and West of Scotland and in
London, whose members included the responsible senior executives
of the Bank and non-executives, usually the heads of prominent local
businesses. Another board shadowed the international department.
They would scrutinise lending propositions, using their business
expertise and local knowledge to challenge the executives. The main
board also discussed lending proposals in a process known by the
Victorian term 'homologation'. The board, drawn from the captains
of the various industries with which the Bank dealt – oil, property,
engineering, shipping, investment – would closely question executives
on what they were doing. 'The idea,' remembers one board member,
'was not to second-guess the executives, but to make sure we understood what they were proposing and also to make sure they understood
it too.'

The Bank board of the 1970s–1980s, exclusively male – white,
middle-aged, middle-class with the occasional member of the aris-
tocracy – would not pass muster today. 'It was non-PC,' remembers
one executive, 'but it worked.' In a small country like Scotland
conflicts of interest must also have occurred frequently, with board
members sitting in judgement on the business plans of their competitors. But standards then were different. Directors were expected not
be partisan or further their own interests and trusted not to do so.

In the UK, the Bank's success in oil and management buyouts was
increasingly bringing it into London – although with typical Edinburgh disdain Tom Risk categorised it as 'an inefficient place to do a
day's work'. In the late 1980s came the 'Big Bang'. The deregulation
of financial services allowed clearing banks to move into previously
prohibited activities. There was a wholesale rush of banks buying
stockbrokers, fund management firms and merchant banks. Names
which had been a fixture of the City for decades or even centuries
disappeared into huge financial conglomerates and the city gents who
had been partners in these firms retired with wealth unimagined even
by their accustomed comfortable standards. In their place came a
new breed of younger, sharper, better educated and more aggressive

operators. 'My word is my bond', the motto of the Stock Exchange, gave way to *caveat emptor*. Long lunches gave way to sandwiches at the trading screen. Bank of Scotland stayed aloof from this movement, preferring to stay as a pure banking operation and in a statement of its defiance, contributed to a capital-raising by Cazenove, the Queen's stockbroker and the most conservative of the city institutions, which had decided to remain independent. The Bank and 'Caz', led by its senior partner, the patrician David Mayhew, appeared to share a similar ethos.

The Bank also refused to be drawn into the increasingly fashionable proprietary trading of derivatives or other complex financial instruments which were forming a growing large part of banks' profit-generating strategies. A treasury dealing room had been set up in London, but Pattullo always regarded the operation, which lent and borrowed in the inter-bank market, as a service department. Its job was to ensure that the Bank always had sufficient liquidity – that it never ran the risk of running out of cash. If there was a shortfall in customer deposits, Treasury had to make up the deficiency as cheaply and effectively as possible by borrowing on the wholesale market. It also bought and sold currencies on behalf of the Bank's customers. What it was not there to do was take unnecessary risks – which the Bank's board regarded as gambling – even if this meant it might miss out on profitable opportunities.

There was one fashion, however, which it did not shun. The Bank's entry into the mortgage market at the end of the 1970s had been a great success. There was an increasing demand from couples to own their own homes and the Conservative Government, headed by Margaret Thatcher, encouraged the trend and offered a tax incentive which made mortgage interest payments more attractive than paying rent. By 1984 home loans made up 10 per cent of the Bank's lending[3] and its advertising campaigns were producing more leads than it could handle. This was low-risk business. Borrowers knew that they could lose their homes if they failed to meet the repayments and would tighten their belts elsewhere rather than default on the monthly mortgage. The Bank carefully screened applicants to satisfy itself that they had steady incomes and could meet the repayments even if the economy turned down. It also took security over the house, or over an endowment life assurance policy. Besides the loan, there were other gains for the Bank: it insisted that mortgage customers open a current account to channel their monthly payments and tried to sell them insurance, on which it earned a commission. The loans themselves were very profitable: the Bank not only charged a premium on the interest rate, but a set-up and administration fee as well. The problem was that home lending was growing much faster than the Bank could attract deposits. It wanted to do more, but how was it to find the money to lend?

The answer was to sell the loans on to someone else, a process now known as 'securitisation'. The Bank formed syndicates with other banks and they parcelled up thousands of mortgages together. They now represented a very large amount of lending, which was being repaid in regular and predictable instalments. The risk was low, partly because the Bank had taken care to vet the borrowers, but also partly because of the diversification effect of this huge portfolio which was spread over different parts of the UK, different ages and types of homes and borrowers, whose occupations and incomes were different. It was very unlikely that many of them would default at the same time. These packaged mortgages could be sold to life assurance and pension companies which had cash to invest and needed predictable, reliable incomes to meet monthly pension payments.

The Bank kept the fees it had charged to borrowers and took a small share of the interest payments to cover the cost of continuing to administer the loans, collect the repayments and process any early redemption of loans when borrowers moved house. It also kept the risk and undertook to buy back any outstanding loans at the end of seven years.

Borrowers were oblivious to any of this. As far as they were concerned, their loans were with Bank of Scotland, to whom they continued to make their repayments and to whom they addressed any queries. But with the money it received from selling the mortgages, the Bank was able to make new loans, collecting set-up fees and a margin on the interest payments each time. As long as the demand was there it could carry on doing this indefinitely.

Had he been able to see 300 years into the future, William Paterson would have approved; this was near to his ideal of a bank benefiting from interest on money it was creating out of nothing. Some of the Bank's board, however, did not approve.

'Who were these mortgages being passed on to and what responsibility did we have?' one director remembers wondering. 'We asked these questions, but they were never satisfactorily answered.' The non-executives were uneasy about the whole process. Their concerns were quietened by assurances that the Bank carefully vetted the borrowers, retained the risk and would buy back any outstanding loans at the end of the process, but doubts remained. 'If you can pile up loans and get them off your balance sheet and believe you have no responsibility for them, whereas the people who took out the loans believe you are still responsible – that is not good business. However, it became very fashionable and everyone was doing it the same way, so we did it.'

The practice did not last long. The Bank decided that mortgages were to become an important part of its lending and should stay on the balance sheet. It would be years before securitisation was attempted again.

5

The Cultural Revolution

By the end of the 1980s the Bank's performance was attracting attention. Pattullo had exceeded his ambition of doubling its share of the UK market and of making it the best-performing bank, in the UK at least. Bank of Scotland's growth – 20 per cent per annum in the previous four years[1] – had propelled it into the top 100 companies listed on the Stock Exchange. Its cost/income ratio, a measure of its efficiency, was 10 per cent better than any of its London competitors and was heading lower as it continued to find new ways to increase its earnings and hold down its expenses.

Investment institutions, which a decade before had regarded the Bank as a safe but unexciting utility, were now looking on it as a growth stock. In contrast to its bigger rivals, which were seen as poorly managed, it had strong leadership and a clear strategy for continuing to take market share from its bigger but slower London competitors. *The Times* noted that Bank of Scotland 'still enjoys the highest prospective multiple in the banking sector, which points to a high tolerance by investors for the Bank's flair for innovation'.[2] Professional investors were starting to focus on new measures where the Bank excelled, like return on equity (shortened by professionals to RoE and expressed as a percentage).

The *Financial Times*' influential 'Lex' comment column became a regular fan. In 1989, commenting on a profit rise of 36 per cent, it berated investors for growing 'tired of Bank of Scotland's refrain: strong management, even stronger balance sheet and novel strategy for growth'. Its shares had lost some of their premium over the troubled English banks, but the newspaper added, 'If the market thinks that the Bank has lost its deft touch in these matters, there is surely no sign of it in yesterday's results.'[3] A year later the Bank again posted record results, together with a sharp fall in its cost/income ratio and a return on equity of 25 per cent. Lex commented: 'Coming less than 24 hours after the grim warning from Midland, Bank of Scotland is a refreshing reminder of what well-managed banks can achieve even when times are tough.'[4]

Before I go any further I should include a brief and very simplified explanation of bank finances. Confusingly for lay people, banks call the sums of money they hold – the deposits of their customers – 'liabilities'. They are liabilities because the banks do not own the cash and one day it will have to be repaid. But in the meantime they can use this money to lend and earn profits from. The money they don't hold – the cash they have lent out – banks call 'assets'. They are assets because the banks expect the money to be repaid and in the meantime it is earning interest.

'Equity' is the capital its shareholders subscribe for shares, plus the profit retained in the business, which belongs to the shareholders. Banks make money by lending out the funds entrusted to them by their depositors. The equity owners, the shareholders, get the profit on this lending, but in return they take the risk. If some borrowers cannot repay – usually the case in a recession, for example – it is the equity owners who lose their money (or should be), not the depositors. Banks need a certain minimum level of equity as a cushion against the risks of lending. How much equity a bank needs is partly determined by what sort of business it does – some forms of lending are more risky than others – and partly by how it thinks the economy will perform. You can look on equity as 'rainy day' insurance. How much you need depends on how likely you believe it is to rain and how hard.

In the days of William Paterson governments had very little to say about how much capital a bank needed to hold; it was up to shareholders and depositors to make up their own minds about the level of risk. But numerous bank failures in the intervening three centuries have persuaded governments to specify a minimum capital level. (There will be more about government and international regulation later, but thirty years ago it was a lot simpler than it is today.) Above this statutory minimum it is a matter of judgement for a bank's executive and board how much equity it needs.

There is more than one way a bank can increase its RoE. It can, of course, increase its profits (the return) by growing its business and managing it efficiently. But it can also flatter the apparent return, thus making the ratio look larger, by reducing its equity, or at least not increasing it as fast as its lending is increasing.

In the 1980–90s Bank of Scotland was achieving high levels of RoE, but not by reducing its equity cushion. The Presbyterian ethos of the Bank prevailed and as its business increased it had no hesitation in going to its shareholders to raise new capital to maintain its capital ratio, which was already higher than many of its rivals. This was not a reflection of the riskiness of its lending – its bad debt levels were low – but of its cautious approach. The 1980s had seen recession as well as economic boom and the Bank ran its business on the assumption that between the good times there would always be bad ones. After declaring record profits and an increased dividend in 1984, the Bank raised £41 million, another £81 million the following year and a further £191 million in 1991. 'This is a capital-hungry business,' Pattullo explained. 'I believe the strong are going to get stronger and the weak are going to get weaker.'[5]

The Bank was riding high, but instead of gloating or greed there was a rectitude bordering on Calvinism. In 1991, with a recession starting to take its toll and the first reverse in profits for years, senior executives and the non-executive board decided to take no pay increase. Of the other British banks only Midland, then in its last difficult days of independence, followed suit.

It also had a policy of supporting its customers through bad times, particularly industrial and commercial customers who had been with it for a long time. In the Bank this was known as 'staying at the table', a metaphor derived from gambling which seems inappropriate for an institution still characterised by its moral rectitude. Justifications for this policy were varied and sometimes vague. There was a feeling of social responsibility: if the Bank forced a company into receivership, jobs might be lost and communities might suffer. There was also a more pecuniary motive: by supporting a company through hard times the Bank might be able to get more of its money back than it would by an immediate default. But occasionally there was also a loyalty to the business owner which seems naïve by today's standards. One executive explained it to me at the time: 'It would be very hard for someone who had been a loyal customer for years to see his business transferred to someone else because the Bank had called in the Receiver.'

This policy was not without its critics. Where Bank managers could defend it by pointing to flourishing businesses which would not exist had the Bank not held its nerve when things were apparently going wrong, others could assert that had the Bank called in the receiver earlier a business which had eventually collapsed might have been saved by a new owner with fresh ideas and new capital.

Whatever the motivation, sometimes the Bank stayed 'at the table' too long and it acquired an odd assortment of businesses by default during the 1980s and 1990s, including office blocks, a half-completed golf resort which it went on to finish before selling it, a part-share in the Magnet Joinery business, and the Balmoral Hotel at the end of Edinburgh's Princes Street, which it let to the management company of Rocco Forte for five years before selling it to him. In fact, at one stage it was said to own so many hotel rooms that wags named it 'the largest hotelier in the UK'. This practice of supporting customers was not unique to the Bank; its main rival, the Royal Bank of Scotland, acquired the airline Loganair by the same process and operated it for 15 years before selling.

Progress at the Bank was being watched not only in London, but much nearer to home too. During the 1980s Royal Bank of Scotland had struggled with many of the same problems of poor management and an unwieldy structure which had hobbled the Bank a decade before. Despite being larger than Bank of Scotland and having a greater presence in England through its subsidiary Williams & Glyn's, it lagged in efficiency, innovation and performance. Several of the Royal's non-executive directors were becoming concerned that its slumping share price could make it vulnerable to collapse or takeover and persuaded the board that new blood was needed to bring new energy and ideas. Sir Robin Duthie, chief executive of the tent maker Blacks of Greenock, had been chairman of the Scottish Development Agency (SDA), and pushed the name of its Chief Executive, George Mathewson.

Mathewson was not a career banker. He had been born in Perth and after studying electrical engineering at university to doctoral level, he had worked in the US for an electronics company and taken an MBA degree there. He came back to Scotland at the beginning of the oil boom to work for the investment bank ICFC (now called 3i), rising to become a main board director based in London responsible for a portfolio of a thousand companies. He returned to Scotland as the second chief executive of the SDA, and transformed a bureaucratic government body into a nimble, dynamic organisation focused on industrial investment, urban regeneration and the attraction of investors from the US and Japan. At the end of his five-year term he was considering an offer to run the New Zealand electricity company when the call came to move to the Royal Bank.

Mathewson was fiercely competitive and combative – he played club rugby into his fifties – but also a team builder. One young subordinate remembers fierce arguments which would get steadily more heated up to the point where 'George would remember that he had hired you and that he was never wrong, so maybe you had a point'. He was also an inspirational leader with strong self-belief. Another manager remembers coming away from a meeting at which George Mathewson had set a seemingly unachievable goal and had inspired the team to believe they could reach it by saying: 'I will get there and I have never failed.' It was only after the meeting that the manager had remembered all the instances in which George had failed. 'But at the time he said it he believed it to be true and we all believed him too.'

He had managed the transformation of the SDA with a small group of bright young men, mostly recruited from outside the agency. When he moved to the Royal Bank as strategy director he brought the team with him. These were not time-served bankers, but intelligent, ambitious people, many with postgraduate degrees and the arrogance which comes with being young and highly educated. Their analysis of the problems of the bank showed contempt for the ponderous management structure and complacent attitudes. Society and business had changed rapidly, but banking had not kept pace with it. With a handful of like-minded second-tier executives from within the bank, Mathewson began a series of weekly meetings to plot an internal takeover and oust the senior management.

Their chance came with the recession of the early 1990s, which cruelly exposed the bank's poor lending record. At the end of 1991 the Royal's bad debts soared and group profit collapsed by over 80 per cent. The retail bank managed a contribution of less than £6 million, but only by finding every legal means it could to flatter its accounts. Bank of Scotland also suffered from the economic downturn, but still managed to increase its pre-tax profit to £140 million.

Mathewson was helped by the fact that George Younger had recently resigned from the Cabinet as Defence Secretary to become chairman of the Royal Bank of Scotland. The two men had worked closely together when Younger had been Secretary of State for Scotland and had given Mathewson the political cover he needed to run a successful interventionist industrial policy at the SDA which ran counter to the ethos of Mrs Thatcher's government. The move had paid off. Reversing the pattern of decades, Scotland had started to do better in the league tables of economic performance and prosperity than many of the English regions. When there were riots in English cities in protest at the harsh austerity being imposed from Westminster, Scottish cities had remained calm.

Younger's relaxed manner and urbane charm disguised a decisive mind and a shrewd judge of character. The two men were to become as effective a combination as Tom Risk and Bruce Pattullo at the Bank. Mathewson and his team made a presentation to the Royal's directors and argued that only a radical transformation could save the bank. The board decided in his favour. He was installed as chief executive shortly afterwards and cleared out the old guard from the top jobs.

The effect on the Royal was dramatic, but the most radical changes were yet to come. Mathewson split the bank into three – a wholesale bank to service corporate customers, retail for smaller businesses and personal customers, and an operations division, to provide shared services such as property, computer services, now renamed 'Information Technology', and personnel, which was renamed 'Human Resources' following the fashion of the time. The 17,000 staff were also divided into three – those whom the new management wanted to keep, those whose attitudes or skills did not fit the new regime and those who were to be given the chance to change.

The retail bank went through fundamental change. Under the code name Project Columbus, Mathewson's team identified numerous failings, including poor organisational design, poor-quality people in key positions, lack of vision and investment in IT, unreliable lending and pricing policies, unimaginative products and low priority given to customer service.[6] The solution, it was decided, was to reinvent branch banking and it called in the international management consultancy McKinsey to help it.

Hundreds of branch managers now found themselves either facing early retirement or having to be interviewed for their own jobs. 'The golf courses of Edinburgh were full,' quipped Mathewson. Compared to the gradual evolution which Pattullo had encouraged at the Bank, the upheaval at Royal Bank was more like Mao's Cultural Revolution. It was a shock not only to the Royal's staff, but to the whole of

Scottish banking, which had regarded entry into one of the banks at the age of 18 as being the passport to lifelong employment. From now on people 'who had done nothing wrong' could find themselves out of a job.

It gave rise to a gallows humour:

Question: What is the definition of an optimist?
Answer: A Royal Bank manager whose wife irons five white shirts on Sunday evening.

The changes signalled the end of the branch manager as a territorial potentate, the local representative of the bank to any customer, whether that was a firm employing a thousand people, or a widow eking out her meagre savings. In his place came the 'Relationship Manager', whose geographic area was much less important than his (or her) understanding of the needs of the customer. It now became possible to say 'or her' because although women had been entering banking in increasing numbers they had not progressed to branch manager status. Project Columbus cleared out a raft of older male employees and in their place promoted women who previously had been confined to clerical or branch teller jobs. (The exception in the Royal Bank being 'The Ladies Branch' in Edinburgh's Princes Street, which was entirely staffed by and exclusively for women.) Despite the fact that girls frequently topped the prize list in Institute exams, very few made it beyond middle management to the top grades of the Royal Bank. The same was true of Bank of Scotland and the Clydesdale Bank.

Mathewson also slaughtered a few sacred cows. His bright young PhDs showed that Charterhouse, the upper-crust London merchant bank bought a few years before over dinner at an IMF meeting in Washington, was not earning its keep. Mathewson sold it and fell out with its suave Chief Executive, Victor Blank, who had also been a main board director of Royal Bank.

The top jobs in the reorganised groups did not necessarily go to experienced bankers. Although Mathewson put Tony Schofield, a long-serving bank executive in the Royal's English subsidiary, in charge of the retail bank, he brought in Iain Robertson to run the corporate bank, based in London. Robertson was an accountant by training, but had spent years in the civil service and had followed

Mathewson as chief executive of the SDA. When he joined the Royal he had only a couple of years experience at NatWest.

Changes were also occurring at Head Office. No longer were time-served bankers with their Institute exams acceptable as heads of specialist departments like finance, marketing, computing or personnel. In came professionals with no banking experience at all, but university degrees and professional qualifications in accountancy, marketing, information technology or human resources. The effect on the Royal's performance was rapid and profound. From coming last in surveys of customer satisfaction, the Royal now regularly came top. With its new confidence it expanded in America, developed its insurance arm, began to innovate in technology and started to challenge the Bank in corporate lending and structured finance – even poaching one key manager, much to Pattullo's annoyance. Profits zoomed. By 1994 they were ten times what they had been in 1991. By the end of the decade they were over £1 billion.

The staff who survived the upheaval benefited. They liked being part of a winning organisation, one lauded for its customer service rather than castigated for its failings. Their numbers increased rapidly, as did their remuneration. They were now in an environment where their progression depended on their performance, rather than length of service or 'Buggins's turn'. The non-financial benefits of working for the bank increased and care was taken to ensure that the premises in which they worked were pleasant and efficient. Staff wanted to share in the success which they were helping to achieve. Staff bonuses began to be earned regularly as targets were hit or exceeded and it began to be commonplace to take annual payments in shares rather than cash.

But other consequences were less apparent at the time. Collegiate management was now a thing of the past. Senior managers did not have time to dine together every working day, nor to take coffee together. Common values and problems discussed over coffee or lunch gave way to analysis, feasibility reports and business plans. Broad experience conceded to narrow expertise. The new HR professionals wanted to control management education of new recruits, not to outsource it to an arm's-length body like the Institute of Bankers in Scotland. They were looking to create competitive advantage, not to have their key managers go through the same courses as their competitors, so they began to organise their own training and education courses. Enrolments for the Institute's banking courses declined and with them its financial viability. It began to be regarded not as the bedrock on which Scottish banking expertise and reliability was founded, but as a fusty old institution which needed the dust blown off it. To survive, the Institute began to offer new shorter courses, like modules in mortgage appraisal and telephone selling. The old concept of the well-rounded banker who had studied all aspects of the craft was disappearing.

From its lofty perch on The Mound, Bank of Scotland contemplated these changes by its upstart rival – a stripling yet to reach its 270th birthday, whereas the Bank was preparing for its tercentenary. The older guard thought some of the changes flashy, dangerous and bound to end in tears. Younger managers looked on in awe and realised their revolution had not gone far enough.

6

The most boring bank in Britain

In 1988 Bruce Pattullo had split the top job at the Bank in two. He took the new title of Chief Executive, concentrating on growing the group by acquisition. His old title, Treasurer, which went back to the early days of the Bank, was now effectively managing director of the domestic banking and finance operation, and he gave it to his brightest lieutenant, Peter Burt.

Burt, like Pattullo, was middle-class, having been educated at Merchiston, one of the more academic Scottish public schools, and St Andrews, smallest, oldest and most exclusive of the Scottish Universities. After graduating he had taken an MBA degree at the prestigious US Wharton business school and started his career with Hewlett Packard, one of the new breed of successful computer companies where the management style could not be more different from that of Scottish banking. Hewlett Packard had open-plan offices and its shirt-sleeved employees called each other by Christian names no matter how junior or senior. Even the founders were known as Bill and Dave. Chains of command were short and hierarchy was not important. Innovation and experimentation were encouraged and so was teamwork. Returning to Edinburgh, Burt had worked briefly for a high-tech spin-out company and then for the merchant bank Edward Bates, putting together financial deals for the North Sea oil industry.

Bates had collapsed in the secondary banking crisis in the 1975, throwing Burt and his colleagues out of work. He was unemployed for three months – not a long period by today's standards – but he had recently married and had his first child and he felt the anxiety of uncertainty and repeated rejection acutely. I wrote about him during the 1990s and played down the episode in my article, for which he rebuked me. The experience had marked him and it was not something he wanted to hide.

47

In his search for a new job he had been interviewed by Bruce Pattullo, then running the Bank of Scotland Finance Company, who had not had a vacancy, but had been impressed enough to send Burt up to The Mound, where he had been hired in the new 'Special Duties' department of the International Division. It was a period when the Bank of England was restricting sterling lending so Bank of Scotland was exploring ways to lend in foreign currencies. The Bank's reputation in the oil industry was growing and Burt worked on some of the major North Sea field financings. Through ability and hard work he had worked his way up, becoming a divisional general manager in 1983 and general manager leading the international department two years later. His brain and drive made him the obvious successor to Pattullo.

Like his boss, Burt was a tennis player, but his sporting enthusiasm lay elsewhere. He was an exceptional amateur golfer and drove himself as hard on the tee as he did at work. An interviewer once asked him why he played golf and got a rhetorical question in reply: 'Why did I turn to banking?' The interviewer concluded: 'Despite him putting golf on the same level as banking, you get the impression that one is a passion and the other a job that enables him to follow his love. In golf, he says, 'You are competing against yourself, nobody else – and every so often you hit a perfect shot and there is no reason, other than human frailty, why you shouldn't do it every time.'[1] Human frailty was not something Peter Burt allowed to hold him back in banking any more than in golf. His *annus mirabilis* came in 1993 when he achieved two personal goals – getting the Bank's cost/ income ratio below 50 per cent and taking the amateur record at the championship Muirfield golf course with a round of 69, which stood for many years.

He had a sharp mind and a quick wit which could sometimes wound, not always intentionally. For some this made him difficult to work with. One non-executive director remembers that although Burt was never a bully, his rigorous reasoning could intimidate subordinates into not standing up to him or putting counter argu-ments in case a flaw was found in them. Burt was an admirer of the Hewlett Packard style of 'management by walking around', but his own style was not exactly pedestrian. David Jenkins, the Bank's Economist recalled seeing him running down the first floor corridor at the Bank's international division, tripping at the top of the stairs and falling head-over-heels right to the bottom, where, to the amazement of those watching, he sprang up and continued running to his next appointment. Jenkins was one person who was not intimidated by Burt's intellect, but admired and liked him. The two men became close colleagues and Jenkins used his sense of humour to turn Burt's barbs aside and tell him home truths if the occasion demanded. When Jenkins retired (and, sadly, died shortly afterwards), his counsel was missed.

In 1990 Tom (now Sir Tom) Risk retired and Bruce Pattullo took his place as Governor, but continued as Group Chief Executive. While Peter Burt ran the domestic banking business, Pattullo tried to find acquisitions to expand the Bank abroad. It had opened a New York branch and had long had a representative office in the Texas oil capital of Houston. Gradually it opened small offices in other large US cities, but it hankered after a slice of the huge American domestic banking market. With over 15,000 registered banks, there was no shortage of opportunities, but America had been a graveyard for British banks. One by one the Big Four London banks had bought US subsidiaries, only to fail to make them profitable and be forced to dispose of them at a loss. Even with this history, Pattullo was keen to buy a US bank, but his Scottish caution kept getting in the way.

Bank of Scotland had good contacts in Texas through its work in the oil industry. The dramatic rise in oil prices following the Middle East war had prompted a massive boom in the state, particularly in property. But a rapid plunge in the price in 1986 brought about a collapse in the market and Texas banks, which had over-extended themselves, failed at a rate unprecedented in US history. In all, 506 commercial banks went bust, including seven of the ten largest banks in Texas. The job of cleaning up the mess fell to the Federal Deposit Insurance Corporation, which restructured banks, injected new funds into those which were salvageable and offered them for sale. Bank of Scotland joined two auctions, the first in 1987 for First City Bancorp and again two years later for 20 banks, part of the Dallas-based MCorp. Either deal could have transformed the fortunes of the Bank, but it was unsuccessful in both. Pattullo later regretted his caution: 'The Presbyterian instinct means that you don't pay top dollar at the table.'

The Bank did take a minority stake in a Greek banking venture, but sold it again a couple of years later when it disapproved of the way the management were stretching their mandate. It also entered into a joint venture with a German department store group to offer credit cards, but it found Europe difficult and the US too expensive. It turned to the other side of the world. New Zealand was a small country like Scotland, spoke English and had a similar legal and financial system. In 1987 the Bank took a stake in Countrywide Building Society, taking full control in 1992. The country's financial markets were deregulating and the Bank applied its skills and balance sheet to grow the business.

It was a modest and cautious purchase, but Pattullo felt emboldened by the experience to go further. Two years later he splashed out £437 million to buy BankWest from the Government of Western Australia, which had rescued the bank in the late 1980s. Such a bold move was out of character and the stock market reacted badly, marking down Bank of Scotland shares. But Pattullo had thought it through and six months later sold 49 per cent of the new subsidiary on the Australian stock market.

The year 1995 saw Bruce Pattullo receive his knighthood and the Bank celebrate its tercentenary. The *Financial Times* Lex column marked the occasion by calling the company 'the most boring bank in Britain' which had made dullness a virtue. 'The business's steadiness helps explain 300 years of consistent profitability and more recently how the Bank has outperformed the sector by nearly 100 per cent since 1980.'[2]

Pattullo, in a piece published at the time, gave his own view of the Bank's longevity and recipe for success: 'The culture in any corporation is important and can help a bank to ride out the [trade] cycle. I would also argue strongly – and my friends in the City of London would be disappointed if I resisted the temptation to make the point – that not having one's headquarters within the Square Mile makes it slightly easier to resist some of the herd instinct and cyclical pressures to over-extend advances and rashly build up new directions . . . Bank of Scotland's Tercentenary in 1995 reminds us that our canny forebears must have resisted temptation many times over those 300 years.'

Then in a passage which emphasised the Bank's distinctive culture, where the institution was more important than the individual, he added: 'Mistakes are more likely to occur in corporate life, especially in a bank, where one individual is anxious to achieve too much in too short a space of time. There is no substitute for good old-fashioned common sense.'[3]

The following year saw the Bank again produce record profits and a return on equity of an unheard-of 36 per cent, but the market punished it for allowing its cost/income ratio to rise over 50 per cent again – although it was still the lowest of any UK bank. Pattullo was unrepentant and upbeat. The Bank had been investing in its computer systems, refurbishing its branches and boosting its finance house subsidiary. He stated, 'The point is you must not fall in love with having a low cost/income ratio if there are investment oppor-tunities and income streams to be generated, otherwise you inhibit growth for the future.'[4] Lex found his bullishness hard to take, asking: 'Is Bruce Pattullo losing his grip?' and pointing to the unaccustomed optimism of the legendarily bearish Pattullo and dour Peter Burt. It quoted an unsettled stockbroker as saying: 'We are all used to emerging from our conversations with them plunged in gloom.' There was no gloom for the next five years as the Bank rode the boom in the UK economy and increased its profits by an average of 20 per cent a year.

If there was an outward show of optimism, it was masking deeper concerns. Despite Bruce Pattullo's exhortation to his managers to pull in the deposits, they could not keep up with the Bank's success in lending. In 1978 it had been able to fund over 90 per cent of its lending from retail deposits – the savings of its customers – and a large proportion of these were in current accounts, which did not pay interest. By 1985 the amount of lending covered by branch deposits had fallen to less than half.[5] This trend had serious implications, but it would not be easy to reverse.

The Bank's deep roots in Scotland and its branches in every town and city meant that it was a natural home for the savings of thrifty Scots. Its expansion, however, had been fastest in the south of England where it did not have a branch on every high street and was not a known and trusted brand. The success of non branch-based savings products like the Money Market Cheque Account and HOBS, which had a savings account facility, could pull in amounts in thousands or even tens of thousands per customer, but lending, whether it was in mortgages or corporate loans, was in much larger sums. Competition for savings was also much fiercer than it had been 20 years before. The deregulation of building societies in 1986 had spurred a number of the larger organisations to follow aggressive expansion policies, which included competing strongly with the banks for deposits.

Another factor was that British households were saving less. Unsurprisingly the proportion of incomes which went into savings fell during the recession of the early 1990s, but worryingly for the bankers even in the relatively good economic position of the late 1990s the savings ratio was dropping rapidly – from nearly 12 per cent of household incomes in 1995 to less than six per cent five years later.

The effect on Bank of Scotland was to make it much more reliant on the wholesale money market, where banks and other financial companies and institutions lent and borrowed on a daily basis. Banks would forecast how much money they would need to meet their obligations and lend out any surplus to other banks for days, weeks or even months. Other institutions, such as pension funds and investment managers might lend for longer periods, months or years. Brokers were also active in the market, lending and borrowing on behalf of a wide range of clients from financial institutions, to governments, local authorities and other public agencies, private corporations and wealthy individuals. By the mid-1990s the ability to trade electronically had made this market wide and deep – hundreds of banks and other financial companies were active across the world, trading in many currencies as well as government and corporate bonds and 'derivatives' such as futures contracts and more esoteric products. The market functioned 24 hours a day and was continually liquid with untold billions (in whatever major currency you liked to name) moving hourly.

To borrow in this market you needed to be 'a name', meaning that you were known and trusted. Your standing determined how willing others were to lend to you and what interest rate they would charge. The Bank, with its high capital ratios and its reputation for prudence, would have no difficulty in raising the finance it needed.

But the wholesale market was capricious. Interest rates could vary widely and the perception that a bank was becoming dependent on it could affect both its credit rating and its share price. Analysts began to ask questions about the Bank's strategy and whether it could sustain the remarkable record it had achieved in increasing its lending. The question mark over how the Bank would fund itself in the future became a weakness and in the minds of Pattullo, Burt and the board it made the Bank vulnerable to takeover and the possibility of losing its independence just as it was celebrating its 300th birthday.

These fears were heightened by the shock decision by Standard Life in May 1996 to sell the one-third stake in the Bank it had acquired a decade previously from Barclays. Up to this point the Bank had been able to ignore the threat of takeover, confident that its close relationship with the life assurer would protect it. The two companies were twin pillars of the Edinburgh establishment and had representatives on each other's boards. Any potential acquirer of the Bank would have to deal with Standard Life and it was tacitly assumed that nothing would be done to jeopardise the independence of Scotland's largest company.

But times were changing and the 'squalid Scottish stitch-up' which Tom Risk had been able to pull off ten years before was no longer possible. Local loyalties and the necessity of avoiding embarrassment in the New Club, the exclusive gentlemen's club overlooking Edinburgh Castle in Princes Street, cut no ice with the professional fund managers running Standard Life's equity portfolio. The insurance company had done well out of its Bank of Scotland shares, but it represented a disproportionate element of its equity holdings and if the Bank's performance in the future faltered, the shareholding could drag down the fund's return. The announcement came without warning and immediately promoted speculation that the shares might be sold to a potential predator, such as one of the London Big Four or a foreign bank wanting to enter the UK market. The *Financial Times* Lex column declared that the decision had 'put Bank of Scotland into play'[6] and the share price jumped on speculation of a possible future bid.

The decision caused uproar in Scotland and spilled over from the business world to the political. The day after Standard Life's announcement Bruce Pattullo met Michael Forsyth, Secretary of State for Scotland in the Conservative government, who issued a statement emphasising the importance of the Bank to the Scottish economy and saying that he hoped there would not be a hostile bid. Alex Salmond, leader of the Scottish National Party, called on the Government to refer any future bid to the Monopolies and Mergers Commission. Pattullo was embarrassed and angry that he had not been given prior warning and to show his displeasure at the way the announcement had been made, he immediately quit the board of Standard Life, delivering his resignation letter in person to their offices. He said he had been affronted at the way the news had been allowed to become public and he owed it to the 18,000 employees of the Bank to show where his loyalties lay.

The speculation continued in the Scottish newspapers for a month until Standard Life placed its shares in the stock market, selling them in small lots to many different buyers rather than as a lump to a single purchaser.

There was relief on The Mound, but it did not answer the underlying problem of what to do about the increasing reliance on wholesale funding. The Bank commissioned the management consultancy McKinsey to report on its strategic options, but it confirmed what was already feared. If it carried on growing at the rate it had been, increased reliance on the inter-bank market – and therefore increased vulnerability – was inevitable. The alternative of putting the brakes on growth could have the same effect: the share price would fall, making the Bank an easier target. The only answer was to get access to a new, large source of deposits and do it quickly.

In 1997 the Bank signed an agreement with the supermarket chain Sainsbury's to create Sainsbury's Bank, which offered savings products devised and operated by the Bank, but branded and sold by the supermarket to its customers. There were no branches, customers used the telephone (and later the internet) to access their accounts and carry out transactions. It was the first such venture in the UK and within months it brought in several hundred million pounds in deposits which Bank of Scotland effectively lent to itself – useful, but not nearly enough.

So Pattullo and Burt began a series of journeys through England talking to building societies, which typically had high deposit ratios, trying to interest them in being bought or entering into a merger. Burt joked that he had eaten a 'rubber-chicken' lunch or dinner in every sizeable town from Bristol to the Scottish border. But again the Bank's cautiousness held it back. It was not the only suitor looking for a mate and the Bank balked at the prices being paid, so found itself standing on the edge of the dancefloor while others swept away the most attractive partners. Lloyds took over the Trustee Savings Bank (TSB) in 1995 and Cheltenham & Gloucester Building Society in 1997; in the same year Bristol & West Building Society was taken over by Bank of Ireland and in 2000 Barclays bought the Woolwich. The Royal Bank had also tried to form an alliance with the Midlands-based Birmingham Midshires society, only to find itself jilted when Halifax, the largest former building society and now a retail bank, bettered its offer and made off with the prize.

Bank of Scotland already had working arrangements with Halifax– a team of 20 from the Bank had been seconded to the building society for a year to help sort out problems in its commercial property lending business and the Bank, through its successful credit card processing operation, provided the back office for Halifax's Visa Card. Trying to build on this relationship, Pattullo and Burt had on two occasions tried to interest the building society's management in a closer tie-up, but both had come to nothing. On the first, Jim Birrell, chief executive of Halifax until 1993 and a dyed-in-the-wool building society man, dismissed any idea of a merger with the Bank. His successor Mike Blackburn, a former banker, did see the logic in putting Halifax's huge savings base to work with Bank of Scotland's skill at lending, but could not get his board to see it the same way.

In the end Pattullo had to admit defeat – all the lunches and dinners had been for nothing. He retired at the annual shareholders meeting in 1998 at the normal Bank retirement age of 60. In nearly two decades at the top he had transformed an inefficient and complacent company into one which was admired for the quality of its management, its talent for innovation, its growth and its prudence. The final set of results he presented to shareholders delivered another 20 per cent increase in dividends – the 26th consecutive annual increase – and showed that costs were again below 50 per cent. The Bank's shares had been the best-performing in the FTSE 100 over 1997, having achieved an 85 per cent rise in the year.

In his valedictory message he warned: 'The fast ongoing rate of change in the volatile financial services sector means that success can only flow from a pragmatic blend of opportunism tempered with experience. We are particularly wary of grandiose designs. The corporate scrapheap is already littered with other players' comprehensive blueprints that were found to be inappropriate even before they could be implemented.'[7]

He set three challenges for his successors: stay independent, with a headquarters in Edinburgh; be judged the best, even by your competitors; and 'evolve and develop the business in such a way that future generations of management always inherit the stewardship of a sound and stable business organisation with further capacity for ongoing expansion'.

7

A dark land – we need to pray for them

Pattullo's place as Governor was taken by Sir Alistair Grant, who had been on the board for five years. Grant had been born in Scotland at Haddington, a village in East Lothian a short way south of Edinburgh, but had grown up in Yorkshire. After school he had entered the retail industry and had risen to become the right-hand man of the Scottish entrepreneur Jimmy Gulliver at Argyll Foods. While Gulliver provided the energy, flair and single-minded drive, Grant was credited with bringing competence and unflappability to the relationship and with tempering his partner's impetuousness and irascibility. The two were beaten by Guinness in the highly controversial takeover of the Distillers Company, but their consolation prize was the purchase of the British arm of the Safeway supermarket chain. When Gulliver left, Grant took over as chief executive and turned it into one of the most successful retail brands in the UK.

Grant's business life had mostly been in London and his years at the top of Safeway had made him a familiar face in the City. This was one of the qualities which recommended him as Governor. Now that the Bank no longer had the comfort of knowing that a third of its shares were owned by a friendly Edinburgh life assurance company, establishing good relationships with financial institutions, fund managers and stockbrokers' analysts would become essential.

The Bank's shares were still more highly valued than those of other banks, but the shine had come off them and investors did not immediately see how it was going to overcome its funding problem and continue its phenomenal rate of growth. The *Financial Times* Lex column had reprimanded the Bank: 'If you cannot be bothered to explain, you can hardly complain if people don't understand. Bank of Scotland's sub-par rating is a legacy of years of neglecting investors when Standard Life owned nearly a third of the shares. That position has changed and the Bank has been talking more, but the message still has not been getting through.'[1]

Peter Burt had assumed the role of Chief Executive a few years earlier and had promoted Gavin Masterton to Treasurer and Chief General Manager. In 1997 the two began a reform of the structure of the bank, following a similar format to that adopted by its main rival, the Royal Bank. The old geographic fiefdoms – east, west and London – were abolished and in their place functional divisions were created – branch banking, corporate banking and risk and compliance.

The Bank was still growing, but the funding worry would not go away. Having failed to buy a building society, a couple of tentative approaches had been made to London banks, essentially suggesting that a merger could inject Scottish management expertise into a much larger under-performing balance sheet. While still Governor, Bruce Pattullo had met Robert Alexander, then chairman of Nat-West, who had dismissed the idea as 'Scotland 4, England nil'. A few years later when Barclays was going through one of its recurring changes of chief executive, Peter Burt's name had been mentioned as possible leader. He had met the chairman, but it never went any further because Burt would not come alone – making him chief executive would lead to the reverse takeover of the under-performing Barclays by the much smaller Bank of Scotland. In any case, Burt was not a member of one of the founding families, who still wielded influence in Barclays. Some executives might have been frightened by his very active management style, which contrasted with their more *laissez-faire* approach.

On the positive side, Sainsbury's Bank had proved to be much more successful than even the Bank had expected. Six months after launch it had taken £1 billion in deposits and had 500,000 customers, most new to Bank of Scotland since Sainsbury's had predominantly a south of England network. Two years later this was up to £2 billion. Opportunities to pull the same trick again in the UK were obviously limited: other major UK retailers were already joining up with other banks (e.g. Tesco with the Royal Bank of Scotland). But having been rebuffed in its attempt to buy a bank in Texas, perhaps the US would be more fertile ground? The concept of telephone banking was still novel there and the Bank began to scout for a suitable partner, one which already had a large customer base, but was not already either providing finance itself or linked to a financial institution.

The seemingly ideal partner came in early 1999 via an unlikely route. The Catholic Archbishop of New York introduced the Bank's head of US operations to Dr Pat Robertson,[2] who appeared to have everything the Scottish bankers could wish for. He was an established and successful businessman with a reputed personal fortune of $200 million and a law degree from Yale, and he had built up a private television channel with 55 million subscribers. He thus not only had the potential customers for the new venture, but a means of promoting financial services to them through his own show on his own channel. On top of that he was already familiar with the UK as a non-executive director of the fashion retailer Laura Ashley.

The Bank plunged in. Mindful of the fact that although Sainsbury's Bank had been very successful in customer acquisition, high initial start-up costs had meant that it took two years to break even, a deal was structured to reduce initial outgoings. A US company was formed – New Foundation Bank to be based in Hartford, Connecticut – with Bank of Scotland taking 60 per cent of the shares, Robertson 25 per cent and a Milwaukee company, Marshall & Ilsey, holding the remaining 15. The Bank was to provide the expertise and up to $50 million of seed capital, while Robertson did the marketing and Marshall & Ilsey processed the accounts. The bank planned to launch within six months with a massive advertising campaign. The initial target was to take $300 million in deposits, rising to $3 billion after three years – a modest aim if the Sainsbury pattern could be replicated. The deal was initially greeted with enthusiasm in the US, with the *Milwaukee Journal Sentinel* claiming that it would create 300 new jobs in the city.

Robertson was to chair the new bank and commented that 'by a nice coincidence' his ancestors had left Scotland for America in 1695, the same year in which Bank of Scotland had been conceived. The three partners made applications to the relevant US Federal and State authorities for a banking licence.

What the Bank had not realised was that Robertson was a very controversial figure. It was already known that besides being a businessman he was a pastor in a Baptist Church based in South Virginia and that he led an organisation known as the US Christian Coalition. He had been an unsuccessful Republican candidate for the Presidency and his television station was the overtly religious Christian Broadcasting Network. What had not been appreciated was that Robertson was a man of divisive views who expressed them regularly and forcefully on his own television show. In particular he condemned homosexuals, but he was not much in favour of feminists or members of religions other than his own.

The Bank announced the venture in a low-key press release faxed to newspapers at the beginning of March. Although it used the headline 'Moneylenders in the Temple' in its first report *The Scotsman*, the Bank's local daily in Edinburgh, was broadly complimentary, calling the deal 'low risk with plenty of upside'.[3] But the news alerted gay rights groups in the US who were quickly in touch with their UK counterparts, complaining about the unsuitability of a man with Robertson's views becoming a partner of the hitherto upright Bank. Before long the Jewish Anti-Defamation League had joined the protest, citing several speeches and remarks Robertson had allegedly made. By the following day *The Scotsman* was calling Robertson 'a far-right zealot' and boycotts and pickets outside Bank offices were being organised.

Momentum developed with surprising speed; a day later *The Scotsman* was reporting that customers were closing their accounts. Journalists were digging up quotes from Robertson not only criticising homosexuals and Jews, but Hindus and Muslims as well. On the fourth day the newspaper carried a leading article under the headline: 'The lure of the false prophet.' It declared that Robertson was not just a maverick, but a deliberately offensive man who had equated homosexuality with Satanism and Nazism and believed that liberals were involved in a worldwide Masonic conspiracy to subjugate mankind to the devil. 'In a British context his views are insane. It is hard to understand how a significant minority of Americans can take his views seriously.'[4] Robertson's flair for business was unquestioned, the paper added, before asking pointedly of the Bank: 'Does one of Scotland's most prestigious institutions really feel comfortable that it is now intimately associated with a man who earnestly insists that homosexuals want to destroy Christianity, that feminists kill their children and practise witchcraft and that the United Nations is an evil organisation?'

That afternoon, the Edinburgh *Evening News* reported that a meeting of students at Edinburgh University calling for a mass withdrawal of accounts from the Bank had attracted 70 people. The *Daily Mail* in London joined the attack and the Scottish tabloid *Daily Record* urged

'Don't bank with hate peddling preacher Pat'. Only the *Financial Times* offered the Bank any support, saying that although at first the unlikely alliance of the outspoken Southern Baptist and the taciturn Scottish Presbyterians sounded like a hoax, Robertson offered arguably as strong and trusted a brand in the US as Sainsbury did in the UK.[5]

The Bank's public relations department was completely unprepared for the row and didn't know how to react. On top of that the Bank's two top executives, Peter Burt and Gavin Masterton, were reluctant to speak in public and the Governor, Sir Alistair Grant, had other more pressing concerns. He was fighting cancer, a battle which was later that year to force him to step down from the post and hand over to one of the Deputy Governors, Sir Jack Shaw. Burt was nonplussed by the furore. Describing Robertson, he declared: 'He is a charismatic personality. He is not a hellfire and brimstone preacher and he is not a John Knox. He is of Scottish origin and not like the traditional image of the Scottish preacher damning the faithful from the pulpit. I would say he comes across as a very kindly man.'

But the controversy would not die down. Academic staff called on Edinburgh University to close its account, trade unions, local authorities, charities and the Anglican Bishop of Edinburgh joined the protest and a group of MPs talked about lodging a protest with the Comptroller of the Currency in the US. Gay protestors picketed the Bank of Scotland stand at the Ideal Home Exhibition in London. In April the Bank unveiled another set of record profits and a dividend rise and a defiant Burt told the annual meeting: 'I quite understand that some people feel uncomfortable, but from a commercial point of view I don't think we have any alternative and an individual's personal religious views don't form the basis on which the Bank makes its business and commercial judgements, nor should it.' He added that the Bank had received 'a few hundred letters, but not one church, or trade union or university has registered a complaint'.

The attempt to quieten the row proceeded on two fronts. A lawyer acting for Pat Robertson sent a strongly worded letter to newspapers marked 'not for publication' and warning them of consequences should they describe him as 'an extremist, bigot, racist or anti-semite'. *The Scotsman*, undaunted, printed the letter together with a catalogue of quotes from Robertson illustrating its charges against the preacher. Meanwhile a crisis management specialist hired by the Bank to beef up its public-relations effort organised a trip to the US for Scottish journalists, paying $3,000 a head to fly them to meet Robertson in person. He received them on his 700-acre wooded estate at Virginia Beach and told them in emollient tones that he was frankly appalled at the attacks on him coming from the British media. 'Suddenly to be described as a Bible thumping fundamentalist is something I don't understand,' he said. 'I am a man of integrity and honour.'

The Bank dearly wished the row to go away. It was overshadowing everything else it was doing, including selling the small New Zealand subsidiary it had bought, making £175 million profit on the deal, and launching banking services via 5,000 Australian pharmacists, which passed off unnoticed.

For a while it looked as though the strategy was working. Press comment died down and protest groups struggled to keep it in the headlines. The crisis might have passed had Robertson not decided to use his TV show to investigate the current state of Scotland. He sent a reporter to the country and commented on the unflattering picture which came back. Scotland, he said, was a 'dark land' and the contrast with the glorious history of the country was 'kinda frightening'. He went on: 'In Europe the big word is "tolerance". You tolerate everything. Homosexuals are riding high in the media and in Scotland you cannot believe how strong the homosexuals are. Heroes of the calibre of John Knox no longer exist, spelling possible doom for the nation. And that could happen. It could go back to the darkness very easily. It used to be called Christendom and the Church of Scotland was so noted for their piety. The Edinburgh University was a great cultural centre of theology. I don't know, we need to pray for them . . .'[6]

Predictably the programme, widely reported in Britain in the press and on television and radio, provoked a renewed onslaught on the Bank. The Church of Scotland, the Roman Catholic Church, the Scottish TUC and even the Scottish Tourist Board, fearful perhaps of losing the business of God-fearing Southern Baptists, joined the chorus. The charities ActionAid and Guide Dogs for the Blind threatened to pull out of their commercial relationships with the Bank. Newspaper interest which was dimming, was suddenly reignited. Under the heading 'No place for intolerance', *The Scotsman* leader on 1 June linked Robertson's views to those of football bigots and declared that there was no place for either in modern Scotland.

The Bank issued a typically cautious statement: 'We have reviewed the content and the context of the broadcast made by Dr Robertson and are considering the position.' Bank of Scotland shares fell by 4 per cent.

Clearly the game was up. Reputational damage was outweighing the potential upside and rumours began to circulate in the stock market that the deal would be killed. On 3 June Peter Burt flew to the US for a showdown with Pat Robertson in a hotel in Boston and Bank of Scotland shares rose modestly on the news. Two days later it was confirmed that the deal was dead; the Bank bought out Robertson's shares for a reported $10 million and chalked it up to experience.

The *Financial Times in* an editorial under the heading 'God's Bankers', said there had been a distinct element of comedy about the affair and pointed out the irony that despite Robertson's characterisation as a country of sexual licence, Scotland had waited 13 years after England before legalising homosexual activity between consenting adults in private. 'In the goldfish bowl of world business anonymity is impossible. Mr Robertson knows his market – it would scarcely pay him to tailor his views for a small country in Northern Europe. Partnership is all very well, but the trick is to ensure that there is an identity of interest and balance of power.'[7]

Peter Burt rejected any suggestion that heads should roll because of the fiasco. 'If you try to do things, sometimes you get it wrong, but if you execute everyone who tries something and gets it wrong pretty soon you have no one who tries to do anything. That is exactly the wrong way around.'[8] At the annual general meeting a week later acting Governor Sir Jack Shaw made the same point: 'Our judgement was wrong and we apologise, but the Robertson decision was reviewed by the board over a year – any idea that we should be seeking scapegoats is totally foreign to our nature.'

8

No turning back at Derby

In November 1745 a Scots army led by Bonnie Prince Charlie crossed the border and headed for London. They had been victorious in their native land, defeating an English army at the battle of Prestonpans. They easily captured Carlisle and pressed on southwards, so that by 4 December they had reached the bridge over the River Trent at Swarkestone, near Derby. There self-doubt began to overtake them. Rumours had been building of a massive English force waiting for them and after a day of arguing with his council of advisers, the Prince reluctantly led the retreat back to Scotland.

In fact there was no English army. London was in panic at the imminent arrival of the feared Scots and King George II's courtiers were loading his possessions onto a ship ready to flee. What might have been had Charles Edward Stuart not turned back at Derby is one of the great 'what ifs' of Scottish history. As it was, although he captured Stirling and achieved one more victory at Falkirk Muir, his retreat gave the Government time to regroup. His army was destroyed at the battle of Culloden and he spent the rest of his life in embittered alcoholic exile.

More than 250 years on, the bankers on The Mound were determined not to turn back before London. What was preoccupying Peter Burt and Gavin Masterton after the Pat Robertson debacle was something much more important and dramatic than an American telephone banking venture – they began to contemplate a move which had the potential to double the size of the Bank at a stroke.

Having failed to find a partner among the building societies, Bank of Scotland had also tried to forge a friendly alliance with one of the London Big Four. Two approaches to NatWest had been rebuffed and talks between Peter Burt and Peter Middleton, Chairman of Barclays, had come to nothing.

A dramatic way out of the impasse was suggested by Will Samuel, who, as head of corporate finance with the long-established and revered London merchant bank Schroders, was an adviser to Bank of Scotland. He also had a personal link; his sister Lesley Knox was a non-executive on the Bank board. If NatWest could not be interested in a friendly merger, suggested Samuel, why not launch a hostile bid?

This was a radical suggestion. Hostile bids were never easy in any industry, but especially not in banking. The Bank of England, which had overall responsibility for the banking sector, was known not to look kindly on such moves and the last openly hostile full bid – by HSBC for Royal Bank of Scotland 18 years before – had been blocked by the Government. There was also the difference in scale. Bank of Scotland was less than half the size of NatWest. There was no way it could raise the resources for a cash bid, so it would have to persuade NatWest's institutional shareholders – the professionals who managed investments on behalf of pension funds and insurance companies – to accept Bank of Scotland shares in payment. In effect Burt and Masterton would be asking the City of London to trust them to make a much better job of managing NatWest's assets than it could itself. They had proved they could do it in Scotland, but would the City accept that they could operate at three times the scale in the less familiar English market?

Samuel argued that NatWest's management record had been so awful for so long that shareholders would be ready to take the risk. The London bank had lurched from crisis to disaster with amazing regularity. After nearly going bust in the secondary banking crisis of the 1970s, during the following decade it had become embroiled in a financial scandal which resulted in an investigation by the Department of Trade and the resignation of several board members, including the chairman. Ill-judged acquisitions in Canada and the US had not worked and been sold at a loss, and the domestic banking business in the UK was slow and inefficient. In an astonishingly arrogant move, the bank had built the NatWest Tower, an ostentatious headquarters in the City of London, which until the development of Canary Wharf was the tallest building in Britain. The building had a footprint in the shape of the bank's logo and an art gallery at the bottom which housed its extensive picture collection. (It was only occupied for a few years before Irish terrorists severely damaged it with a bomb.) The latest disaster, losses uncovered in the investment banking business, had again led to calls for top resignations.

By 1999 NatWest had a new chairman in Sir David Rowland, who had made his name leading the Lloyds of London insurance market, but also a long-serving chief executive, Derek Wanless. He was regarded by the City as undoubtedly clever – he had studied maths at Cambridge and was a qualified statistician as well as a banker – but far too nice. He lacked the ruthlessness to deal with the bank's inflated costs.

Peter Burt was convinced not only that Bank of Scotland's management could run NatWest, but also that he had a sporting chance of convincing the City to back him. But the London bank would be a huge mouthful to swallow. Samuel suggested a plan which he thought would halve the risk and double the chances of success, so in August 1999 Burt walked down The Mound from the Bank's headquarters in the Old Town, crossed Princes Street into the New Town and called on his main rival, the chief executive of the Royal Bank of Scotland – now Sir George Mathewson, after his knighthood in the New Year's Honours List. Burt's proposal was that they should co-operate in a joint attack.

On paper the plan looked watertight. Both Scottish banks were much smaller than NatWest, with the Royal Bank being slightly larger than Bank of Scotland, but together they were roughly equal to the London bank. Bank of Scotland had a 20-year record of management competence and superior financial performance behind it and, since the Mathewson revolution, the Royal could easily match it. By contrast NatWest was a serial under-performer. The plan was essentially to capture and dismember NatWest, injecting a double dose of strong Scottish management to drive down costs and boost sales.

Mathewson had transformed the performance of the Royal Bank, but faced the same problem as Burt: how to a make step change and secure a bigger share of the English market against the entrenched hegemony of the Big Four – LloydsTSB, Midland (now owned by the international group HSBC), Barclays and NatWest. He too had held talks with Barclays' chairman Peter Middleton, but had come away with the same answer as Burt. Mathewson believed Barclays and NatWest were in the same position that the Royal Bank had been in a decade previously, with the difference that they did not want to take the steps necessary to pull themselves out of it.

He was sufficiently interested in Burt's joint bid idea to want to explore it further and small groups of top executives from both banks started meeting in secret to plan the attack and the division of the spoils.

At the same time, each bank individually began to work out how it would manage its share of the acquisition. Gavin Masterton, for the Bank, was already planning his moves and for the Royal Mathewson's new recruit, Fred Goodwin, was doing the same. Masterton had worked his way up through the Bank in the time-honoured fashion. He had joined the old British Linen Bank straight from school, taken a correspondence course to get his certificate from the Scottish Banking Institute and been moved around by the bank to gain experience. He had joined Bank of Scotland when it acquired British Linen and progressed quickly up the management chain. Recognising his potential, the Bank had put him through Harvard University's Advanced Management Programme.

Goodwin, by contrast, was one of the new breed of late entrants to banking from other professions. He had read law at Glasgow University and then trained as an accountant, rising quickly to become a partner in the international firm Touche Ross. His sharp forensic mind had made him the ideal candidate to lead the liquidation of the Bank of Credit and Commerce International (BCCI), a vast sprawling multinational which had collapsed after a complex fraud. His skilled handling of that job had convinced National Australia Bank to hire him to head their two UK banking operations, Clydesdale and Yorkshire Bank, where his cost-cutting had earned him the nickname 'Fred the Shred'. He was being lined up to move to Australia and the top post in NAB when Mathewson lured him to the Royal Bank as his number two.

Both Scottish banks were ambitious to continue their expansion, but to do that they needed access to the English market, which was ten times the size of Scotland. In particular they coveted the vast deposit base which NatWest had garnered through its 1,700 branches. The Royal Bank had 200 English branches, but the Bank had only 25. Dividing the NatWest total between them would enable each of them to leap decades of organic growth.

The talks continued for a few weeks but as they began to work out the detail it became clear to both sides that the joint bid idea had a fundamental flaw – they both wanted the same parts of NatWest and neither was willing to allow the other to take the largest share or the best bits. However united they might be during the bid battle, afterwards they had to become competitors again. The talks ended in failure. Mathewson wanted Burt to agree not to bid alone; Burt was unwilling to do so, but he still faced the problem of convincing his own non-executive directors to go ahead with a lone bid.

In a board meeting Burt told his colleagues that the Bank was too small to survive on its own. It lacked the scale necessary to invest enough in technology, marketing or management to be able to compete and would sooner or later be swallowed up by a larger predator. 'Whatever we thought of Peter's analysis, we had to admit that it was well researched and the board accepted it,' recalls one director. 'But we still had questions over a bid for NatWest. Did we want it? If we did, could we get it, given that it was over twice our size? On that we were very much in the hands of our advisers. If we went for it and failed to get it would we be in play ourselves? If we got it, could we manage it?'

On the last question, Gavin Masterton, whom Burt had proposed to run the combined bank, told the board he had already identified 100 key managers from within Bank of Scotland and his first priority would be to do the same in NatWest. They would form the core team to lead the integration of NatWest into the enlarged group and the transformation of its performance.

Board opinion was moving in Burt's direction – 'We were thinking, "if we don't do this now we will never do anything" ' – when NatWest made the decision for them. At the beginning of September 1999 the London bank announced an agreed takeover of the insurance giant Legal & General at the high price of £10.7 billion. This was a now-or-never moment for Bank of Scotland. NatWest at twice the size was already a big pill to swallow; if it were to succeed in acquiring the insurance company it would become more than three times Bank of Scotland's size and well out of reach. But the announcement also created an opportunity. Institutional investors did not like the Nat-West proposal and began to criticise it openly: the London bank was paying too much, previous acquisitions had not been well-managed and had destroyed value rather than creating it, and NatWest's management should be concentrating on getting their existing business right before taking on new ones. They showed their displeasure by selling NatWest shares and over the next two weeks the value of the bank on the stock market fell by more than a quarter, making it more digestible for the Bank.

If they were going to move, the Bank team did not have much time. NatWest had called a special shareholders' meeting for early October to approve the Legal & General deal. To persuade NatWest's investors to reject it, Bank of Scotland had to be ready to make a public announcement of a credible and detailed alternative proposal. The Bank's internal team had done some work, but there had been little thought about the technical aspects of an offer. What was the right price? It would have to be high enough to convince shareholders to back the Bank, but low enough to be affordable without compromising future performance. How was the bid to be funded? Mostly it would have to be a share-for-share offer: investors would be asked to swap their NatWest shares for Bank of Scotland shares, but it would not be a straight swap and the question of how many new shares investors would get for their old shares would determine the balance in the new enlarged group. NatWest shareholders would inevitably end up with the majority of the shares, but would it be 60, 65 or 70 per cent? If they got too much, the Bank's existing shareholders might feel cheated and not support the deal.

The answers to these questions would come partly through doing the arithmetic, but the rest had to be 'gut feel'. This was where the Bank's investment banking and stockbroking advisers were expected to earn their large fees. Their knowledge, contacts and experience would help judge the mood of the market and pitch the price at the right level, but the Bank would not have Will Samuel on its side. Schroders was acting for Legal & General and so was compromised.

A bid would not be attractive without some cash in it and the amount was another issue needing fine judgement, but whatever the level it would be a whopping sum for the Bank to raise. To do so it would have to issue loan notes – a way of borrowing from the stock market. Shareholders would want to know that the Bank could do this before accepting any offer, so the issue would have to be underwritten. A group of investment banks would be persuaded – for a fee – to guarantee to buy the loan notes and provide the cash if, for some reason, the Bank could not sell them in the market.

In addition to these high-level decisions there was a huge amount of routine work to be done in the preparation of documents, the fulfilment of regulatory, legal and accounting requirements, preparation for making the announcement, presentations to be made to investors and stockbrokers, public relations strategies and so on. The clock was already ticking. Peter Burt virtually moved into the Canary Wharf offices of Credit Suisse First Boston, the international investment bank which was to be one of the lead advisers.

Planning a massive hostile takeover is like planning a military campaign. The generals have a team working out what their moves should be, but they also have a shadow team role-playing the management and advisers of the victim company. How will they respond? What will be our reaction to any counter-moves they make? There may also be third or fourth teams playing the parts of other companies which might be provoked by the bid into joining the fray, either on the side of NatWest as so-called 'white knights' or as opportunists attempting to snatch the prize for themselves. At the back of everyone's mind was the thought that London banking had been too cosy and too complacent for too long and that a bold move like this from Bank of Scotland could signal the start of a wave of consolidation within the sector which would bring other, possibly bigger and better resourced, opponents into the battle.

As in any military campaign, surprise is a valuable tactic. So preparations have to take place under strict secrecy, with special passes to get into parts of the adviser's offices and codewords used for predator and prey. The timing of the announcement is also important. You want to choose a time convenient to you, but one which would wrong-foot your opponent and any possible counter-bidders. As it happened, an ideal opportunity was coming up at the end of September. The annual meetings of the International Monetary Fund and the World Bank in Washington are usually attended by the chairmen and chief executives of all major commercial and central banks and the events that go on around them, dinners and receptions, are fertile ground for informal networking and deal-broking. Everybody who is anybody in banking would be there. Peter Burt and Sir Jack Shaw were due to attend, but quietly they cancelled their air tickets and persuaded Sir Bob Reid, one of the Deputy Governors of the Bank, to go instead. Discreet inquiries were made to find out when Sir David Rowland and Derek Wanless, NatWest's chairman and chief executive, planned to cross the Atlantic: Sunday 26 September.

Most contested takeovers do not come completely out of the blue. They are preceded by talks between the boards of the bidder and the target aimed at trying to secure agreement. Only when those talks break down does the previously friendly and coaxing bidder turn hostile. In this case NatWest was given no warning. A board which had already cast itself as predator with its own bid for Legal & General was hardly likely abruptly to swap roles and accept the part of prey. In any case, Bank of Scotland had already been rebuffed twice in the recent past and was not going to subject itself to the third rejection.

Initially the announcement of the Bank's bid was planned for Thursday 23 September, but the supporting documentation was not ready and it had to be put back for a day. There followed 24 hours of intense nail-biting, waiting to see if the news leaked, but the security held fast. That evening Burt left the investment bankers, lawyers and brokers working on the documents and went to bed early, but he could not sleep. The adrenalin was already pumping around his body and his feet were so cold that he had to put on two pairs of socks. He was told by his doctor brother later that this was usual in people in a heightened state of expectation and was the origin of the phrase 'to get cold feet'. But there were to be no cold feet and no turning back.

Takeover announcements have to be made before the Stock Exchange opens in the morning and dealers get to their screens. Traditionally, the first news is delivered in a call from chairman to chairman and the contacts books of the top city advisers contain the ex-directory home numbers of every FTSE chair and CEO. At dawn on Friday 24 September Sir Jack Shaw psyched himself up to make an historic call. He would announce the largest-ever takeover bid for a British bank and torpedo NatWest's planned takeover of Legal & General, which was acknowledged to be Sir David Rowland's idea. At the very least it would ruin Rowland's day, but it had the potential to cut short his banking career.

At 6.30 a.m. Shaw dialled Rowland's home, only to be told that Rowland had gone out for an early morning run and would call back. The *Financial Times* later reported that in fact Rowland was still in bed, trying to decide whether to go for a run or not, but in any case a few minutes later he returned the call and Shaw delivered his bombshell.[1]

By 6.45 a.m. Rowland had called Wanless, who called his senior executives and summoned them into the office for an urgent meeting. For most it was merely an early commute, but for Bernard Horn, NatWest's head of group operations, it meant a scrambled return from Lake Como, where he was celebrating his wife's birthday. Also called was Terry Eccles, the senior executive of the investment bank J.P. Morgan, which was advising NatWest on the Legal & General deal.

At 7.15 a.m. first news of the bid hit dealers' screens.

At 9 a.m. there was a hastily arranged meeting between Bank of Scotland's senior team and their NatWest counterparts. The Scots outlined their proposal, the English listened politely, but were non-committal and the meeting ended quickly. Another part of the ritual over.

Peter Burt then hurried to a meeting of stockbrokers' analysts. These were key people, experts in banking and finance who followed every major company in the sector, dissecting figures and trends, assessing strengths and weaknesses, predicting future performance. They would all write notes to their clients on the merits of the bid and eventually, when the campaign was nearing its end, would make recommendations to accept or reject. They were not decision-makers, but they were key influencers and their reaction on this morning could determine the course of the battle. One of the requirements for their job is that they take nothing at face value and they tend to cultivate a professional cynicism. They are not often given to collective enthusiasm.

The Bank of Scotland chief executive gave a presentation which was characteristic: it was detailed, thorough, dense with facts and evidence and driven by a remorseless logic, spiced with occasional touches of humour. Afterwards the analysts asked questions and then, unexpectedly, at the close of the meeting they rose to their feet and gave Burt a standing ovation. In his haste to get on to the next event he had already left the room, didn't notice and had to be told about it afterwards, but the campaign could not have had a better start than this.

9

Morituri te salutant*

The City loves big hostile takeovers. Contrary to the impression given by films such as *Wall Street* and *Margin Call*, much of the daily grind in the financial sector is routine, predictable, boring and repetitive – relieved by a long Friday evening session in the wine bar. Unsolicited bid battles, which can run for months, bring a period of unpredictability and excitement and everyone can join in. Some will be closely and directly involved. The companies on either side will have one or perhaps two principal advisory firms from among the handful of investment banks which comprise the global elite. The team directing the campaign may be fairly small, but everyone on the staff will feel they have a part in it, down to the receptionist at the door. Bids mean fees and fees mean bonuses. Then there will be one or two stockbrokers, big City firms of lawyers and accountants and, of course, public relations companies. The battle will be fought at many levels. These days the skirmishes take place on computer screens, but in the late 1990s they still happened in the financial pages of the newspapers and magazines which carried stories every day.

At any one time there can be dozens or perhaps hundreds of people working full-time on each side of a bid. And this is only in London. If the bidder or the target company has interests abroad or its shares are traded on markets in New York, Paris, Frankfurt or Tokyo, there may have to be teams in those cities too.

The fees are huge. In 1999 Bank of Scotland was budgeting for £82.5 million, with a further £105 million on top to go to the Government in stamp duty should it be successful. The money goes to boost corporate profits and annual bonuses for the City's stars, but it also trickles down a long way. Specialist financial printers get extra for rush jobs done under strict security, newspapers get an

---

* We who are about to die salute you – motto of the gladiators of Ancient Rome.

unexpected surge in advertising revenue, courier companies have cyclists and motorbike riders on standby, even contract caterers benefit from the sandwich meals brought in to be consumed in overheated rooms in the middle of the night. These events are so essential to the well-being of a major financial centre like London that the top advisory firms try to stimulate them into happening whenever possible by sliding a list of possible bid targets across the desks of their clients. Not for nothing are the most successful corporate financiers known as 'Rainmakers'.

There were ironies in the teams lined up on either side in this bid. Schroders, who had advised the Bank on its earlier approaches to NatWest, was now in the opposite camp, as was Cazenove, whom the Bank had backed when it decided to stay independent. The firm had told the Bank then 'We will never go against you.' Now they were. On the Bank's team, advising in the US, was the Wall Street investment boutique Gleacher, run by Peter Burt's old golfing partner Eric Gleacher. The firm had previously been owned by NatWest and Gleacher himself still had a large personal holding in the London bank.

When a bid happens everybody tries to get aboard the bandwagon. The advisers to firms not directly involved will call suggesting that they keep a watching brief – for a modest retainer of course. Other big banks and newly demutalised building societies were consulting their brokers and investment bankers. Analysts and fund managers who are normally reticent and guarded in print are able to let themselves go when called by a journalist for an unattributable quote. Some may be close to the action, but even those who are not feel entitled to an opinion. Those not important enough to be telephoned will find an audience for their views propping up the bar in Balls Brothers, Corney & Barrow or El Vino on Friday evening.

At one level takeover battles are governed by strict rules. The stern watchdogs are the Stock Exchange and the City Takeover Panel, who insist that form is followed, that documents are issued, that statements are supported by evidence, that rigid timetables are adhered to and that there is no mischief-making in the form of companies suggesting they might bid, when they have no intention or lack the wherewithal to do so. The Takeover Panel cannot send anyone to prison, but woe betide any investment banker, stockbroker or lawyer hauled before it for a reprimand. His – or, extremely rarely, her – chances of getting the next lucrative deal will be severely damaged.

Formal documents have to be prepared – at least an offer document from the bidder and a formal response from the target – but perhaps more if the terms of the offer are changed or another bidder enters the battle. These are not 'easy reads'; comprising multiple A4 pages of dense text unrelieved by colour, illustrations or eye-catching design, they conform to a set format, with information in set places. Every fact and assertion stated has to be checked and supported by evidence. This is policed by a team of lawyers.

I was once on the receiving end of this process. Each executive from my company was summoned in turn into the boardroom where the legal verification team (soon known throughout the building as the 'Spanish Inquisition') demanded documentary proof of every fact proposed for the draft document, even down to the three-line biography of each of the directors. The insistence that I support my claim to qualifications resulted in a floor-to-attic search which eventually revealed that the 'empty' cardboard tube my wife had thrown into the recycling bin actually contained my degree certificates. For one of my fellow managers it was not so simple. He failed to provide proof of a claimed university degree and was quietly dropped – not only from the document, but also from the board.

This is the formal process and is usually unseen by spectators not actually involved. But the contest also takes place at another level in a series of one-to-one clashes – chairman against chairman, chief executive against chief executive, investment banker against investment banker – and mob struggles of one PR company against another. This is the gladiatorial spectacle the City loves, fought in wordplay rather than swordplay in the columns of the newspaper financial pages and the one-line flashes on the newswires. The press likes to personalise the process and often reduces it to a macho hand-to-hand struggle between chief executives. For those fronting the bid it can become a time of intense public exposure. They are in the public eye and expected to produce a new accusation or a new rebuttal every day. Some thrive on the experience, others find it extremely stressful.

For those most directly involved it is a long and exhausting process with no let up. Mondays to Fridays will start with early breakfast meetings with advisers to review the progress of the battle and assess the latest move by the other side. Then there will come a relentless round of press conferences, meetings with analysts and endless presentations to shareholders and investors. I went through a similar process a few years before the Bank of Scotland bid and, with two colleagues, made 60 one-hour presentations in two weeks. We started by trying to vary what we said to add some variety and interest, but by the end we were on autopilot, mechanically saying the same words in the same order in the same monotone each time.

In the biggest battles there may have to be teleconferences with the Far East in the early morning and with New York in the evening. On Saturdays PR advisers will be pressing for new lines for the Sunday papers and on Sundays they will be hassling for newer lines for the Monday papers. The principal combatants are sustained throughout the campaign on a cocktail of adrenalin, testosterone (there are still very few women involved, and were even fewer in 1999) and caffeine. Meals are often taken on the move or during meetings. Alcohol dulls the senses and is not taken until the nightcap whisky before a thin, exhausted sleep.

Bank of Scotland's timing was impeccable. The IMF and World Bank meetings would not start until the Monday, but many senior bankers were either already in the US on Friday 24 September or on their way. The Royal Bank's Sir George Mathewson had taken a few days off and crossed the Atlantic early to watch the opening of the Ryder Cup, the annual golf tournament between Europe and the United States. That morning he was among the crowd on the edge of the green at the Country Club, Brookline, near Boston. Club rules dictate that all mobile telephones must be switched off during play, but Mathewson had never been one to follow rules and took the call telling him of the Bank's bid. He cut short his vacation and flew back for a hurriedly arranged meeting with The Royal Bank's City advisers, Goldman Sachs and Merrill Lynch. They were, he told his colleagues later, 'gagging for us to make a counter bid'. Mathewson, however, decided to hold his fire. He was not the only one to catch an early plane home. Peter Ellwood, LloydsTSB's chief abandoned the IMF meetings and flew back that Sunday.

The bid sent a shockwave through the City. An early morning flash from Reuters declared: 'Bank of Scotland has torn up the handbook on how to achieve a British financial services merger and thrown the pieces to the wind.' An unnamed analyst was quoted as saying: 'This is about as hostile as you can get without going up and punching the other side in the face. The law of the jungle now presides.'[1]

Meanwhile the war of words had started. Bank of Scotland's team were busy undermining the record of the NatWest management and rubbishing their future strategy. Peter Burt called NatWest's plan to buy Legal & General an expensive and ill-judged diversion from the urgent work the English bank ought to be undertaking to improve its core banking business and reduce costs. Bank of Scotland would offer shareholders a real choice between its own 'value adding' proposals and NatWest's 'value destroying' plans. If successful it would sell NatWest's peripheral businesses, the fund management group Gartmore, Ulster Bank and the American investment bank Greenwich, and return the proceeds to shareholders. This would enable it to concentrate on the basic banking business.

For NatWest Sir David Rowland hit back, describing the bid as unsolicited, unwelcome, ill-thought-out and undervaluing NatWest. Peter Burt, he declared, was long on rhetoric and short on substance. There was a big difference, Rowland declared patronisingly, between running a corner shop and running Tesco.[2]

Analysts friendly to NatWest were roped in to say that the bid was opportunistic. 'I don't think this is a sincere bid,' said one anonymous source. 'It is a spoiling tactic against the Legal & General bid and a PR exercise following the Pat Robertson fiasco.' A more measured and perceptive comment was given by Justin Urquhart-Stewart of Barclays Stockbrokers, who, as a Scot, knew the Bank pretty well. 'This move is almost as defensive as it is aggressive and it is a good strategic play by a medium-sized bank. One reason they are doing this is as a pre-emptive action, it moves their share price and it shows they are aggressive and gives out a clear message to anyone who might be thinking of them as a takeover target.'

Most comment, however, favoured the Bank. The financial news service of Reuters said that the bid had 'stunned and delighted' the City. 'A David of British banking has taken on one of its Goliaths and the delighted spectators think it can win.' The following morning's newspapers were equally enthusiastic. *The Times* said the bid had been timed to perfection and the paper contrasted the return shareholders had received from Bank of Scotland over the past decade with that from NatWest. A hundred pounds invested in the Bank at the beginning of 1989 was worth £1,515 a decade later, whereas had it been invested in NatWest it would be worth less than half that at £745.

The *Financial Times* Lex column said it was hard to feel sympathy for NatWest and when it came to a comparison of the management of both banks it was an easy choice. The Sunday papers were also almost unanimous in being equally complimentary. Only the Glasgow *Sunday Mail* came up with an original line, first reporting that Gavin Masterton had taken Saturday afternoon off from the bid battle to see the 'Pars' (Dunfermline Athletic football team, where he was on the board) get beaten 2:1 by Ayr United, and then warning that if Bank of Scotland succeeded in winning NatWest it would inherit Coutts, the exclusive private bank, and with it the overdrafts of Sarah, Duchess of York, and Elizabeth, the Queen Mother (reputed to be £4 million, said the paper, run up on horse racing and fine wines.)

Over the next few days the Bank gave details of how it would transform the performance of its target. A massive £1 billion a year was to be taken out of costs by eliminating duplication between the two banks and reducing the number of processing centres from 54 to nine. Most of NatWest's branches were to be moved from Victorian or Edwardian buildings to shopping malls and there was to be a much more aggressive sales policy. Gavin Masterton let his guard slip when he told journalists that Bank staff were trained so that as soon as a customer entered a branch he or she was 'targeted'. He quickly corrected that to 'approached', but the message was clear: under Scottish management NatWest would be driven much harder. The underlying principle of the Bank's new management style, he added, would be 'focus, focus, focus'. Brandishing his Scottish credentials, Peter Burt said that NatWest's bloated and expensive head office would be reduced to a brass plate in London. The combined bank would be run from Edinburgh.

The Bank team attacked the philosophy behind NatWest's proposed tie-up with Legal & General – the alleged benefits which would come from 'bancassurance', a fashionable manufactured word to describe putting banks and insurance companies together. In retaliation NatWest leaked to the newspapers the fact that Peter Burt himself had had dinner with the Legal & General chief executive to discuss some sort of tie-up. It was true, Burt admitted, the two had met, but he had decided that it was not worth pursuing. 'You don't have to own a cow in order to sell milk' – you did not have to own an insurance company in order to sell its products through branches.

When NatWest issued its response to the Bank's formal bid there was a distinct feeling of déjà vu. It was now promising to sell exactly the same subsidiaries as Bank of Scotland had said it would sell; it would give its branches a makeover, cut costs by freezing recruitment and salary rises; the art gallery in NatWest Tower was to be closed and the bank would end its sponsorship of an annual art prize. To answer criticism of its management, it would recruit a number two to chief executive Derek Wanless. Burt described the new strategy as a 'copycat' defence and the City was distinctly underwhelmed. Nat-West had no answer to the question that if these were such good things to do, why had it waited until Bank of Scotland had suggested them before proposing them itself? It was too little, too late and it left Derek Wanless in charge – a man associated in the City with NatWest's years of underperformance.

The special meeting of shareholders called by NatWest to approve the Legal & General purchase went ahead on 8 October. It was a mournful affair. Professional investors holding the vast majority of NatWest's shares did not bother to turn up and the handful of small shareholders who did attend were thanked by Rowland for coming as, he added, it would have been a bleak occasion had the hall been completely empty. They heard the formal announcement of what the City had known since the morning of the bid – the L&G deal was dead. After the meeting the NatWest non-executive directors met with David Mayhew, senior partner of Cazenove. Executive directors were pointedly excluded. Wanless was to be thanked for his service and summarily sacked. He was a nice man but in the gladatorial arena there is no place for sentiment. Rowland assumed the role of chief executive as well as chairman, and as his number two he was to bring in Ron Sandler,[3] who had fulfilled the same role in Lloyds of London. The City was again unimpressed. Wanless had gone, but now there were two insurance men running the bank, with not a banking qualification or a year of banking experience between them.

Yet not everything was going Bank of Scotland's way. Since the bid had been announced the Bank's share price had been rising, but NatWest's price had been rising faster. The stock market signals its intentions through share price movements and the soothsayers who read the entrails declared that this meant one, or possibly, two things: Bank of Scotland would have to raise its bid; and/or another bidder would enter the contest.

With its collective minds telepathically united, the City now tried to will these events to happen. Reuters reported that investors were salivating at the prospect of a counter-bid emerging and the newspapers started to speculate on who the bidder might be. LloydsTSB, HSBC and Barclays were ruled out on competition grounds – they would surely be blocked by the Monopolies and Mergers Commission – but the former building societies Halifax, Alliance & Leicester and Abbey National were possibilities, as were foreign banks wanting to enter the UK market. And it emerged that the Royal Bank of Scotland had put down a marker with the Takeover Panel on the day George Mathewson had arrived back in London. It did not mean they would bid but it did mean they were not excluded.

Takeover Panel rules are clear but careful wording can stay on the right side of them. Peter Burt had declared the Bank's bid 'full and fair'. He had not said it was 'final'. NatWest's share price had stayed irritatingly ahead of the value of the Bank bid and at the end of November the Bank bowed to the inevitable. Jack Shaw again telephoned David Rowland before dawn to tell him that Bank of Scotland had made an improved offer, there was to be more cash, meaning higher borrowing for the Bank, there was to be a special dividend of £2 billion for shareholders as an extra inducement and, crucially, NatWest shareholders were to get more of the combined group; now they would own 70 per cent as against 68 per cent under the first offer. 'Peter Burt, BoS' chief executive, insisted that his original offer was "full and fair", implying he would not open his sporran again,' reported *The Economist*.[4] Rather sheepishly, he described the new bid as 'fuller and fairer'.

The whole package now valued NatWest at £24.3 billion – a colossal sum – but it was not enough. NatWest's share price continued to rise and by the end of the day was above even the value of this increased offer. The market was expecting even more and the Bank would be stretched to breaking point to provide it.

10

'The next thing he does has got to work, otherwise he's toast'

The Royal Bank launched its attack on NatWest on Monday 29 November. This time Sir David Rowland received his pre-dawn call from Sir George Younger, the urbane and genial former Cabinet minister who was chairman of the Royal Bank. It hardly came as a surprise to Rowland or to anyone else. The weekend papers had been full of stories of talks between George Mathewson and Rowland, with the Royal trying to win approval from the NatWest board so that its offer would be friendly and recommended, rather than a second hostile attack. The talks had broken up on the previous Friday and Rowland had gathered his board together on Saturday for a brief meeting, but there was not much to discuss. NatWest had decided it wanted to remain independent, there was to be no deal. The fight would now be a three-cornered contest.

The Royal Bank's team, which had been working on the detail of their offer for weeks, had had to do some last-minute tweaking when Bank of Scotland announced its increased offer; nevertheless, the new bid had a very familiar shape. The headline value was slightly higher than that offered by the Bank and the promised cost savings were £165 million more, but otherwise the recipe was the same. Non-core subsidiaries were to be sold, there was to be a closer focus on the core business. The Royal contrasted its financial performance against the record of NatWest and compared NatWest's management to its top team – chairman Sir George Younger, chief executive George Mathewson and Fred Goodwin, who was designated as the man who would run the bank. One of the factors which may have discouraged Rowland from endorsing the bid was that the Royal Bank had made it clear that if it won there was to be no place for Rowland or Sandler in the merged group. George Younger had announced the date of his retirement and the Royal Bank's board had agreed that Mathewson would succeed him as chairman, with Goodwin becoming chief executive.

Mathewson's caution in not rushing into a bid had given him a number of advantages. He had seen how the City had greeted the Bank's bid, he knew the size and structure oi ᴜie competing offer and, crucially he had waited until the Office of Fair Trading had ruled that a takeover by the Bank would not produce a monopoly and would not have to be referred to the Competition Commission. The Royal Bank would have to get similar clearance, but it could use the Bank of Scotland decision to bolster its own case. Although the Royal Bank team had been working intensively on their bid before going public, they were now coming fresh to the fight, whereas the Bank management had already been at full stretch for more than two months. Also the delay had given the Royal's PR team time to leak out favourable news, such as the decision by the Spanish banking giant BSCH (now Santander), which was a shareholder in the Royal Bank, to back the bid and contribute cash.

In public Peter Burt was philosophical: 'I would prefer not to enter into a pitched battle with a company so close to home, but the Royal will do what it believes is in the best interests of its shareholders and so will we.' But the Royal's move was a bitter blow. At one time the team from The Mound might have hoped to have declared victory before Christmas and gone home to their families; now it would continue at least until February and they would be fighting on two fronts. Even for a man of Burt's prodigious energy, this was a sapping experience and it was tying up around 150 senior employees in the company. It is a tribute to the depth of management that the Bank was still able to turn out double-digit growth and announce new ventures, but it was a big distraction.

The bid would now also run through the end of the millennium, which was supposed to be a time for celebration but was overshadowed by the 'millennium bug' or Y2K – possible flaws in computer programmes which it was feared could cause everything from the controls on nuclear power stations to aircraft guidance systems to crash. The problem was taken seriously enough for the United Nations to establish a taskforce and individual governments around the world to formulate action plans. The Scottish banks had redesigned their computer systems relatively recently and were well

advanced in checking millions of lines of code for parts of programmes which had to be rewritten, but there was always the chance
that some other part of the financial system would fail, bringing down
the whole network. In the event there were no serious difficulties and
opinion was divided between those who said the expensive remedial
work had averted catastrophe and those who said the whole issue was
just hype to bring work to IT consultants.

Meanwhile the confrontation ground on. NatWest responded to
the Bank's improved offer ('still inadequate, shareholders will not be
hoodwinked by an illusion') and were answered in kind ('painfully
lame, repeating the same weary rhetoric, NatWest management has
thrown in the towel'). For the first time Burt had to acknowledge
publicly the possibility of defeat when he was asked whether failure
would lay the Bank itself open to takeover. He dismissed the question,
adding that if the price of NatWest rose too high, Bank of Scotland
would walk away 'without a backward glance'.

But the tension was obviously getting to him and, against the advice
of his public relations managers, he succumbed to the temptation to
attack the Royal Bank's management, recalling Fred Goodwin's
nicknames of 'Fred the Shred', and 'Fred the Impaler' and drawing
attention to the fact that many of the Royal's top executives had been
brought in from outside, without much banking experience. 'I'm
struggling to think of an executive of RBS who came up through the
ranks. If Fred Goodwin falls under a bus, who is going to run the
bank?' George Mathewson briefly replied in the same negative style,
drawing attention to the age of Burt's number two, Gavin Masterton
(58, less than two years from normal bank retirement age) and Fred
Goodwin's 41. It was left to Goodwin to bring the temperature down.
'We think logic and fact will win this. It needs to be done on a more
professional footing, rather than slagging each other off.'

The long drawn-out fight was also producing tensions within the
Bank of Scotland board as some directors began to question the
wisdom of having made the bid in the first place and spoke among
themselves of having been railroaded into it by the executives.
Counter to this was the feeling among the executives that they
had not had strong enough leadership from the board. Was Sir Jack
Shaw, who had been propelled into the post by the illness of Sir
Alistair Grant, the right man for the job? He was able and committed
but he lacked the guile of a practised City operator or the personal

connections which might have swayed investors. The man who should have filled Sir Alistair's shoes, some argued, was Sir Robert Smith, who as chairman of Deutsche Bank Asset Management, was well-known and respected in the Square Mile and as a former corporate financier was a veteran of bids and deals, but he had only been on the board a short time.

As the contest ran its course, both bidders added refinements to their offers in the hope of making them more attractive to share-holders, and NatWest announced that it had poached Gordon Pell, a senior executive at LloydsTSB, to join them. This went part way to answering the criticism that, however able Rowland and Sandler might be, they lacked banking experience. Pell had it in spades.

Rowland's defence tactics, which had previously looked piecemeal and borrowed from his tormentors, now began to look plausible. By adopting virtually the same programmes as the Bank and the Royal – sell peripheral businesses, concentrate on core banking and reduce costs – he had removed strategy as a basis for deciding the bid. If all three banks – the Royal, Bank of Scotland and NatWest – had the same strategy and were roughly offering to return the same value to shareholders, it was a question of which management team could best deliver. His argument was that the incumbents had the best chance, since they knew the business best.

As the bid moved into its final days in mid-February opinion swung between the three possible outcomes. One or two analysts now suggested that NatWest might – or indeed should – remain inde-pendent and it began to look possible that both bidders might fail. There was a fillip for Bank of Scotland as the influential *Financial Times* Lex column recommended that shareholders accept its bid, but slowly large institutional shareholders began to declare themselves for the Royal Bank. Now the peculiar logic of the stock market began to show itself. As the Royal Bank began to look the likely winner, its share price fell, whereas the price of Bank of Scotland shares rose on the prospect of it being the loser. By the Thursday of the last week the Royal Bank's shares had fallen 18 per cent from the level at which it had made the offer, meaning that its bid was now worth less than the Bank's bid and less than the value at which NatWest shares were trading on the stock market.

At lunchtime on Friday there was enough good news to convince Peter Burt that he had won, but the afternoon was still taken up with a hectic round of investor meetings. In the evening the Bank's team, Burt, Masterton and George Mitchell, head of corporate banking, were invited for champagne by Richard Lambert, editor of the *Financial Times*, which had been a consistent supporter. As they filed into his office Burt asked Lambert what was it to be: congratulations, or commiserations? The latter, replied Lambert, enough institutional shareholders had now declared for the Royal Bank to guarantee it at least 51 per cent of NatWest shares. The three men drained their glasses, cancelled their remaining scheduled meetings with investors and caught the last flight to Scotland. Burt put on a brave face: 'We saw NatWest as an opportunity, pure and simple. Someone was on the other side of the street holding up a £100 note, we crossed over and offered them £90 for it, but someone else made a better offer.'

In the following week NatWest gave up the fight and the Royal Bank mopped up the remaining shares. George Mathewson felt strangely deflated after his stunning victory. A decade before, his bank had been on the edge of falling into loss, now he had tripled its size and made it a major force in UK banking. He had fought a short, but extremely hard campaign, tirelessly presenting to investors, not only in London and Scotland, but flying to New York to woo NatWest's American shareholders. He'd taken the supersonic service on Concorde to save time, but had to spend frustrating hours at Heathrow Airport when the flight was delayed. After months of lack of sleep and living on adrenalin, fatigue and depression overcame him. 'It took me weeks to recover,' he told friends, 'and I won!'

The loser succumbed to 'flu and had to take a week off work – an almost unheard-of event for Burt – but he knew he could not afford to give way to exhaustion. A week after conceding defeat, and after numerous post-mortems, he admitted to being bitterly disappointed, but determined to carry on. 'We must do something. We don't necessarily have to acquire something, but we must drive the business forward because if we don't we will not only be seen to be vulnerable, we will be vulnerable and deservedly so.' It was a sentiment widely shared. Despite the Bank continuing to report sparkling profits growth, in the harsh judgement of the City Burt was now seen as having had two failures in a row, the Pat Robertson affair and NatWest. 'The next thing he does has got to work, otherwise he's toast,' one unnamed banker told the *Financial Times*.[1]

The feeling of despondency in the Bank extended from the board-room to the branches. Six months' work had crumbled in 24 hours and there was no alternative to swallowing hard and carrying on, but the concern that the Bank could now become a victim persisted. Takeover speculation swirled around for the following six months, with newspapers vying with each other to produce more names of banks said to be running their avaricious eyes over Bank of Scotland. The rumours had been enough to keep its share price at a premium level but they were baseless and when Burt reported a 14 per cent rise in profits for the half-year he commented that despite the stories, there had been a 'distinct lack of bids'. Slowly the speculation died down and the share price subsided.

The old problem, however, would not go away. Bank of Scotland's growth was being propelled by its success at lending, which was growing at 20 per cent a year, but it was only generating new capital at 13 per cent a year.[2] To fill the gap it was increasingly being thrown back on the wholesale funding market. It badly needed access to a larger deposit base. Burt had received a tentative approach from National Australia Bank and had spent some weeks talking to them but the discussions had come to nothing.

Another opportunity was not long in coming. A call came from Abbey National, a former building society which had demutualised and turned itself into a bank. The fit looked reasonable. In contrast to Bank of Scotland, Abbey had deep roots in the north and south of England, with only a small branch presence north of the border. It was predominantly a deposit taker and a mortgage lender, with only a modest corporate or small-business lending book, although it had moved into pensions and life assurance. Abbey was headed by another Scot, Ian Harley, whose insistence that he be the chief executive had scuppered previous deals, according to press reports. He was not an easy man to talk to – even Abbey's own chairman, the former Tory politician Lord Tugendhat, described him as 'a bit dour', before adding, 'but he does deliver'. But Burt got on quite well with him and did not feel he was an obstacle to a merger.

Talks continued with Tugendhat enthusiastically urging them on: 'Bank of Scotland has been extolling the virtues of this for some time – it is self-evidently a good deal.' But more than personalities were getting in the way. Peter Burt favoured a merger of equals – Abbey was bigger, but Bank of Scotland was better, a more comprehensive organisation with a broader range of skills and superior performance. Abbey, however, was unimpressed and saw it as a straight takeover: 'We will be acquiring and we will decide how it goes forward,' its spokesman told the press. Recognising that a takeover by an English company, of a bank which had been part of the Scottish firmament for 300 years, might not go down too well north of the border, Abbey's PR department tried to make some conciliatory noises, promising extra shareholder gatherings and board meetings in Scotland. There would also be Scottish directors – 'It will be a pretty tartan board.'

Despite this patronising tone, the negotiations progressed, with Tugendhat and his deputy Charles Villiers meeting Sir Jack Shaw and Sir Bob Reid for the Bank. Advisers also met, but in the way of mercenary armies some had now switched sides. Morgan Stanley, which had been on the Bank's side in the NatWest struggle, was now aiding Abbey National. A deal looked do-able. Bank of Scotland thought it could generate £400 million more in profit from Abbey National's branch network and estimated that £350 million could be taken out of costs. Abbey began to talk enthusiastically about becoming a fifth force to challenge the hegemony of the Big Four London banks, but the Bank team began to have doubts. Abbey's corporate lending book did not look good but the Bank of Scotland team was not allowed to see the figures.

The Bank was on the verge of walking away when, almost on the anniversary of the date on which the Royal Bank had launched the bid which had snatched NatWest away, LloydsTSB announced an offer for Abbey. The predator was now the prey and although there was a certain referral of the bid to the Competition Commission on monopolies grounds, meaning a six-month delay, investors put pressure on the Abbey board to end its ambitions to tie up with Bank of Scotland and support the LloydsTSB bid. Lloyds' branch network had considerable overlap with Abbey. If it could hold on to the customers while closing branches it would be able to make massive cost savings. It was a trick it had pulled off twice before with its acquisition of TSB (the Trustee Savings Bank) and the former building society Cheltenham & Gloucester.

In the spring of 2001 Gavin Masterton retired as group managing director and was succeeded by George Mitchell, who like Masterston was a Bank lifer, having joined straight from school. A quick learner and a safe pair of hands, he had led the Bank's operations in Hong Kong and New York before being given a mess to sort out in the international treasury department and then heading corporate banking. Life had to go on and the Bank pressed ahead with an acquisition in Ireland and a deal with insurance company Zurich to offer loans and credit cards to its customers.

Peter Burt, tired after years of trying to solve the Bank's strategic problem, had taken his family for a skiing holiday to Chamonix in the French Alps when he took a call from David Mayhew, senior partner at Cazenove. The Old Etonian had been against the Bank in the NatWest battle, now he was asking whether Burt would be willing to meet James Crosby, chief executive of Halifax.

The former building society had undergone a transformation since Bank of Scotland had last approached it to discuss a possible merger. Mike Blackburn had retired as chief executive to be succeeded by the man he had brought in to run Halifax's insurance business. Crosby was young (45 in 2001), energetic and fiercely intelligent. After reading mathematics at Oxford he had trained as an actuary with life assurance company Scottish Amicable, before moving into fund management with Rothschild Assurance. He looked the archetypal egg-head and it was joked that he was bald because his brain was so big it had pushed his hair out. In the six years since he had taken over the top job he had made a series of bold moves designed to transform Halifax from being a one-product mortgage bank to a more rounded financial institution. He had spent £1 billion buying the life assurance business of Equitable Life to add to Halifax's Clerical Medical subsidiary; he had poached Scotsman Jim Spowart from Standard Life to set up a new telephone and internet bank named Intelligent Finance; he had bought into the wealth management business St James's Place Capital and he had gone into partnership with Peter Wood, the man who had set up Direct Line insurance.

To manage Halifax's retail business, Crosby had recruited Andy Hornby, who was even younger (34 in 2001) and just as bright. He had followed a First in English at Oxford with an MBA from Harvard, where he graduated top of his year. His brief working career had seen him make a rapid ascent, from the Boston Consulting Group, to Blue Circle Cement to the supermarket group Asda, where he had become Retail Managing Director, overseeing 36 stores and 14,000 employees, and joined the Management Board at the age of 32.

Halifax was the biggest mortgage lender in the UK and had a truly gigantic deposit base, with over 11 million saving customers. For decades it had been run very conservatively, with the result that its vast mortgage book was solid and secure (in the jargon of the industry it had a low loan-to-value ratio). It was also very profitable. Until Mrs Thatcher's government started deregulating the mortgage business in the 1980s, building societies, of which Halifax was the largest, could charge virtually what they liked, knowing that there was little price competition and that customers, once signed up, were unlikely to leave. Now all that had changed. Borrowers were being enticed away from traditional providers like Halifax by banks which were keen to get mortgage business and were prepared to offer cut-price deals. New competitors were also entering the market, offering loans over the telephone or the internet. Hornby, using the retail skills he had learned at Asda, had taken the fight to the enemy, offering existing customers new incentives to stay and trying to extend Halifax's market-leading share further by competing fiercely for new loan business.

Together Crosby, Hornby and Dennis Stevenson, who had become chairman in 1999, had revived investor confidence in Halifax. For years the share price had languished below the level at which the company had first floated on the Stock Exchange when it demutualised; now it was rising strongly again.

For Bank of Scotland, Halifax made a much more attractive partner than Abbey National. It was bigger and appeared to have few of the management hang-ups which had dogged the Abbey negotiations. It had no corporate lending to speak of, but its problem was the reverse of the Bank's. It had – in the words of one Bank executive – 'deposits coming out of its ears', the difficulty was where to lend them profitably. Peter Burt played it cool with David Mayhew on the telephone, but conceded that, yes, he thought it might be worth making time to speak to James Crosby.

11

Peter's Last Supper

When Peter Burt arrived at Halifax's London corporate flat in St James's, he was surprised to find James Crosby with his foot in plaster after a fall, but the meeting went well enough. Secondary to finding an escape from the Bank's strategic straitjacket, one of Burt's objectives was to keep the headquarters in Scotland, which he believed was key to retaining the organisation's independent spirit and keeping together the formidable management team he had built up. A fear always in the back of his mind during the NatWest bid had been that, despite the intention, the economic pull of the larger organisation would have steadily moved the focus of decision-making to London. That was much less of an issue this time. Whatever the merits of the Yorkshire town, if it came to a choice between Halifax and Edinburgh from which to run a UK financial services group, the Scottish capital would come out top on most criteria.

The shape of the deal proposed by Mayhew was that Halifax would provide the chairman, and Bank of Scotland the chief executive. Although variously described in the press as 'excitable' and 'eccentric', Dennis Stevenson had an established reputation in the City. When approached to lead the board at Halifax he was already chair of a Top 100 company, the publishing group Pearson, which owned the *Financial Times*. There he had surprised everyone by picking as chief executive an American woman who had been running the group's *Economist* subsidiary and was well down the management pecking order. In doing so he bypassed the handful of able male executive directors who had expected that one of them would get the top job. It had proved to be an inspired choice. Marjorie Scardino was not only the first woman to head a FTSE 100 company, but had gone on to transform the group with a series of bold strategic moves and won the admiration of the men over whom she had leapfrogged.

Stevenson was also an assiduous networker with fingers in many pies. He had been chairman of the Tate Gallery, a member of the Takeover Panel and was a director of the top-drawer merchant bank Lazard Brothers. He moved easily in business and political circles. At the age of 26 he had been picked by Peter Walker, Housing Minister in the Conservative government, to chair the Newton Aycliffe and Peterlee New Town Development Corporation, but it was under Labour that he came into his own. Describing himself as an 'unreconstructed *Guardian*-reading liberal', he was a long-time friend of Peter Mandelson, one of Prime Minister Tony Blair's closest advisers. Under Labour Stevenson had first received a knighthood and then 18 months later a peerage. Blair chose him to head the committee which was choosing the new 'People's Peers' to sit in the House of Lords. 'Dennis had "New Labour" written all over him,' recalled one Bank executive on meeting him for the first time. 'When he came out to greet you he was always in his shirt-sleeves, signifying that there was work to be done and he had rolled up his sleeves to do it.' He had the added bonus of being a Scotsman, although having been born in Edinburgh and educated at Glenalmond, after Cambridge his career had been almost entirely in England.

Peter Burt was to be chief executive, although on the understanding that he would not go on beyond his 60th birthday, which was less than three years away, and that he would be succeeded by Crosby. Not to lead the new group from the beginning was a blow to the younger man, who had been chief executive of Halifax for only two years, but one he was prepared to accept to get the deal done. The problem was what to do with him in the meantime – there was no obvious job description for an 'heir apparent'. Bringing the two management teams together would mean that the key divisional posts would go to able and strong-minded men who would not take kindly to having Crosby floating around without a clear role.

To further the discussions Burt organised a dinner for the top management teams from both companies in the dining room of the Bank's head office on The Mound. The room has one of the most impressive views in Britain, taking in Edinburgh Castle, with the city spread out below it. But the diners' minds were on other things and the meeting did not go well. Crosby was ill at ease and there were personality clashes across the table. The Bank men, on their home ground surrounded by the history of the Bank, were older, more experienced, confident that they understood what was possible and what had to be done. The Halifax team seemed younger, smarter and in a hurry. There was a danger that disagreements might derail the discussions altogether but it was Andy Hornby, the most junior in age by a decade, who worked to calm tempers and find common ground.

Burt was insistent that, despite Halifax's larger size, the deal should be seen as a partnership of equals. They would form a new holding company and carry out what was known in the City as a 'nil premium merger', that is shares in the new group would be swapped one-for-one with existing shares in Halifax or Bank of Scotland. The two brand names would be retained, although Halifax might conduct its retail business under the Bank name north of the border. In the corporate market, the brand name would continue to be Bank of Scotland. Unlike Abbey, which thought it should have the upper hand, Halifax was content with this arrangement, which was simpler and meant that its shareholders would end up with most of the combined business, 63 per cent against 37 per cent for the Bank shareholders.

Top posts would be allocated on merit but the split was roughly equal. Mike Ellis, Halifax's chief operations officer, would fill the role as finance director of the new group, Andy Hornby would take charge of retail and personal banking, and Phil Hodkinson would look after the insurance and investment business. From the Bank, George Mitchell would run corporate banking, Colin Matthew business banking, concentrating on the smaller end of the market, and Gordon McQueen would merge the two treasury operations. It all looked pretty straightforward, there was very little overlap either in skills or branch network. There would be few redundancies: costs could be saved, but that was not the basis for the merger. Seizing opportunity was to be the driving motivation.

Burt and Crosby, joking that Yorkshire thrift had met Scottish parsimony, spent little time and no money on deciding the name of the new holding company, which was to be Halifax Bank of Scotland. Since it would inevitably be shortened to initials, Burt had no hesitation in agreeing that the Halifax name should come first – HBOS may not be elegant, but it was preferable to BOSH. The choice of name upset the Herne Bay Operatic Society, which had called itself HBOS for years, but the PR men straightened that one out. The corporate logo, sketched out on a piece of paper, was a combination of Halifax's 'X' and Bank of Scotland's saltire and coins.

Within the Bank the merger was being sold as an equal partnership, but a different impression was being given to Halifax's top management. At an away-day at Bolton Abbey, Wharfdale, a handful of top managers were told about the talks, but not given the name of the intended partner. 'It was referred to as "Project Linwood" and there was great speculation at dinner as to who it might be, but it was obvious from the way they spoke that Stevenson, Crosby, Ellis and Hornby were to get the top jobs. No one else mattered,' one Halifax manager remembered.

The Bank of Scotland board could see the logic of the union but was still nervous at giving up its independence and of Halifax's true intentions. 'They always used soft language,' said one director. 'They talked all the time about merger but there was always the implied threat that if our board didn't agree, they would bid for us.'

At the end of April 2001 the news that the two companies had been talking leaked and both share prices leaped up. Comment was generally favourable.

Newspapers calculated that the merged group would have a combined market value of nearly £28 billion and be the 11th largest bank in Europe, employing 61,000 people and making £2.8 billion in profits. It would still be smaller than the London Big Four (with the Royal Bank now being in control of NatWest), but it would be able to give them a run for their money. In contrast to the Abbey National talks, which had dragged on for months without getting very far, the courtship between Halifax and the Bank was positively whirlwind; the two sides had been talking for only a few weeks.

Halifax had made a point of moving its annual general meeting around the country to give its customers who had taken shares at the time of demutualisation the chance to hear and question the board. By coincidence it was due to hold its AGM in Edinburgh on Tuesday 1 May. On the Sunday evening before the meeting, Stevenson, Crosby and their adviser from Lazards, met Burt and Mayhew for dinner in a private room in the Caledonian Hotel, Edinburgh. In the last few days Peter Burt had been thinking hard about his position. He was tired, not physically, but years of mental strain wrestling with the problem of the Bank's future and dragging up and down the country to proposition potential suitors had been draining. He had had fruitless talks with a dozen companies and come close to securing NatWest, only to have the prize taken from him. Now at last he had found a solution.

The Bank had been growing at 20 per cent compound for 20 years. It was a record no other bank had equalled, but it was a tiger from which it was impossible to dismount. If its performance was seen to falter, its share price would fall and it would be vulnerable to takeover. More than 300 years of independence and the unique culture which the Bank had fostered would be lost. With access to Halifax's large balance sheet and capital strength, the Bank could continue with its phenomenal lending growth.

He wanted to see the merger through, to oversee the integration and then to retire, having achieved what he set out to do. After a dozen years leading an FTSE 100 company he had no will to go on indefinitely. The more he thought about it, the more it seemed logical that he should not become chief executive of HBOS. He talked to David Mayhew about stepping down altogether, but Mayhew warned him that if he did that the whole deal might fall apart. At dinner, Burt announced his decision: he would take the title executive deputy chairman and concentrate on making the integration of the two companies as smooth as possible, leaving the way open for Crosby to become chief executive immediately. When news of the meal leaked out, cynics in the Bank described it as 'Peter's Last Supper'.

As Stevenson and his board arrived at the Edinburgh International Conference Centre for the shareholders' meeting they were met with placards demanding 'Don't Sell Us Out', and 'Don't Cave In to Tartan Tantrums'. It was a stunt organised by the Halifax *Evening Courier*, but a reminder that Yorkshire sensitivities were at stake as well as Scottish ones. In a post-industrial world the town of Halifax did not have a lot going for it and the bank which bore its name provided 3,500 high quality jobs – one in six of the working population – in the monumental 1970s stone and glass headquarters building which dominated the centre. During the meeting the chairman had to steer a careful path between pleasing his largely Scottish audience – telling them he had been born in nearby Ainslie Place – and the readership of the West Yorkshire local paper – 'We are proud of our 150 years of Yorkshire heritage.'

Speculation was now so strong that a deal would be done that there was pressure to get the final details agreed and an official announcement made to the Stock Exchange. The Bank postponed the announcement of its annual results and the two management teams met again. The following day the boards of the two banks met separately to approve the deal in principle and teams of lawyers and brokers met in London with Crosby and Burt to work through the night on the detailed agreement. It was 6 a.m. on Friday 4 May before the work was finished; the statement was issued and a press conference was called for noon. Burt was in jovial mood, telling journalists that a Yorkshireman was just a Scotsman with the generosity squeezed out and pointing up the group's cost-consciousness with the statement: 'Just think how difficult it would be to come between a Yorkshireman, a Scotsman and a pound note.' Crosby showed signs of fatigue when a slip of the tongue made him say that Halifax was merging with the Bank of England, but he recovered to threaten: 'We intend to generate as much pain as possible for our competitors. It is nothing personal.'

The merger was mostly well received inside the two companies. Only 2,000 jobs would be lost through reducing duplication, a fraction of those already lost in the Royal's takeover of NatWest, and these were to be achieved by natural wastage rather than compulsory redundancy. Yorkshire would retain the headquarters of the retail bank, but the corporate head office was to be in Edinburgh and Burt had secured a safeguard – more than half of the board would have to vote in favour before the HQ could be moved. Since the board was to be made up equally of directors from each side, it looked like an effective Scottish veto.

There was a north-south divide in the way the merger was viewed from the outside. Crosby stressed to *The Herald*, Glasgow's daily newspaper, his love of the city, in which he had lived for many years and where his wife had been born. To the *Yorkshire Post* he emphasised his Yorkshire birth and his family home at Ilkley. There was scepticism about the company's assurances on the headquarters. Nationalist and Conservative politicians in Scotland sought assurances that The Mound would be the head office in more than just name, while the Halifax *Courier* ran a banner headline: 'Betrayed'.

Bank of Scotland published its results on the same day, revealing that profits were up 12 per cent and had topped £1 billion for the first time. The share price of both companies rose, taking their combined worth over £30 billion, but the argument that the new bank would succeed by boosting sales rather than cutting costs did not please everyone in the City. One analyst was doubtful that the strategy could succeed: 'We like slash-and-burn deals. The more people who get fired the better.'[1]

A few weeks later the Office of Fair Trading cleared the merger on competition grounds. HBOS would have a market-leading share of 20 per cent in mortgages and not far short of that in savings accounts, but its position in other markets such as current accounts, business and corporate accounts was tiny compared to the Big Four – underlining the fact that there was a lot to go for. As far as the balance of power in the new organisation was concerned, it was fairly clear where the weight lay. Not only were Halifax providing the chairman, chief executive and finance director, but nearly half the profit would be generated by the retail business controlled by Andy Hornby and a further quarter by the insurance activities run by Phil Hodkinson, who was brought in from Zurich Financial Services at the time of the merger. Taken together these five top executives had no banking qualifications and only a few years of banking experience between them. Little more than a year earlier, Peter Burt had criticised the top management of NatWest for the same failing. Now he had handed over his Bank to them.

It was announced that James Crosby and Mike Ellis would have offices in The Mound and both men rented flats in Edinburgh. Ellis worked out of his office except when group business took him elsewhere and quickly won respect from the Bank of Scotland management for his professionalism, experience and the hard work he put into mastering the new business. Crosby was seen in his office much less often. He admitted to the *Independent* that he would only visit once a week and was immediately branded the 'once-a-week Scot'. He would continue to live in Yorkshire, where three of his four children were at school. He was recognised as very intelligent, but not an easy man to talk to or to read. With Hornby based in Halifax, the days of the close corporate collaboration of the Bank of Scotland general managers with offices grouped together on the same floor of The Mound were gone. It was much more difficult to get an overview of the business or a sense of shared values and mission.

Non-executive directors for the combined board were chosen by the executives – who issued invitations to five from each side. The Bank provided Deputy Governor and former Shell executive Sir Bob Reid, Sir Ron Garrick, former chief executive of the engineering group Weir, John Maclean, an accountant who had been in shipping,

Brian Ivory, who had run a whisky company, and Lord Simpson of Dunkeld, whose stewardship of the electronics group Marconi, which was facing collapse, was coming under sustained attack by workers and investors alike. He lasted less than a year before resigning under shareholder pressure. Notable among those not asked to serve as an HBOS director was Lesley Knox, who had a reputation for asking pointed and difficult questions on the Bank board. She also had experience in corporate finance and asset management, working for an investment bank. In the years to come her expertise would be missed.

There was also a lack of banking experience among the former Halifax directors. They were Charles Dunstone, the founder of Carphone Warehouse, Tony Hobson, who had been finance director of the life assurance company Legal & General, Coline McConville, who was in advertising, Louis Sherwood, whose background was television and retail, and Philip Yea from the drinks industry.

Bank of Scotland had got by without ex-bankers among its non-executives, but the process of 'homologation' – the cross-examination of executives on specific initiatives, including major lending decisions – meant that they had built up a detailed picture of how the Bank ran and where the pitfalls might be hidden. Those directors who moved to HBOS found that the board was expected to operate in a very different way. 'Stevenson didn't see the point of close questioning the executives,' one director recalls, 'but there was a point. Over time you could see a growing over-confidence: we lent money and we were never wrong. The board lost the habit of challenge.' HBOS was on a different scale to Bank of Scotland and a much more complex organisation. The formal governance demands on boards had also grown, with new regulations and new City codes. 'Board papers were inches thick and if you asked a question at a board meeting an executive could always point to a report of 156 pages and tell you that your question was answered on page 144. You had never got to it – there just wasn't time to read it all.'

Another director recalls: 'The HBOS governance structure was well thought through, they had taken external advice and on paper it looked very strong. In practice Dennis, James and Andy were a very tight team and they ran the company. We thought Peter would be part of it, but he wasn't.'

Yet despite the misgivings there was a feeling that the Bank had found a way out of its long-standing funding dilemma. But had it? Despite the fabled strength of its balance sheet, Halifax had not completely eliminated the reliance on wholesale funding markets. In its last year as an independent company, Bank of Scotland had lent £66 billion and been able to cover 54 per cent from customer deposits. Although HBOS could cover 66 per cent of its lending from deposits, it was still reliant on the wholesale market for a third of its advances and, worryingly, there was no significant business area where deposit growth was keeping up with the rise in lending.

Responsibility for keeping the group funded fell to Gordon McQueen, who had merged the two treasury operations. Bank of Scotland had always been conservatively run, never venturing into proprietary trading, but seeing itself only as a service department for the Bank and its customers. Since demutualisation Halifax had started a small trading business, which, although it involved some risk, was well run and profitable, but McQueen closed it. Treasury was expected at least to cover its costs from the prices it charged corporate customers and the lending businesses within the group for the capital they needed, but McQueen wanted to go further and use higher internal pricing to force the retail, business and corporate banking operations to target deposit growth as well as lending increases. The proposal was vetoed by Crosby. To do so would hold the whole business back, he said.

However, there was nothing to fear on the wholesale funding market. The combined group had a strong balance sheet and was viewed as low-risk by those who lent to it. The rating agencies graded 99 per cent of its investment portfolio as A or better, and 86 per cent was graded AAA – the highest level. For Bank of Scotland's continued growth in corporate lending the outlook was good: following the merger its senior debt had been upgraded from A+ to AA by Standard & Poors, one of the leading ratings agencies.[2] This was a mark of approval and meant that the Bank would be able to borrow at lower rates, making it more competitive in its drive to take business from its London rivals.

12

A clash of cultures

HBOS shares made their debut on the London Stock Exchange the day before the attack on the Twin Towers in New York in September 2001. The market was already in a grim mood fearing a recession and the FTSE index suffered a major fall, but the new bank's shares bucked the trend and rose more than three per cent on the day, a good omen. The previous few months had seen the deal approved by both sets of shareholders in ballots and at special meetings. Sir Jack Shaw and other Bank of Scotland directors who were not joining the HBOS board bowed out and more than three centuries of independence for Britain's oldest commercial bank had come to an end.

The vote of Bank shareholders had produced a final example of the personal attention to detail for which chief executives of the Bank had been known. A small shareholder, Dr George Fieldman, complained that because of an administrative error he and others like him who held their shares in a tax-free savings plan had been denied a vote. After complaining, getting no satisfaction and threatening to take it further, he was surprised to receive a telephone call from Peter Burt.

'He seemed a very polite and thoughtful individual and said he had heard that there was a problem. I explained how I and many other customers holding BoS shares in a BoS Personal Equity Plan had been disenfranchised and that the Bank had actually profited by failing to meet its obligations. I outlined how they must have saved money by not having to pay for the necessary paper, printing, postage and processing for the vote which failed to take place. Mr Burt said: "All true but what can we do about it?" I suggested he should add up the total amount that the Bank had saved by dint of its mistake and give the equivalent sum to charity. He asked, "Which charity?" I said, "You choose." He suggested "Save the Children", and I agreed. Shortly afterwards I received a letter, dated 3 September 2001, from Peter Burt informing me that he had sent a cheque for £4,000 to the

Save the Children Fund, and so a degree of satisfaction was obtained.'[1]

A few weeks later Bank of Scotland reported half-year results – its last as a separate company. Profits rose by 7 per cent on lending, up by nearly a quarter, but HBOS shares fell on the revelation that bad debt provisions had risen by 27 per cent – a portent of the harsher economic times which were coming.

HBOS's first annual report laid heavy stress on partnership. The cover, with the caption 'The New Force', showed two shirt-sleeved arms with hands clasped in friendship. One set of cufflinks bore the cross of St George, the other the saltire of St Andrew. In his chairman's introduction Lord Stevenson promised 'shared values, shared vision and an ambition to seek out new opportunities'. The speed at which the merger had been agreed and concluded was testimony to the closeness of view of the two sides. 'This was a merger of equals where relative size was always secondary to the shareholder value that teams with a shared vision can create.'

The overview of the group's activities highlighted its strength in various areas through a very selective use of the numbers. Retail banking was number one in mortgages and savings, the report trumpeted. There was no claim for market position for insurance, merely that it had £1.1 billion of life, pension and investment premium income. Similarly the document reported £19 billion of business lending (a figure which would have put it fairly low down the list of lenders to small and medium firms) but claimed HBOS was market leader in the UK in management buyouts, bank finance for social housing and public-to-private financing. To round it off it was also a 'major sterling money market presence'.

In his narrative, James Crosby emphasised the bank's solidity and its intention to be a consumer champion. For personal customers he promised realistic pricing and transparent charging coupled with 'pro-consumer PR work'. For corporate banking he described the 'old world' character of the lending book – and indeed the Bank of Scotland portfolio was old world. It had avoided the excesses of the new economy's 'dot.com' boom and bust and preferred to lend to traditional industries like engineering, manufacturing, construction and property and have its loans backed by real-world assets like land, bricks and mortar. In an echo of the traditional Bank philosophy of 'staying at the table', he promised, 'We also pride ourselves on having the flexibility, whenever realistic, to see customers through the bad times as well as the good. After all a bank that pulls back at the first whiff of trouble does not deserve the partnership we seek with each of our corporate customers.'

You had to look deeper into the accounts to spot some of the less satisfactory aspects of the group's performance. In retail, the area run by Andy Hornby which made up half the total group business, profits had declined despite increased lending. Costs and provisions against bad debts were up and interest margins were lower. It was insurance, which was benefiting from the acquisition of the Equitable Life salesforce a year earlier, and corporate banking, which saw lending increase by a third and profits by even more, that provided the group's growth.

Deep inside the report, it was revealed that the merger had been the occasion for substantial increases in salaries for the top management. James Crosby saw his total remuneration (salary plus bonus) leap from £690,000 to over £1 million, a rise of 56 per cent and a sum which made him better paid than the chief executive of LloydsTSB. Peter Burt was not far behind, seeing a rise from £682,000 to £994,000. Mike Ellis received 55 per cent more, Andy Hornby 64 per cent more and the three former Bank executives, Gordon McQueen, Colin Matthew and George Mitchell more than doubled their total takings. Even the part-time chairman, Lord Stevenson, saw his remuneration jump from £265,000 to £363,000.

The extra pay would not stop with the end of employment. Since bank employees enjoyed pensions based on their final salary at age 60 – typically at two-thirds – the HBOS executives could look forward to retirements considerably more comfortable than they had been expecting before the merger.

The late 1990s and early years of the new millennium saw a rapid explosion in top corporate remuneration, serviced by a new specialism – corporate pay consultants. These experts could produce tables of comparative salaries paid by other companies in the same sector showing why boards had to agree to match remuneration for fear that they would lose top talent to competitors, although actual instances of the highest level executives moving from one bank to another were comparatively rare. Rates also had to keep up with those paid in other countries, especially the United States, although movement between countries was even rarer. In 2001 the only recent immigrant to the

highest echelon of British banking had been the Canadian Matt
Barrett, hired by Barclays as chief executive. Barrett brought with
him an expectation of higher pay and immediately set a benchmark
for other bank chiefs. Boards were bamboozled by the calculations
produced by the top pay experts and cowed into accepting their
arguments. 'We didn't like it but we found it impossible to resist the
consultants and go against the tide,' commented one director.

Consultancies also devised complex bonus structures including
short-term incentives, long-term incentives, cash payments and the
award of shares or options to acquire shares at a later date at a fixed
price. These awards were granted on an assessment of performance
against a cocktail of measures including earnings per share (EPS),
return on equity (RoE) and profit performance. To make the whole
process 'transparent', to use the jargon of the time, extensive notes to
the accounts purported to explain each scheme. Ten pages were
devoted to the report of the remuneration committee of the board in
the 2001 HBOS accounts. Even for a professional shareholder,
working through that volume of words and figures to determine
whether the exalted salaries and bonuses were being earned or not
was a daunting business.

A simpler and cruder calculation illustrates how the pay of top
executives had changed. In 1990 Bruce Pattullo, as the highest-paid
director in Bank of Scotland, earned £176,000, 16 times the average
salary of all staff in the Bank. There was no bonus, although these
began to be introduced a few years later. By 2000 Peter Burt's salary
as chief executive and highest-paid director had risen to £426,000,
some 18 times the average. One year later James Crosby's basic pay
was 25 times the average. If you add in his bonus – which nearly
doubled his total remuneration – he was paid more than 43 times the
average HBOS employee.

These increases did not go totally unremarked, particularly among
small shareholders who expressed their disquiet at the group's first
annual meeting, with one questioner calling them 'obscene'. A long-
term bonus scheme which could have seen Crosby and Burt earn up
to £7 million more over the following three years came in for special
condemnation, with even some institutional shareholders voicing
concern. But small shareholders discovered the limit to their power
when the chairman revealed that he already had votes in favour from
institutional investors representing three-quarters of the total share-

holding. The meeting also illustrated a sharp difference in style between the old days of the Bank and the new HBOS. Stevenson's easy, casual approach contrasted sharply with the formal manner of Sir Jack Shaw and his predecessors as Bank Governors and upset at least one small shareholder who demanded an end to the 'Andys, Bobs and Georges' and a return to formal titles.

Inside the Bank Stevenson's familiar style and eclectic mind divided opinion. Some saw him as a breath of fresh air, to others 'He was a right plonker'.

The job of integrating the two organisations had now begun in earnest and was felt in some areas much more than in others. In corporate banking it was almost business as usual. Most of the staff and management had come from Bank of Scotland and they were still trading under the same name, with the only difference being that they had more firepower at their disposal, but in branch banking the difference was felt acutely.

Bank of Scotland staff had been through a half-revolution of their own. With Gavin Masterton as Treasurer and Chief General Manager there had been much more emphasis on sales, with counter staff being expected to ask customers what more the Bank could do for them, rather than waiting for the customer to volunteer the information as in the old days. But the transformation had only been partially completed. 'We were trying to downsize the branch network because of the costs and the old idea of customer service had to change. We had to move to relationship banking. But people were used to having the same manager for three or four years – when they found they had three different managers in 12 months, they got pissed off,' recalls one executive.

The upheaval not only discomfited customers, there was also resistance from staff. 'Everyone realised that things had to change, that our network was old-fashioned, but a lot of people were steeped in their ways and didn't like change with the result that the transformation was not done as well as it should have been. There were teething problems – we would have got them fixed, but before we knew it we were into the merger.'

Bank of Scotland employees had not been prepared for the sales-driven culture which Andy Hornby, using the retail experience and skills he had learned at Asda, had introduced into Halifax. Staff were expected to sell products rather than provide a service and were given targets to reach, and training in how to achieve them. Branch premises were also undergoing a makeover, doing away with mahogany counters and bandit screens and making them into bright, modern retail outlets. If they weren't in the right locations they were closed and new premises opened in shopping malls and other high-footfall areas.

Older, more traditional bank customers were unsettled and to make matters worse, the switchover of computer systems did not go smoothly. Personal customers had their accounts moved from the Bank system to the Halifax network, being given a 'roll number', a traditional building society identifier, in the process. Business customers stayed with the Bank system. This was a physical severing of the old Bank principle of seeing the business relationship as an extension of the personal relationship and created problems where customers had personal and business accounts with HBOS. I was one of many customers to experience difficulties when I unwittingly paid cash into my personal account in a branch which was connected to the business banking computer network. The money disappeared without trace, my account went into unauthorised overdraft and the bank started refusing to pay my standing orders and direct debits. It took me ten days to sort out the mess, with bank staff apparently powerless to help me. The threatening letters from the gas, electricity and telephone companies went on for much longer. I ended my 20-year relationship with the Bank. A personal apology from Hornby was sent to all Scottish account holders and staff, but by that time it was too late. Many loyal customers had left.

The determination with which the Halifax way of working was imposed on the Bank was reflected in the nickname given to the men from Yorkshire, which compared them to the religious fanatics of Afganistan – 'the Haliban'. Some senior personal banking managers from the Bank transferred to the Halifax retail headquarters in Yorkshire, but found they had little or no influence in determining direction. 'Andy had four or five people around him who were clones of Andy Hornby. They didn't have much latitude. They could hear us bleating about things, but they weren't going to change the model for one little bit of the market north of the border. Back in Scotland we couldn't go out socially because of the constant complaints from friends.'

The differences in the new approach went deeper than style.

Experienced retail bankers were at a loss to understand the logic behind Hornby's strategy. With its history of being a building society only a few years behind it, Halifax was still predominantly a home loans and savings institution. It had a dominant market share in mortgages. This was a low-risk and solid business on which it made an excellent return – in fact almost half the profit from the new group came from mortgages. But it was under sustained assault from other banks, building societies and new entrants to the market, such as the telephone and internet banks Egg, Direct Line and Standard Life Bank. They were offering much finer deals, not only to new borrowers, but to existing home owners to persuade them to switch.

It made sense to hang on to as many mortgage customers as possible by offering those who showed signs of wanting to leave a better deal. However, the original intention of the merger, as far as Bank staff were concerned, was to lessen the group's dependence on this big, but threatened, market share by diversifying away from mortgages, particularly into corporate and business banking. Hornby showed no signs of allowing this to happen. As the corporate lending book grew, he expanded the mortgage book, competing hard, going head to head with competitors to offer the best deals. Each new loan was less profitable than an old one, but would also eat up some of the bank's capital and liquidity (funding), meaning that it couldn't be used to support lending elsewhere.

The drive also upset existing Halifax customers, many of whom had been loyal for a long time. They now saw new borrowers being offered interest rates lower than they were paying. Complaints began to be received and the Financial Ombudsman stepped in, fining HBOS, along with several other banks, for treating existing customers unfairly. The Bank agreed to pay £7 million compensation to 30,000 customers who had complained, but said it would not similarly recompense a further 400,000 who had not yet registered a complaint. This grudging attitude, which contrasted with that of competitors like the building society Nationwide which had put up £200 million to compensate all its customers, brought a torrent of criticism down on the Bank. BBC Radio 4's *Money Box* programme commented: 'Halifax, the high street bank, is fighting for its reputation this weekend after an unprecedented onslaught in the press and an accusation by the Financial Ombudsman of misleading its customers.'[2] The programme's presenter, Paul Lewis, listed the adjectives used to describe the Bank: 'Shameful, pitiful, bizarre, penny pinching, a blunder, descended to the gutter, are just some of the terms used against Halifax Bank of Scotland, which likes to call itself a new force in banking. After this week "new farce" might be closer.' So much for Crosby's promise in the annual report of being the consumer's champion.

To compound matters, Halifax had also started its own internet and telephone bank, called Intelligent Finance (IF). To lead it the bank had poached Jim Spowart, a veteran banker who had started his career with the Royal Bank of Scotland, but already had done two start-ups with the insurers Direct Line and Standard Life. IF had been phenomenally successful in its first year, gaining 155,000 customers, grabbing a 9 per cent share of new mortgages and lending £5.2 billion. Add this to the success of the main Bank and HBOS was winning nearly a third of all new mortgages. Its dependence on the housing market was becoming more rather than less.

Another puzzling aspect of the strategy was the campaign to win more current accounts. As a former building society, Halifax had a relatively small share of this market but traditional bankers from both sides of the merger were not over-keen to increase it. Current accounts were the necessary evil of retail banking – in supermarket terms they were loss leaders. Cheques, still the main form of bill payment in 2002, were expensive to process and although customers might have high cash balances on pay day, the average in an account over the month was much less and canny customers withdrew spare cash to put it into interest-earning deposit accounts. At one time banks had charged fees on current accounts in order to break even but competition and government pressure had forced them first to introduce free banking and then to pay a grudging amount of interest on credit balances. The going rate was a measly one-tenth of 1 per cent. Halifax went all out to grab a larger share of this business, with a market-beating promise to pay forty times as much interest – 4 per cent.

Traditional bankers looked on in disbelief. No wonder retail profits were down; it was estimated that paying the extra interest cost Halifax £100 million a year.[3] Extending that to customers of Bank of Scotland, which already had a much larger share in its own market north of the border, could increase this cost by £50 million – and all to gain accounts on which it would be hard to earn any profit. The theory

Left. Sir Walter Scott broods before the former Bank of Scotland headquarters in Edinburgh. It was the heart of the Bank for nearly 200 years; now it is just another office of the Lloyds Banking Group. (Ray Perman)

Below. Covenant Close, off Edinburgh's Royal Mile, once housed the Cross Keys Tavern, where in 1695 shareholders, quaintly called 'Adventurers,' first subscribed for Bank of Scotland shares. (Ray Perman)

An early Bank of Scotland note. The directors feared that rivals would hoard notes, then present large quantities for payment in coin at short notice, provoking a run on the bank. (Courtesy of Lloyds Banking Group plc Archives)

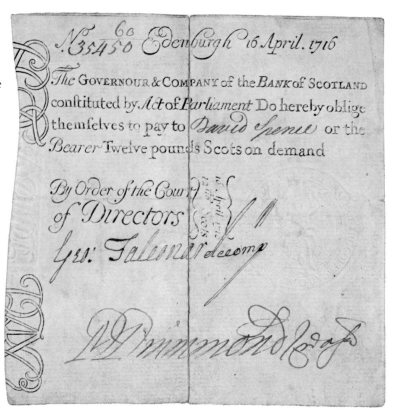

The Bank of Scotland board in 1995. Newly knighted Governor Sir Bruce Pattullo stands in the centre of the front row, with Jack Shaw (on his left in glasses), later to become Governor. Directly behind Pattullo's left shoulder, standing on the stairs, is Sir Alistair Grant, who succeeded him as Governor, but died of cancer shortly afterwards. In the second row, behind Pattullo, is Sir Bob Reid, a deputy Governor who was selected to join the HBOS board, and next to him Lesley Knox, who was not. (Courtesy of Lloyds Banking Group plc Archives)

The Bank of Scotland crest outside The Mound, its former headquarters. The Latin motto 'Tanto Uberior' approximately translates as 'so much the more plentiful.' (Ray Perman)

Peter Burt (left) and Halifax's James Crosby announce the merger which formed HBOS in 2001. Burt surprised everyone with his decision not to take the chief executive post. (Press Association)

Above. Bank of Scotland's Gordon McQueen (left) would head HBOS treasury, with George Mitchell (right) leading corporate banking. Burt (centre) took the title executive deputy chairman, but resigned after less than two years. (Press Association)

Right. George Mitchell was a lifetime banker and considered a safe pair of hands, but he resigned from HBOS after losing out to Andy Hornby to become chief executive after James Crosby's early departure.

Above. The HBOS board in 2006 in the old Bank headquarters, after its controversial refurbishment. Lord Stevenson, the chair, is fourth from the left. Peter Cummings and Andy Hornby stand in front of the pot plant at the back. On the far right is Benny Higgins, who resigned after a year as head of retail banking, but was later proved right on his mortgage pricing strategy. (Courtesy of Lloyds Banking Group plc Archives)

Left. Under Peter Cummings, corporate banking became HBOS's top profit earner, but he faced continual pressure to produce more. (© Paul Raeburn)

There was an outcry when HBOS refurbished The Mound, closing the branch which used to operate there and removing the offices of the Governor, chief executive and general managers to be replaced by 'hot desking.' (Press Association)

Sir Philip Green, a talented businessman and retailer, was Cummings' key contact. He did big deals, risking his own money alongside the Bank's, but always repaid his debts in full, ahead of time.

Vincent Tchenguiz with his brother Robert were among the high-rolling 'FOPs' – friends of Philip Green – who did big property deals backed by Bank of Scotland corporate. (Press Association)

Former Rangers Football Club owner Sir David Murray introduced the Bank to Tom Hunter. The Bank also part-funded several of his property deals.

Entrepreneur Tom Hunter took his first big deal to Bank of Scotland, but later the Bank began to approach him with invitations to participate or lead deals which they would fund. (Scotsman Publications)

Graeme Shankland was one of Cumming's key lieutenants. He lead on the Arcadia purchase, and after the collapse of the Bank helped to recover value from some of the HBOS deals.

Andy Hornby (front) initially thought he had put together a great deal with Lloyds' chairman Sir Victor Blank (right), but as the real state of HBOS became more apparent the value received by shareholders was progressively reduced. (Press Association)

Above left. Hornby's negotiations with Lloyds' chief executive Eric Daniels (right) were heated and dragged on into the early hours before agreement was reached. Both men were fooling themselves about the deal, but neither yet realised it. (Press Association)

Above right. Sir James Crosby resigned as deputy chair of the Financial Services Authority after Paul Moore, the former head of regulatory risk at HBOS, gave evidence to the House of Commons Treasury Committee. (Press Association)

Right. Lord Stevenson, former HBOS chair, claimed in evidence to the Treasury Committee that the closure of wholesale markets was the principal reason for the collapse of the Bank. (Press Association) was that once acquired, current account customers could be sold other products – insurance, savings, loans – but that was in the future.

To make things worse from the traditionalists' point of view, Hornby was undeniably superb at marketing and selling and even the former Bank of Scotland board members were impressed. 'Hornby was a most able and most likeable marketing person. His ability to get things on TV and to sell was amazing. When you saw him in action with his people and his charts and all his modern thinking, it was difficult to believe there was anything he could not do.'

His great innovation was to allow his advertising agency to launch a television and press campaign which turned traditional stereotypes on their heads. Instead of using celebrities or actors the ads featured ordinary members of the HBOS staff singing and dancing in front of the cameras. Although there were Scottish staff north of the border, the most popular by far of these amateur stars was Birmingham-born, bald, bespectacled Howard Brown, who sang specially written lyrics around the theme of 'Who gives you extra?' to well-known hits such as Tom Jones' *Sex Bomb* and *Who Let the Dogs Out* by Baha Men. Brown became extremely popular and HBOS used him extensively, adapting hits such as Rod Stewart's *Sailing*, with the word 'Saving' and Aretha Franklin's *Think* with the title-word changed to 'Extra'.

Brown became so well known that he was recognised in the street and the Bank sent him on a tour of branches so that customers could meet him face to face. He made guest appearances in television shows but the novelty wore off and the over-exposure of Howard began to provide irritation rather than delight. The Bank withdrew him from public performances and for a while gave him a job in the public relations department, but eventually he left banking and went back to his previous trade as a locksmith.

Meanwhile the bank was trying to boost its presence in the small- and medium-sized business market under a new department headed by Colin Matthew. This was a lucrative sector, with profit margins more than twice those in personal banking. Bank of Scotland led this market in Scotland but without a branch presence in the south had found it difficult to break the stranglehold of the London banks. The plan was to pilot new business banking services in 15 Halifax branches in England and then roll them out to 100 more. Matthew announced that he would recruit 1,500 experienced staff – mostly from other banks – and HBOS would match its offer to personal customers by paying interest on cash held in business accounts.

But the initiative got off to a disappointing start. Branches were geared towards personal customers and business people were not keen to discuss their company's problems in busy, noisy retail malls. Halifax branch staff were unused to dealing with commercial customers and did not understand their needs. They were also not equipped to handle large volumes of cash, particularly coins. The campaign received a major setback when, after a training session in an open-plan branch in the Trafford shopping centre in Manchester, a flip-chart was left in full view of customers. It listed all those businesses that Halifax did not want and that staff should discourage. They included new business start-ups, taxi drivers, window cleaners, market traders, shops and supermarkets. *The Sun*, the largest selling daily newspaper in Britain, got hold of a photograph of the chart and ran a story on its front page under the heading 'Halifax couldn't give a XXXX'.[4] It went on to quote affronted taxi drivers and window cleaners and carried a cartoon, which Bank of Scotland staff felt 'captured all our frustrations'. *The Daily Mail* called HBOS 'The bank that likes to say "no" to small business'.

The hapless Bank tried to explain that it was merely discouraging those businesses with cash-handling requirements which it could not yet meet, but the impression that it was rejecting a whole class of basic small businesses proved hard to shake off. Other newspapers took up the story and small-business associations made loud complaints. James Crosby had to admit to a major embarrassment over the gaffe but its campaign to break into the smaller end of the market received a blow from which it was hard to recover. Persuading small firm owners to change their bank had always been a long job, involving them in considerable upheaval and disruption to their business. Now it looked even harder.

The flip-chart incident was bad enough, but there was a starker illustration of the change in culture to come. A cabbage was placed on the desk of a cashier who had not hit targets in a branch in Glasgow, while in Paisley a cauliflower was the brassica which was chosen to represent under-achievement. The banking union was horrified and the incident provided another reason for the press and broadcasters to criticise selling methods in financial services. The company's apology looked lame.

13

Room at the top

With the embarrassment of the 'no taxi drivers' story still ringing in his ears, James Crosby delivered another bombshell when he went back to HBOS shareholders to raise £1.37 billion in new capital. The market did not take it well and the share price, already trailing that of the Bank's competitors, fell 8 per cent on the announcement. Officially HBOS explained that it was having to put more money into its life assurance and pensions business because of changes in regulatory rules, but the feeling inside and outside the company was that it was being driven too fast, particularly in selling new mortgages and corporate loans. Adding new business was sustainable if it could be done profitably so that some of the surplus generated could provide extra capital. The worry was that new mortgages were being sold which were not profitable, or not profitable enough, and that the fast pace of growth Crosby was setting would lead HBOS corporate banking into lowering its standards.

Newspapers voiced the fears of some City analysts:

It is not hard to see why HBOS' share placing should have sent investors reaching for the panic button. Banks have squandered shareholders' money so often that it is almost a core activity – think of the billions that have been lost in Latin America, the US, property or investment banking, to name but a few follies of the past two decades. HBOS chief executive James Crosby insists that if it cannot find a profitable way of investing the cash, he will hand it back to shareholders. While that might please the City advisers, who would generate yet more fees from such a deal, it is hardly reassuring. The general rule is that banks with money to burn inevitably find a way to do so. The real concern is that the money will be channelled towards Bank of Scotland's corporate banking business. Under Peter Burt, that bank was a model of probity and Scottish parsimony. While everyone fretted that it did not have enough capital to fund its rapid growth, Burt set about delivering it year after year, apparently on a shoestring. It has not taken Crosby long to destroy that reputation.[1]

Crosby also fuelled the fears himself when he admitted that HBOS could not fund its own expansion. 'We are growing too fast to do that. Three years ago the bank had surplus capital and no growth. Now we have got the strongest growth seen at a bank for years. I know it costs a lot to raise the money, but when you need money you have to ask for it.'[2] Crosby had set demanding targets for the group and all its divisions. He wanted a return on equity of 20 per cent – a stretching goal at the best of times but made more difficult by the decision to raise more equity. He also wanted each division to meet the return criteria and achieve a share of 15–20 per cent of its market. Retail could already claim that in mortgages and deposit accounts but in other respects HBOS was still a small player. To 'eat the lunch' of the Big Four as Crosby promised, it would have to run very hard.

The pace of growth was causing strains inside the company too. 'The annual budgeting process was quite tense,' remembers one senior manager. 'The divisional chiefs would draw up their budgets and send them up to Mike Ellis [finance director]. When they came back they had been pushed up, but were then carved in stone and you had to deliver. If you were to compete, you just had to lend more.' The feeling among former Bank of Scotland people was that HBOS was being pushed by men with little experience and no understanding of banking and the row boiled over at a board meeting. 'George Mitchell [head of corporate banking] lost his temper and shouted across the table, "We joined you on the basis that you had a lot of assets – but now you are throwing those assets away." '

Peter Burt retired in January 2003 after 27 years with the Bank. He had been knighted in the New Year Honours List. His internal titles, now largely honorific, were passed on. George Mitchell became Governor and got his name on Bank of Scotland banknotes, and Sir Ron Garrick stepped up as deputy chairman, although without executive responsibilities. The market had an inkling Burt was about to announce his departure when he sold £2 million of HBOS shares. He had gone a year before his normal retirement age but still received a pension of £334,000 a year from a total 'pot' of £5.4 million. *The Daily Telegraph* reported that he also received a bonus of £347,000 in his last year and retained 529,414 shares – worth about £3.5 million.[3] The annual report was careful to say that he had 'elected to retire' and that no severance payment had been paid, but added: 'Sir Peter Burt's pension was based on his accrued benefit with no actuarial reduction for early payment. The cost of waiving the actuarial reduction was £614,000.' A pay-off of two-thirds of a million pounds is more than the vast majority of people can expect when they leave their jobs, but this was not an exceptional amount in banking and, hidden away in the notes, provoked little attention.

Other salary increases were modest, except for Lord Stevenson, who saw his remuneration as part-time chairman rise by nearly a third to £472,500, partly paid to him directly and partly through his company, Cloaca Maxima, named after the sewerage system of Ancient Rome.

Gordon McQueen, who had been running the treasury operation, left later the same year, again retiring early. His place was taken by Lindsay Mackay, a treasury veteran who had joined Bank of Scotland in 1982. A big, quiet and serious man, he had a reputation for prudent management and calm judgement, but he was not given a place on the main board, where treasury was represented by George Mitchell. The board also lost Sir Bob Reid, the former Shell executive who had served as a director of Bank of Scotland and had been senior non-executive director on the HBOS board. He had long experience and had not been afraid to speak his mind.

There was still disquiet in Scotland that HBOS had been a takeover rather than a merger and the trigger which turned the concerns into public anger was the decision to refurbish the Bank's 200-year-old headquarters on The Mound. To create a double-height central hall with views over Edinburgh which, it was unwisely announced, would be used for corporate entertaining, the working branch was being closed and moved elsewhere. The public would no longer be admitted into the building, which still had in its foyer the 300-year-old iron-bound wooden chest which had served as the Scottish Treasury. Not only that, but the gallery, a first-floor landing running around the foyer, was also removed. Off it had been the offices of the chief executive, treasurer and six other general managers of the Old Bank. The traditional collegiate management structure had gone, to be replaced by 'hot desking'.

For those who had opposed the merger, this was proof that the Scottish capital had lost an important head office, now being turned from a working building into little more than a dining room. A campaign was launched headed by Hugh Young, a former secretary of the Bank, and it gathered political and civic support, but it could not prevent the remodelling from going ahead. Despite the assurances that the building now housed more working executives than it had done under the old Bank of Scotland regime, it was difficult to believe that the Bank was being run from Scotland in anything but name.

Nevertheless, despite teething problems, the integration of the Bank and Halifax had gone well and the new group made good progress. For 2003 HBOS was able to report profits up 29 per cent, with all divisions contributing. The retail business had been reined in slightly and grew by less than 20 per cent, but insurance and investment rose by over a half, business banking – having put the 'no taxi drivers' row behind it – grew by a third and corporate banking by 21 per cent. It was a substantial result but there were still some doubts. The *Financial Times'* Lex column reported: 'The real question remains bad debts: can HBOS conceivably have achieved this sort of loan growth without jeopardising credit quality? There are at present few signs of serious trouble – non-performing loans remain at 1.75 per cent of advances. But until it is clear that all HBOS's new loans do not carry the seeds of disaster, the market will not give Mr Crosby the benefit of the doubt.'[4]

The following year the group was again able to report strong profit increases, with all divisions contributing. Crosby had to report that he had missed his 20 per cent return-on-equity target – but only by a fraction. The City seemed generally pleased with the way things were going. In its three years of life, HBOS had outperformed other banks, without the feared dramatic rise in bad debts, and had shown that when necessity demanded it was prepared to restrain its instinct to dash for growth.

Crosby dithered for several weeks over whether or not to make a counter bid for Abbey National, which was being bought by the Spanish bank Santander, but the City decided he had made the right decision in sitting on his hands. Mike Ellis, the finance director, retired, to be replaced by Mark Tucker, who came from the insurance group Prudential. The board also lost another link with the old Bank of Scotland with the retirement of John Maclean. Modern governance standards demanded that non-executive directors serve for limited fixed terms. If they stayed too long they were deemed not to be independent any more, but what it meant was that board members seldom stayed long enough to experience a whole business cycle, from boom to bust.

Tensions among the executive directors seemed to have cooled when, in March 2004, it was revealed that Andy Hornby had received an offer from a large retail company to join them as chief executive, and to keep him, HBOS had given him a special incentive worth £2 million. The fact that the company was so keen to stop Hornby leaving clearly anointed him for higher things, but there was no suggestion of any vacancy at the top of the business in the immediate future.

With better results generating more internal capital, HBOS now began to reverse the decision it had made two years before, using its cash to buy back shares from its investors. The effect was to shrink its capital and to increase the share price. In two stages it first spent £750 million, then a further £250 million. Crosby said the policy was designed to make HBOS's assets 'sweat more effectively' on behalf of shareholders. 'We have invested in capacity to self-fund our growth. Now we have got to that point and this allows us to convert that growth into value for shareholders. We have got to make growth work harder for shareholder return.'[5] Reducing the number of the company's shares would also have the effect of increasing its return on equity.

But beneath the surface rivalries in the senior management had been building. James Crosby was still not 50, at the height of his powers and by taking his foot off the accelerator pedal had started to be accepted by the City as an effective manager who could deliver sustainable growth for his investors. Mark Tucker, who had been seen by many as a potential next chief executive of the group, announced in June 2005 that he was leaving after a year to go back to Prudential as its head. The remaining two possible candidates who might eventually succeed Crosby offered a clear choice. George Mitchell, at 55, had nearly 40 years of solid banking experience behind him and had worked in almost every department of the Bank. Personable, but usually undemonstrative in public, he was viewed by those who thought he should be the heir apparent as the safe bet, a practical banker who could consolidate the gains the group had made.

Andy Hornby was almost the exact opposite. Still only 38, he had achieved academic brilliance at Oxford and Harvard, whereas

Mitchell had joined the bank straight from school. Hornby's only banking experience had been in the six years he had been at Halifax/HBOS and then only in the personal banking market. Mitchell's post-school education – studying for the certificate of the Institute of Bankers in Scotland – had been narrowly focused on one industry, banking. Hornby's postgraduate education at the world's foremost business school (where he had passed out first from 800 students) had taught him that management was a generic skill which could be applied in any industry. At HBOS, he had used techniques he picked up in retailing such as weekly sales and service updates.

He was described in glowing terms by the managers he had worked for in the supermarket group Asda. Alan Leighton, Hornby's former boss, said: 'He has brought a lot of Asda stuff into HBOS. He is focused and I know spends a lot of time in the branches talking to people about what is going on and is very good at strategy. As well as being super-bright, he is also likeable.' City analysts were even more complimentary. One said: 'His overall record in the retail business has been exemplary.' Another described him as a 'superstar'.[6] With verdicts like these, it was a surprise to find that Hornby had spent only three years at Asda, his previous jobs being at the Boston Consulting Group and Blue Circle Cement.

Hornby – young, dynamic, energetic, successful and likeable – was the board's favourite, but some of the former Bank of Scotland directors worried about his lack of all-round banking experience and knowledge. They suggested to Lord Stevenson and James Crosby that Hornby should be made chief executive of BankWest, the group's Australian subsidiary. In a few years in a smaller institution and a more benign competitive environment he would encounter a broad range of typical banking problems and be able to return with more experience and enough time still to become one of the youngest chief executives in the UK. The suggestion was rejected without discussion.

In June 2005, Hornby was named Chief Operating Officer – number two in the hierarchy. As well as retail banking he would have overall charge of the insurance and investment division. With this addition he would be responsible for 60 per cent of the group's profit. He was the clear successor to James Crosby, although the chief executive made it clear no change was imminent – he had no intention of stepping down. 'There is no vacancy at the top. I am

49 . . . but it's my job to be thinking about these issues of succession and senior management capability is one of my core responsibilities.'

George Mitchell, the rejected candidate, resigned, although officially he was described as retiring. In the annual report Lord Stevenson said he would be remembered as a powerful advocate of HBOS and a superb business builder. You had to look at the small-print notes on page 81 to find that special financial arrangements were being made for his leaving. There was to be no termination payment, but since Mitchell was leaving ten months short of the 40 years service which would give him his maximum pension, the group was paying £198,000 to make up the shortfall. The pension would be based on his final salary and in the previous year he had received £595,000 topped up with a further half million in bonus and incentives. A salary review in the year he left increased his base salary to £610,000.

To replace Mike Ellis, Phil Hodkinson moved from heading insurance and investment to be finance director and, to replace George Mitchell, Peter Cummings was appointed head of corporate banking and joined the board. He had been with the Bank for 32 years and was not only a capable deputy to Mitchell, but a supremely talented deal-maker, yet some board members had doubts about the appointment. 'Peter was a very able executive,' said one, 'but he wasn't director material. He couldn't see the big picture.'

According to Crosby, the bank was now 'firing on all cylinders', but there were lingering doubts that it could keep up the pace of its expansion over the past three years. Profits had doubled and costs had been cut but could this be sustained? Non-performing loans – mortgages on which the borrowers could not meet their interest payments – had risen, not by much, but enough to raise questions. There was also concern about the creditworthiness of some unsecured personal lending HBOS had made. Six months later, when it reported its half-year results for 2005, the bank did its best to quell fears over its bad debt levels which, although they were up by a quarter, were more or less steady as a percentage of the total loan book, which had also risen by 25 per cent. Deep in the small print some analysts discovered a deterioration in the quality of some personal loans, overdrafts and credit cards, but the market as a whole did not seem worried and the share price rose.

At the beginning of 2006 the HBOS share price hit a record high. The group seemed to have shaken off the doubts about its ability to keep growing and James Crosby was the toast of the City. At exactly that point he announced he was leaving. It was a shock inside and out of the company. He was not being poached to step into another big job, he was not nearing retirement, being still short of his 50th birthday and only a few months previously he had denied that he was stepping down. His decision, which had been discussed with Lord Stevenson, was known to only a few members of the board. Andy Hornby was to be the new chief executive.

Prophetically, the *Financial Times* commented: 'Barring a complete change in HBOS's fortunes in the coming year, [Crosby] is likely to be remembered as the chief executive who walked away from his job long before anyone asked him to leave. "Sustained business success is about an orderly transition from one generation to the next," he says. The next few years will determine whether or not that transition has been a success.'[7]

14

Give me enough debt and
I'll move the world

As any school science pupil ought to know, Archimedes, who discovered the lever laws famously said: 'Give me a place to stand, and I will move the earth.' In the twenty-first century, debt had taken the place of levers in doing the heavy lifting, but there was still a belief that anything could be shifted provided there was enough borrowed money. I will try to illustrate the power of the debt lever with a simplified example from my own experience.

In the 1990s I was a director of a company which bought the *Glasgow Herald* newspaper group from the conglomerate Lonrho for £80 million. Four years later the company was sold for £120 million. Simple arithmetic would suggest the profit was £40 million, or 50 per cent of the original investment – not a bad return in such a short time and certainly much more than would be earned by putting the money on deposit. But that ignores the power of leverage.

Most of the original £80 million purchase price was borrowed. Shareholders – in this case a venture capital company and the management team – only provided £5 million. All the rest – £75 million – was borrowed from banks. The company traded profitably during its four years, but all its earnings went to pay interest on the debt and investment in the company, shareholders took nothing out. When the firm was sold, banks received their £75 million back, plus a further £10 million in fees and charges – a good return for them considering they had been paid interest each year and much more than they would have received under normal commercial lending terms.

This left £35 million of profit to be divided among the shareholders – who had only put up £5 million. Their return was therefore seven times their initial stake, or 700 per cent – the magnifying power of the debt lever.

That burden of debt (more than the annual sales of the company) would not usually be considered for a trading business. A management team would be mad to take it on and a bank would be daft to lend it to them. Banks were willing to lend in this case because the company had a long trading history and they could see that it was capable of generating enough cash to pay the interest, even if the economy turned down (which it did). They charged well above the normal rate for commercial lending and extracted fees on top of that. They would not have been willing to put up the money for a long period, but it was always part of the plan to sell the company within five years to pay off the debt. There are a number of complications I have ignored but the basic principle remains the same. By leveraging its small amount of equity with a large amount of debt, the shareholders were able to greatly increase their reward.

Archimedes' ambition would have been commonplace in the world of corporate leverage. Bank of Scotland was one of the first banks into this market, using the skills it had learned in the 1970s lending to oil field developers to assess the cash flows of a diverse range of businesses. Predicting the amount of money a business could reliably generate was an essential part in reducing the risk for a bank and followed the old banking rule of 'look at the lender, not the asset'. The bank would study the market for the company's products to see how that might affect cash coming in, and would assess the management team to make sure they had the skills and experience to run the company successfully.

The first management buyouts (or MBOs in the jargon) were like our purchase of the newspaper company. In the 1980s and 1990s large conglomerates were selling off basic businesses, often to their managements. Banks were keen to finance these deals because the companies to which they were lending usually had long track records and the people leading the buyouts were usually the same managements who had been running the company previously. They already knew the business and the market and, freed from the control and costs of the conglomerate, they could make the company grow. These were good deals for the banks because they could lend large sums of money at high rates of interest and charge fancy fees. Always implicit was that the debt would be repaid after a few years when the company was sold or floated on the stock market. The bank could then take back its money and start the whole process again, earning more fees and more interest.

The first MBOs were small, in the tens of millions of pounds; then they grew to hundreds of millions, then finally billions. Eventually conglomerates had broken themselves up and there were no more left to sell off subsidiaries so MBOs became less common, but the power of leverage had been discovered and seemed as immutable as the laws of mechanics. Debt in large quantities began to be used in any big transaction – acquiring another company, for example. MBOs became LBOs – leveraged buyouts – and the provision of debt acquired a series of euphemisms, such as 'structured finance' and 'integrated finance'. Bank of Scotland, still operating under its own name even though it was part of HBOS, was an acknowledged leader and its specialist teams based in London or Edinburgh were respected and sought after. Each deal they did added to their stock of knowledge and enhanced their reputation.

The merger with Halifax had given the Bank of Scotland corporate team a lot more clout in the market, but it was still not in the top league. Major multinational companies were unlikely to choose HBOS as their primary banker because it could not offer the full range of services that the Big Four banks could provide. It had only a limited international network and in other specialisms such as treasury and investment banking it was a small player. So it had relatively little of the regular bread-and-butter income that servicing large corporate customers brought to its bigger rivals. HBOS was dependent on one-off transactions for much of its earnings. Although it could take part in financing the very largest corporations, it was unlikely ever to be able to lead these deals and would be a junior partner. It preferred instead to create a niche for itself in servicing medium-sized businesses and entrepreneurs who were ambitious to grow. These were inherently more risky than the very largest businesses but the bank prided itself on its ability to appraise risk and by leading deals it was able to earn arrangement fees.

Because it had relatively little regular income, the corporate team had to position itself to be ready to participate in or lead deals and it became very good at seeking out areas of the economy where there were opportunities to provide debt. These included not only corporate acquisitions and buyouts, but energy, finance to housing associations to build homes and to public/private partnerships to build schools and hospitals.

The corporate department also expanded abroad. Building on the

Bank of Scotland network of offices in North America and the Far East, its BankWest subsidiary in Australia and its growing presence in Ireland, it added offices in European capitals. It also broadened its range of products. Traditionally banks had provided only 'senior debt' – so called because if a company had to be wound up, it was the senior debt providers who would be paid out first and therefore had the best chance of getting their money back. Now it was also providing 'mezzanine' finance – called that because it ranked between the 'top floor' of the senior debt and the 'ground floor' of the equity providers (the shareholders) who would be paid out last and were taking the most risk of losing their money. Mezzanine was more risky than senior debt, but was more profitable. Banks could charge a higher rate of interest on mezzanine and often also received a 'kicker' – a success fee at the end of a transaction, or a small shareholding in the company.

Controversially, Bank of Scotland Corporate (as it branded itself) began routinely taking equity stakes in companies to which it was also a lender. For decades Bank of Scotland had acquired shareholdings in companies but usually through special circumstances. In the oil industry it had been established practice that banks providing debt for oilfield financings might also get a tiny percentage of the ownership. In other industries some shareholdings had been acquired by default: the borrower had run into trouble, usually because of an economic downturn, could not repay the loan and the Bank, rather than write off everything, had accepted ownership of all or part of the venture in exchange for cancelling the debt. It had done this a number of times in South America during the Latin American debt crisis and at home had become the reluctant owner of hotels and golf courses in the same way.

The Bank was never comfortable with this position and looked for opportunities to sell its shareholding as soon as possible. During his period as chief executive, Bruce Pattullo had maintained a rigid policy of refusing to take equity stakes in companies to which the Bank was also a lender, seeing it as a conflict of interest. If a company got into difficulties, the priority for the Bank was to get its money back and that might mean going over the heads of shareholders to call in a receiver while there was still a chance of recovering the loan. That could leave the shareholders with nothing.

When it began to finance MBOs, younger managers started to

question that policy. As the example I gave at the beginning of this chapter shows, equity holders stood to make the biggest gains in leveraged deals. In theory they were taking the most risk, but in practice if a company went down the Bank also stood to lose. Why not get some of the icing as well as the cake? After Pattullo retired, the ban on equity began to be relaxed.

Bank of Scotland Corporate began to offer a 'one-stop shop' to people wanting to do big transactions. Alongside senior debt, it would offer mezzanine and equity finance, earning itself more interest and fees for arranging and structuring the deal. It began to promote itself as the bank which could put together the essential elements of making a transaction happen and it published a regular magazine, *Deal Leader*. Its pages profiled the entrepreneurs it was backing, describing their companies and how Bank of Scotland's cash had helped them grow. It carried a regular feature promoting a member of the Bank's corporate team under the heading 'The Loan Arranger'. A regular section called 'Deals Done Differently' also listed the transactions the Bank had recently completed.

Over the six or seven years following the merger, equity stakes became a major profit source for HBOS. A series of subsidiary companies was set up, all bearing a name derived from the old Bank of Scotland Latin motto *'Tanto Uberior'* (which approximately translates as 'so much the more plentiful'). Uberior Ventures, Uberior Investments, Uberior Equity, Uberior Property and others similarly named held stakes in 70 companies such as health and fitness group David Lloyd Leisure, builder Keepmoat, newsagent group Martin McColl and dozens of property companies including a 22.5 per cent stake in Chelsfield Partners, a 50 per cent stake in a luxury hotel venture with Sir Rocco Forte, a shopping centre joint venture with Warner Estate, a retail joint venture with the Reuben brothers and a petrol station joint venture.

At its height the combined value of these shareholdings was said to top £5.5 billion and the portfolio generated hundreds of millions of pounds of annual income in dividends or the proceeds of sales. Besides providing equity funding, HBOS also lent £4.5 billion to these companies to fund expansion or new developments.

As you might guess from the parties he throws, the retail business-man Sir Philip Green has a liking for the dramatic. He is also a good storyteller. Recalling one of the early deals in which he had been involved – the purchase of the Olympus Sports chain of clothing shops from the British retail group Sears in 1995 – he told the journalist Robert Peston that the message telling him the company was for sale came while he was undergoing a heart operation:

> The only reason I didn't do it myself was that I was in Wellington Hospital in the intensive care unit when I got the call. When I was offered it, I was in the hospital. So I said: 'Can't do it this week, can we do it next week?' I had other things on. Couldn't do it. But it worked out well. Tom did it. Worked well. Everybody won.[1]

Like every good story, it contains some truth, but the actual circumstances of the purchase may be more prosaic. The Tom in question was the Scottish entrepreneur Tom Hunter. When he left university in 1984 Hunter had borrowed £10,000 from his father and the Royal Bank of Scotland and started selling trainers from the back of a van. By 1995 he had built the business into a chain of shops named Sports Division and was making £4 million a year in profit. He was looking for ways to expand when one of his suppliers tipped him off that Sears wanted to sell Olympus. A purchase would more than double Sports Division's number of outlets, but Olympus was losing money. Hunter, then 34, went to see Philip Strong, Sears' chief executive, but was shown the door. Strong did not believe Hunter could come up with the money and would not negotiate with him.

Hunter and Green had met when Green had bought the Glasgow budget retailer What Everyone Wants, so Hunter called him and asked him to front the deal. Green went to Sears and secured an option to buy Olympus. (The call telling him he had the option may have come while he was in hospital.) Hunter received the call from Green saying the deal was on while he was holidaying in Barbados with his family, but now his problems started. To buy the company he needed to borrow £20 million, but the Royal Bank turned him down. Racking his brains, Hunter remembered meeting someone from Bank of Scotland while on a trip to Turin organised by David Murray, then owner of Glasgow Rangers, to see his team play Juventus. He called Murray to be told that the man he had spoken to was Gavin Masterton, the Bank's Treasurer. On his return from holiday, Hunter called Masterton, who sent one of his corporate managers to see him – Peter Cummings.

Hunter and Cummings had a lot in common. Coming from modest beginnings, both had done well in their chosen careers, but had remained rooted in the communities from which they came. Cummings still lived in Dumbarton, Hunter in the South Ayrshire community of New Cumnock. Hunter knew exactly what he had to do to turn Olympus around and took Cummings through his figures in detail. If he could make the new stores perform even half as well as his existing shops he would be able to repay the loan with ease. Cummings had been told by Masterton: 'Be hard, but don't lose the deal.' He fulfilled both parts of his brief. The Bank agreed to lend the £20 million but Cummings demanded security over Hunter's business and his house. Philip Green also extracted a high price for his part – £1 million in cash and 12.5 per cent of the equity – but he was right. It did work out well and everybody did win. Hunter more than met his promise to Cummings and repaid the loan within six months. Three years later he sold Sports Division for £295 million.

The connection between Green, Hunter and Cummings was to be crucial to Green's next big deal in 1999 when he bought the remainder of Sears. Green and Hunter were putting money into the purchase, together with the Barclay twins Sir David and Sir Frederick, who had built up substantial businesses ranging from hotels to shipping. Cummings was handling the transaction for the Bank, but chief executive Peter Burt was taking a close interest, partly because of the importance of the Barclay brothers, whose account he oversaw personally and partly because there was a potential embarrassment for the Bank: its Deputy Governor, Sir Bob Reid, was chairman of Sears. Green, again, told Peston the story:

> It was the night of the deal, Sears. The Barclays were funding. I put in X, they put in Y, we borrowed Z. At five o'clock the night before £150 million of the funding falls out of bed. Bank finance. They couldn't get it done. I called Peter Cummings. I had a relationship with him from Sports Division. I said: 'Peter, I need a favour.'
> 'What do you need?'
> I said: 'I need one hundred and fifty million quid.'
> 'When?'
> I said: 'tonight.'
> He said: 'Is it for what I think it's for?'
> I said: 'yes.'

He said: 'Bit tricky, give me 20 minutes.'

Called back. He said: 'All right, I'm on, on the following basis: boom, boom, boom.'

I said: 'Right, let's go. We did it through the night. So I bought more than my Y. To get it over the line, I got it over the line myself. But it was on a handshake.[2]

You might get the impression that Cummings agreed to lend £150 million to Green on the strength of a telephone call but, again, the truth is less colourful. The banker used that 20 minutes to call his boss, Peter Burt. Bank of Scotland was lending to its long-standing good customers the Barclays, not to Green, and Burt agreed to lend more to get the deal done, but to the Barclays, who had agreed to put in more money. Speed was of the essence, but Burt also called his boss, the then Bank Governor Sir Alistair Grant, to make sure that everyone understood what was being agreed and on what terms.

Like the Olympus deal, the purchase of Sears turned out better than anyone had expected. Green was an extraordinarily talented businessman as well as a retailer. He had paid £549 million, but broke up the group, selling off parts of it which he did not want and recouped the purchase price within three months. Again, the cash the Bank had lent was repaid in quick time and the deal cemented the relationship between Philip Green and Peter Cummings. Green also liked to make a splash at London casinos and from the press reports it could appear that both he and Cummings were gamblers, prepared to take big business risks to win big rewards, but in reality both were detail men. Green had long experience in turning around retail brands and before he made purchases he worked hard to understand every aspect of the business.

Green and Hunter went on to purchase the store group Bhs in 2000 for £200 million, where Green tripled the profits, but it was his acquisition of Arcadia, the Top Shop and Dorothy Perkins company, in 2002 which was his most spectacular. The deal had been planned in partnership with the Icelandic Baugur group, which was going to take some of the high-street brands owned by Arcadia. But in the final stages they ran into trouble and their offices were raided by the Icelandic police.

To get the deal done Green and his family put in £120 million. 'The fundamental difference between me and those tossers running public companies,' Green told the *Financial Times*, 'is that I invest my own money.' Bank of Scotland, by this time part of HBOS, provided the rest – £808 million. The bank also paid £6 million for an 8 per cent stake in the business, effectively acting as a private equity house as well as lending.[3] The deal graphically illustrated Green's maverick approach to business. Arcadia was a public company, quoted on the Stock Exchange, and normal City protocol would have demanded a series of quiet, nuanced conversations between advisory firms before any direct approach was made. Green dispensed with all that and called Stuart Rose, Arcadia's chief executive, himself. 'Why should anyone pay £10–15 million in fees just to find out whether the other person wants to do business?' It was an unorthodox attitude, but the Takeover Panel accepted it.

Green may have been investing his own money but HBOS would be hazarding its depositors' funds. Cummings was closely identified with the deal and was criticised in the press for the scale of the risk he was allegedly running on behalf of the Bank. In fact most of the work was done by a team working under him led by one of his deputies, Graeme Shankland, and the transaction was signed off by George Mitchell, the director then responsible for corporate banking.

But yet again Green proved that he was a master retailer and as good as his word to Cummings. Within a year he had boosted sales in the group and repaid £500 million of the cash he had borrowed. A year after that he had paid off the whole lot. The night before he announced doubled profits, Green hosted a dinner for George Mitchell and Peter Cummings at Les Ambassadeurs, his favourite Mayfair club and casino. The following morning Cummings drank champagne with Green at the Arcadia offices at Oxford Circus, before both of them addressed the staff. It appears to have been a very emotional occasion for them all. As Green spoke, his wife Tina, a tear in her eye, according to the *Financial Times*, held Cummings' hand. But it was Cummings' speech which was most extraordinary and illustrates the very close relationship he had formed with Green.

'As shareholders, stakeholders and bankers, we can only thank you from the bottom of our hearts for delivering a first class set of results. It is outstanding. When you decide to lend money you assess the skill-set of the people in the business: what I see now in this room, is not just a skill-set and competence, but capability to compete with the best.' He went on to describe Philip Green as 'the most conservative and prudent finance manager I have met', and praised his 'integrity by the barrel-load'.[4] His words may have been justified, but his willingness to say them in public was hardly in keeping with the traditional image of the typical Scottish bank manager.

Green had already paid a dividend but as the group rode the consumer boom, there was much more to come. He lived during the week in a London hotel, but had his private jet ferry him back to Monaco at the weekends, where Tina Green was a resident tax-exile. Although Green ran the group, Tina was technically the owner and when Arcadia paid out £1.2 billion in dividend in 2005 – the biggest personal dividend in British history – most of it went to Tina free of tax. HBOS, as the only other shareholder, received £100 million as its reward. To fund the payout Green again borrowed, much of it from Bank of Scotland, which then syndicated the loan to other banks – so the Bank was effectively lending to pay its own share of the dividend.

Cummings was not Green's only supporter in HBOS. In 2004 Green bid an eye-watering £9.5 billion for Marks & Spencer, the UK's biggest clothing retailer, but walked away when the price got too high. Green was prepared to put in £1.6 billion of his family's money and HBOS were to fund the rest alongside other banks. Had the deal succeeded Green had invited Lord Stevenson to become senior non-executive director on the board, an appointment which the Bank claimed would not lead to a conflict of interest because as yet he held no position in M & S and had received no money from the company. The move led to one of the few clashes on the HBOS board when some non-executives objected to the chairman approving the Bank's involvement in the M & S bid. The tense atmosphere was defused by Sir Ron Garrick, who offered to read the papers and make the decision in Stevenson's place.

The Green-Cummings connection was to be a source of opportunities for HBOS which only a select handful of other bankers could access. 'FOPs' – the Friends of Philip – were a small group of high-rolling individuals who were transforming the British corporate landscape with a series of audacious debt-funded deals. The FOPs included Tom Hunter, but also the Reuben brothers, David and Simon, who had made their fortunes in metals, trading and property, the property speculators Robert and Vincent Tchenguiz, Nick Leslau, another property entrepreneur, Alan Leighton the retailer and Bernie Ecclestone, the owner of Formula One motor racing. They worked hard and played hard, often meeting at parties on each other's Mediterranean yachts, in Riviera mansions or London apartments. Green was a spectacular party-giver, but the soirees at Robert Tchenguiz's London home could rival them. Housed in the former Royal College of Organists premises close to the Royal Albert Hall, it boasted two swimming pools, one on the roof terrace, the other in the basement.

The group shared many things in common. They came from modest beginnings. The Tchenguiz family had twice lost everything in Iraq and Iran, before the sons re-established the family fortune in Britain, Leslau had started on a milk round and traded umbrellas on a market stall and Ecclestone had begun his working life dealing in motorcycle spares. They worked outside the establishment. Not for them the tedious formality of normal City convention. They worked directly, took big risks with their own money and understood the power of leverage.

Few bankers were privileged to drink vintage champagne from the bottle in Monaco clubs with this crowd, but among them were Mike 'Woody' Sherwood, of Goldman Sachs, Bob Wigley, of Merrill Lynch, the only woman of the group the American Robin Saunders, and Peter Cummings.

Cummings' appeal came from the impression that he could commit large sums of HBOS money on his own say-so – an idea that Green did little to dispel:

> Goldman Sachs said there's no relationship on the planet that anybody's got [like the one between Green and Cummings]. What flipped Goldman Sachs' lid was that in the middle of the night – in the middle of the night – we were 900 million quid short [on the bid for M & S]. They thought we could not do it. I said: 'why not?' They said: 'Look, we'll do half.' I said: 'Okay, I'll do the other half. Give me ten minutes.' I called him [Cummings] up. He said: 'Right, let's go.' We got a fax inside seven minutes, while they were having meetings, conference calls, meetings of compliance committees.'[5]

HBOS insiders are adamant that Cummings could not and did not authorise big loans on his own. HBOS corporate had a system of credit committees for each part of the business, each chaired by a managing director. Above these was a credit committee for corporate as a whole chaired by the director, although after 2005 this was Cummings himself. This arrangement might have provided a review and checking mechanism while there was a separation between the deal originator and the chair of the committee, but Cummings continued to be personally involved in deal-making while he was in overall charge of the corporate division. If there was no time to put a deal through the committee system, Cummings had to seek authorisation from two other directors and for very big deals from the chief executive. His ability to act fast and make decisions even at night, insiders insist, was because of the short lines of communication within the Bank.

'Peter's clients, without exception, loved him, but he never by-passed the credit committee and when he said "We'll do that" it was always subject to the Bank's safeguards, or he would say, "I'm not going to be able to back that up, we are not going to do it." They knew exactly where they stood,' a board director remembers.

The deals came thick and fast, in retail, properties, leisure and hotels. Then there were the ones that got away. Green tried for Safeway and M&S, Hunter for Alders and House of Fraser, Hunter and Leslau for Selfridges. Sometimes members of the group acted together, sometimes alone and occasionally they were competing against each other. Each time there was 'leverage' – huge amounts of debt, often provided solely or in part by HBOS.

By 2003 Cummings was estimated to have lent £2.3 billion to the retail sector,[6] much of it to men who had become his personal friends. He supported the Barclay brothers in their £750 million purchase of Littlewoods, the stores and pools group, and Tom Hunter's £310 million takeover of Wyevale Garden Centres, with HBOS providing lending and Uberior Investments, one of the group's subsidiaries, buying 20 per cent of the shares. As the economic good times continued the deals got bigger. In 2004 Hunter appointed the merchant bank Rothschilds to find him deals at over £1 billion. There would be no problem in raising finance, he said, to which Cummings commented: 'If the deal was right, that would be correct.'[7]

HBOS was now increasing its concentration on property and property-related sectors and starting to initiate deals and put together consortia to bid for companies. In 2004 it even bought its own headquarters when investors including Tom Hunter's West Coast Capital, Prestbury Investment Holdings and Bank of Scotland Corporate paid £150 million for 33 Old Broad Street, London, the meeting place of the HBOS board and offices of HBOS Group Treasury Services, and the insurance and investment subsidiaries Clerical Medical and Insight Investment. It also lent money and took venture stakes in property transactions led by David Murray, the owner of Glasgow Rangers Football Club and head of a metals business.

But much bigger deals were to come. In 2006, after a contested battle, HBOS corporate bought McCarthy & Stone, Britain's largest builder of retirement homes, for £1.1 billion in partnership with Hunter, the Reubens and Vincent Tchenguiz. As before, HBOS provided the debt and took part of the equity. By now it was also initiating deals, finding the targets and putting together entrepreneurs to front the bids. Shortly after the McCarthy & Stone purchase, Hunter and HBOS acquired the house builder Crest Nicholson for £660 million. There were also big purchases in hotels – a joint venture with Saudi Billionaire Prince Alwaleed bin Talal to buy the Savoy for £220 million and £750 million to buy the de Vere group with a party of eight investors.

The corporate loan book was increasing at an extraordinary rate and outstripping the growth of other banks. In the City some eyebrows were being raised at the speed and scale of HBOS corporate's deal-making, but Cummings calmed fears by describing the Bank's 'aggressive sell-down policy' to pass some of the debt on to other banks. In the 18 months leading up to October 2006 it had originated 14 per cent more deals, but was only holding on to 8 per cent more of them. On one deal, he added, the bank had sold 90 per cent of its exposure.[8] 'German and Irish banks were falling over themselves to buy loans from us,' remembers one manager, 'we had no difficulty in selling down.'

As its reach extended, the corporate division opened an office in Mayfair, separate from the rest of the business. It began promoting itself in European capitals, holding receptions in the Louvre for a thousand French business people and Stockholm's maritime museum for businessmen in Sweden, where it financed a hostile bid for Capio, a Swedish healthcare group. In 2006 HBOS topped the list of debt providers to European buyouts, with 11 deals in the previous six months. The specialist buyout bank 3i came second.

At the beginning of HBOS's life corporate banking was very much the junior partner. It lent £35 billion, only a quarter of the total provided by the retail business, mainly in mortgages. It provided over £500 million in profit to the group, but that was dwarfed by the £1.4 billion earned by the retail business and lagged behind the £770 million earned in insurance and investment. The British economy was in the doldrums in 2002, but corporate banking still managed to grow its lending by a third. As the economy rebounded in 2003 it pushed its lending up to £50 billion and its profit by 21 per cent to £826 million. In time business banking was folded into corporate and the combined group overtook insurance and investment as the second largest contributor to group profits. By 2004 profits topped £1 billion and by 2007 it was making more than £2.3 billion and had passed the retail bank as the group's largest profit earner.

The total amount lent to customers also rose dramatically, from £35 billion in 2001, to £78 billion in 2004 and £109 billion in 2007.

A lot of the growth was coming from the property sector, which accounted for more than a third of all lending. Ideally a bank would want to match its lending to the profile of the whole economy, but as Bank of Scotland was dependent on corporate transactions it was pulled into those activities where most deals were being done. The Bank's risk assessors looked into the problem: 'It was something we were aware of, and we would have liked to redress the balance, but we did not see any need for immediate panic. It was an issue we would get to over time.' The Bank reviewed its portfolio and satisfied itself that it was well diversified between activities – property investment, construction, house building, housing associations, office and factory development. It was not over-exposed to those areas which had been prone to overheating in the past – particularly the London office market. Also its lending was covered by prudent covenants, which specified conservative loan-to-value ratios and strong cash flow from rents. Bad debt provisions were low. The market was past its trough and there was no cause to be concerned.

The first years of the new century seemed a good time to invest in property. Prices had been depressed by slow growth in the economy but interest rates were coming down from their peak. Commercial property, long the Cinderella of the sector, was seen by some investment analysts as due for a rerating and in residential property Britain still suffered from a housing shortage which should continue to support price increases. Over the four years from the low point in the market in 2003, commercial property prices rose by over 40 per cent. HBOS rode the boom, lending to property developers and taking part in developments itself as a joint venture partner. It was not alone. According to Bank of England figures, banks lent an extra £80 billion to commercial property companies during this period, taking the sector's proportion of total lending to an all-time high.[9]

There was no fear of an economic slowdown; in fact the HBOS corporate department prided itself on its counter-cyclical strategy, lending more when prices were low and the competition was backing off, lending less when prices rose and competition intensified.[10]

15

As safe as houses

My wife and I got our first mortgage from the Halifax Building Society in 1976. It was not an easy or a pleasant process. Apart from a few local authorities, building societies were the only source of home loans at that time and they were strictly regulated. The Bank of England turned the mortgage tap on and off to prevent overheating in the housing market, but even when the money was flowing it was not a simple matter to borrow; you first had to negotiate a moral and financial obstacle course.

There was no point in even asking for a mortgage unless you could demonstrate a habit of thrift, which you did by opening a savings account and making regular deposits. Only when you had done this for a period of months, or even years, could you get an interview with the branch manager, who was usually a daunting authority figure. I was working for the *Financial Times* and my solicitor advised that I play to the vanity of the local Halifax manager by asking for his views on the economic outlook before broaching the subject of our application for a mortgage. The ploy worked and he agreed to lend us the money, but that was the beginning rather than the end of the process. The society would lend a maximum of two-and-a-half times my income, plus half my wife's income. They would not take my word for how much I earned; I had to produce my three most recent payslips and even then the branch wrote to my employer to seek written assurance that I was in a permanent job. My wife was a freelance writer, so to prove her income they demanded her latest tax assessment from the Inland Revenue.

The society would only advance up to 85 per cent of the value of the house – the value being determined by a surveyor appointed by them, reporting to them, but paid for by us. The survey came up with a figure which was less than the price at which our solicitor thought we would have to pay to get the house, so to make up the difference we had to resort to subterfuge. My wife told her bank that we had already bought a home and obtained a loan 'to buy furniture'. This had to be hidden from the building society because any suggestion that we were borrowing to provide the deposit would have led to the immediate withdrawal of the offer. The survey also caused another problem. The house was 100 years old and did not have a damp-proof course and the Halifax decided that until we got one, they would withhold one third of the total loan. This was a severe blow. We were already stretched to our financial limit – we could not afford to bridge the gap and pay for the work to be done. We resigned ourselves to losing the house but were saved by an unsolicited temporary loan from my wife's great-aunt.

Thirty years on, the mortgage market had changed out of all recognition. Building societies had been deregulated by Mrs Thatcher's government in 1986. Several of the largest societies had turned themselves into banks and were competing hard for home loan business. The banks themselves had woken up to the fact that mortgages could be very profitable and new specialist lenders and brokers had entered the market. The housing market looked like a one-way bet for both borrowers and lenders. There had been no serious setback in prices for years and from 2000 to 2007 average prices more than doubled. Some areas of the country had seen even bigger rises. In contrast to the tortuous process I had to endure, borrowers were now almost having loans thrust upon them. Without any evidence of saving, it was possible to get an advance of four, or even five times an applicant's annual income[1] and house prices were rising so fast that some lenders were prepared to lend 100 per cent or even more of the value of a house, confident that inflation would restore the loan-to-value ratio to a sensible level. Having to prove that you earned as much as you claimed was not always necessary; some banks offered self-certified mortgages where no evidence was required. Nor did having a bad credit record bar you from getting a loan; several lenders specialised in taking on poor risks.

Halifax was the king of this market, with a dominant market share and an aggressive sales policy aimed at winning more new business each year, but former building societies like Abbey, Bradford & Bingley and, especially, Northern Rock, were out to steal the crown.

Like Halifax, Northern Rock had its roots in the self-help and savings movement of the nineteenth century. Based in Newcastle, it was an important local employer, sponsored the football and rugby teams, and arts events. Through its charity, the Northern Rock Foundation, it supported community and social groups, especially those working with the disadvantaged. After deregulation, it floated on the stock market and under a young, ambitious chief executive followed a strategy of aggressive growth. Adam Applegarth had a lot in common with Andy Hornby. He was clever, joining Northern Rock as a graduate trainee after reading mathematics and economics at Durham University, had a rapid rise through the management ranks and had become chief executive at the age of 39.

Northern Rock was a fraction of the size of Halifax and its market share of existing mortgages did not come close that of its larger rival, but in the fight for new business, it made most of the running. It was heavily involved in the buy-to-let market, where ordinary people without experience or expertise in property letting or the assets to support heavy lending, were encouraged to buy several houses with big mortgages in order to rent them out. It was one of the first lenders to offer 125 per cent mortgages, where an advance of 90–95 per cent of the value of a property was topped up with a further 30–35 per cent as an unsecured personal loan. And it offered self-certified mortgages.

Much of this market was handled by brokers, who would guarantee to get you a loan. The magazine *Mortgage Strategy* estimated that nearly two-thirds of the £200 billion of new mortgages being written by UK banks in 2006 was through brokers. There were some long-established and sound brokerage firms but the house-price bonanza had also attracted a lot of cowboys into the market. A BBC investigation in 2004 found some recommending that applicants should lie about their income in order to get mortgages of five or six times earnings. It was not only brokers who were exploiting the system. The BBC visited high-street branches of HBOS subsidiary Birmingham Mid-shires, where three out of three of the advisers the reporting team consulted offered self-certified mortgages of around six times income for which the team would have had to have lied. One of these advisers boasted of getting a client a mortgage of around ten times income by inflating his salary to over £100,000. The BBC estimated that up to 30 per cent of self-certified mortgages were obtained on fraudulent earnings figures.[2]

My wife and I, having lied about our 'furniture loan', are in no position to criticise the young couples for whom exaggerating their take-home pay was the only way to get a foot on the housing escalator, which was accelerating prices much faster than salaries. Even at the start of the millennium the average cost of a home was more than three times average earnings; by 2007 it was well over five times. But others had more pecuniary motives. Prices were rising so fast in some parts of the country that you could buy a house, hold it for a few months and sell it at a profit, even allowing for professional fees and charges. The bigger the mortgage, the higher the value of the house you could buy and the larger the potential profit.

HBOS, through its Halifax, Bank of Scotland and Birmingham Midshires brands was into all parts of this market, topping up its plain vanilla repayment mortgages – which made up the vast majority of its loan book – with 'specialist' offerings including buy-to-let, 125 per cent and self-certified loans, to the mute astonishment of some board members. The Bank's 125 per cent move was in response to the success of Northern Rock's 'Together' mortgage, which had pulled in more than £8 billion of lending. HBOS also began to introduce 'affordability' as a means of determining how much applicants could borrow, rather than a simple multiple of gross salary. This involved a detailed look at the actual amounts coming into a home each month, versus the outgoings. In theory it was a more accurate measure of the level of repayment applicants could manage. In practice it often led to higher mortgage borrowing. The demand seemed inexhaustible as consumers borrowed to improve their standards of living, not only by taking on mortgages, but also through unsecured personal loans and by buying goods with credit cards. The average debt per household soared by a third during the boom years of 2003–2008 to stand at over 170 per cent of annual income.[3]

After taking over as chief executive of HBOS in the summer of 2006, Andy Hornby set about expanding the Bank's branch network in the south of England, spending £100 million to open 50 new branches in areas where it was relatively under-represented, such as inside the M25. He also announced a new push into the Irish mortgage market, through the Bank's subsidiaries in the republic. However, there were signs that the profit engine of retail banking, which had been one of the main motors of the rapid expansion of HBOS, was starting to falter. Even though economic conditions were still relatively benign, bad debts had risen as consumers struggled to pay off loans – and the share of the new mortgage market was falling.

Retail had increased its profits by only 8 per cent in the previous year, whereas corporate banking had risen by 21 per cent, helped by a fall in bad debts.[4]

To fill his shoes as head of the retail banking division, Hornby recruited Benny Higgins from the Royal Bank of Scotland. Higgins was an outstandingly successful financial services manager, but his colourful private life, leading to stories in the tabloid press, had cut short a career at Standard Life where he had been singled out as a future chief executive. George Mathewson had hired him and he quickly rose to become head of the Royal Bank's retail division. His move after nine years was a surprise, but watchers suggested that his chances of rising to the top job were better at HBOS, even though he was a few years older than Hornby.

Higgins' tenure at HBOS was to be brief and controversial. He fitted the mould of the bright and highly ambitious young managers who were now mostly running the Bank, but some of his actions seemed to run contrary to the fast-growth ethos. He kept the Bank out of 'equity release', a fashionable innovation by some lenders by which home owners with low loan-to-value ratios could borrow more on the security of the unmortgaged part of the value of their property. It was sold initially as a boon to retired people who wanted to stay in their own homes, but lacked a big enough pension to be able to afford to do so. By remortgaging their houses they could obtain cash, which would only be repayable when the property was sold, possibly after their deaths. But unscrupulous brokers and lenders soon turned it into yet another way to borrow for any purpose and people were taking out long-term loans on their homes to buy short-life goods like cars, televisions or refrigerators or, worse, use the money for expensive holidays. Higgins refused to allow HBOS to follow, saying he saw the market as a mis-selling scandal waiting to happen. He also responded to rising personal bad debt provisions by tightening up on credit card lending and wiping £1 billion off the limits of about 600,000 accounts.

But his boldest move was to respond to concerns over arrears in the housing sector by increasing the price of mortgages. HBOS was facing a problem of its own making, in that it had won huge amounts of the new business in 2003 and 2004 by offering ultra-low-start mortgages which would ratchet up in price after an initial three or four years. Faced with a substantial increase in their monthly payments, many customers were now looking to replace those loans with new low-cost deals from other banks. Higgins persuaded Hornby that instead of trying to keep these accounts by again undercutting the competition, HBOS should offer brokers an extra incentive to recommend staying with HBOS. By doing so, he argued, some of the heat would be taken out of the mortgage market, profitability would be improved and competitors would follow suit.

They did not. Rival companies, led by Northern Rock and Barclays, redoubled their campaigns and snatched market share. HBOS had already lost ground, taking only 17 per cent of new home loans in the previous year, against the 20+ per cent it had been used to getting. Now it saw its share halve to only 8 per cent. It was no longer king of the hill and had shown it was vulnerable to aggressive competition. The stock market reacted badly and the Bank's shares fell.

Internally it was also facing a problem. With a smaller volume of new business than budgeted and finer margins, retail would under-shoot its profit target. Heavy pressure was put on Cummings and the corporate banking division to make up the slack. 'We were forcing profit out of corporate to make up for the shortfall in retail,' remembers one senior manager. 'It was push and push in those last few years.' Deals nearing completion were hurried through, bringing arrangement fees and interest payments, and Cummings' policy of regularly taking equity in the companies to which it also lent through the Bank's integrated finance unit now began to pay off. Over six years the equity portfolio produced profits of £2.4 billion. 'It was our piggy bank, but by the end of 2007 it was starting to get empty.' Dividends were taken and holdings were sold to realise profits. Uberior Investments, the subsidiary company which housed many of the Bank's stakes, upped its level of sales to provide more cash for its parent, paying a dividend to HBOS of £290 million in 2006 and £280 million in the following year.

When the Bank reported its annual results for 2007, it revealed that for the first time corporate had passed retail in being the biggest contributor to the group's earnings. Whereas profits from mortgages and personal lending had fallen by 13 per cent, profits from the corporate division had risen by 30 per cent. Even so, HBOS managed only a small increase in overall profits and Hornby's reputation as the sector's whizz-kid was tarnished. Although the Bank scrambled to recover its position by introducing new products and new incentives, analysts and investors wondered whether the housing market could ever again provide it with the fat profits it had been used to, and if it could not, how long the corporate division could go on expanding its loan book without dramatically increasing its bad debts.

Higgins paid the price of the bank's loss of reputation. It was announced in August 2007 that he had 'decided to move on', but analysts were unanimous in their assessment that he had been forced out, a view reinforced by the revelation in the annual report that his basic salary of £655,000 had been topped up to £1.8 million by 'further remuneration'. He had been with the Bank for little over a year but in total he had received more than £3 million in salary, bonus and allowances. Looking back, a member of the HBOS board decided: 'Benny was a hero. He called it right on the mortgage market, but the executive and the rest of the board did not have the courage to back him.'

Higgins' leaving was not the only change among the top management. Phil Hodkinson, who had been finance director since the retirement of Mike Ellis, announced that he was leaving to spend more time on charity work. He was only fifty. The two departures necessitated a reshuffle, with the extensive retail empire that Andy Hornby had once ruled being broken up and distributed to several directors. The surprise was the return of Mike Ellis to resume his former role as finance director. The market viewed his reappearance with puzzlement. He was a safe pair of hands, but what did his recall from retirement suggest for the future – that a firm hand might be needed to steady the ship?

A few months later Hornby scrapped the stretching market share goal that had driven the rapid growth of HBOS over the previous six years. 'We will no longer set annual market share targets for net lending. Instead, we will make judgements on the trade-off between volume and margins on a month-by-month basis,' he said. 'Increased mortgage costs to consumers will inevitably lead to a slowdown in the mortgage market.'[5] It was a significant statement for the man who had once been the arch-competitor and amounted to a tacit admission that the Higgins' strategy may have been right.

There was good reason to be cautious. After a long period of cheap credit, interest rates were starting to rise, bringing financial pain to many people who had over-extended themselves and now found their monthly repayments climbing steeply. Northern Rock had been caught out when it failed to hedge against a rise in rates between the times when it approved fixed rate loans and the money actually being drawn down. The move was going to cost the Rock up to £200 million in lost income and forced the hitherto bullish bank to issue a profits warning. That was not enough to prevent it from continuing to chase new business or persuade its existing customers to stay by offering cut-throat deals to remortgage. 'In two to three years the chances are that interest rates will not be rising and we can retain customers on better margins,' said an ever-optimistic Applegarth. While HBOS' share of the new market again fell to less than 10 per cent, Northern Rock took 19 per cent.

There were some warning signs coming from across the Atlantic. The phrase 'sub-prime' started to be heard for the first time, describing mortgages taken out by people who could not afford to repay them. Millions of these mortgages had been aggregated into large securitised loan packages, which were used as collateral for further borrowing. Now some people were starting to question whether these funds were actually worth what the banks which had issued them claimed they were worth. The investment bank Bear Sterns, not a well-known name in Britain outside the London financial community, but one with an 80-year history on Wall Street, had been forced to bail out two of its hedge funds to the tune of £1.6 billion. It was not a problem which many people believed would have much effect in the UK, but it was unsettling nonetheless.

HBOS was heavily exposed to the property market. At the end of 2007 it had £430 billion outstanding in loans to customers, more than half of it (£235 billion) in residential mortgages. Another £35 billion was lent to construction firms or commercial property companies and a further £8 billion to the hotel and retail trades. Home loans in Ireland and Australia added another £27 billion and lending to construction, property, hotels and retail in those countries and else-where another £24 billion. Add them all together and three-quarters of all lending was secured on land, bricks and mortar.

The board was not unduly alarmed. Nearly half the mortgage book had a loan-to-value ratio of 28 per cent – house prices would have to fall by more than two-thirds before the size of the loan was higher than the value of the property. Of the remainder, only 3.5 per cent was over 90 per cent. The asset cover was there, but what about the lenders? Would they still be able to meet their repayments if there was a downturn? Here there was a worry. A quarter of all mortgages were classed as 'specialist', either buy-to-let or self-certified mortgages – over £60 billion.[6]

The UK housing market which had shown rises of 4–5 per cent a quarter at the height of the boom in 2004, had slowed considerably by 2007, but right up to the end of the summer prices had still been rising. The first fall in the October-December quarter was a little over 1 per cent, followed by a similar decline in the first quarter of 2008. A few doomsayers were claiming that prices could fall by 10 or 20 per cent, following similar plunges in the US, but there were plenty of people taking a more optimistic view. They included Martin Ellis, chief economist at HBOS, who told *Money Marketing* magazine, 'A robust UK economy and the accompanying sound health of the labour market continue to provide strong underpinnings for the housing market . . . there is a fundamental supply and demand imbalance in the UK that simply does not exist in the US.'[7]

16

Ziggy's stardust

In 1997 the rock singer David Bowie faced a problem. He wanted to buy back the ownership of songs he had recorded which were now owned by his manager – including his very successful 1972 concept album *The Rise and Fall of Ziggy Stardust and the Spiders from Mars* – but he did not have the cash to do it. A smart American banker called David Pullman came up with a solution. They would package all Bowie's songs together and sell not the hits themselves, but the future royalties from them for ten years. It was one of the first asset-backed securitisation deals in the music industry and the singer received $55 million when the 'Bowie Bond' was bought by the Prudential Insurance Company of the US.[1]

The concept of selling a stream of future earnings was not new; in fact, Bank of Scotland had tried an early form of it in 1984 when it started to sell mortgages. The loans were grouped into portfolios and sold to a syndicate of banks, which took on the credit risk and received a proportion of the interest payments. The Bank kept the arrangement fees and the remaining interest.[2] The experiment was deemed a success, but the Bank preferred to keep mortgages on its balance sheet and the idea was not repeated until the late 1990s when securitisation started to become fashionable. In the ten years after the Bowie Bond, securitisation issues multiplied exponentially, although in the housing rather than the rock-song market. By 2007 the amount outstanding was estimated at $10.24 trillion in the United States and $2.25 trillion in Europe. Like all new industries it threw up variants and sophistications, produced experts and specialists, inspired PhD theses and spawned its own jargon and initials. There were Asset Backed Securities (ABS), Residential Mortgage Backed Securities (RMBS), Commercial Mortgage Backed Securities (CMBS), Collateralised Mortgage Obligations (CMOs), Collateralised Bond Obligations (CBOs), Special Purpose

Vehicles (SPVs) and Special Investment Vehicles (SIVs), sometimes also called 'conduits'.

For the banks there were two attractions to securitising their mortgages – liquidity and capital. They got their money back immediately (rather than waiting until the loans were redeemed) so they could lend it again; and, because the buyer of the securitisation issue took the risk, it did not have to be counted in the issuing bank's balance sheet and therefore no regulatory capital had to be set aside to insure against default. This was truly William Paterson's Philosopher's Stone: the bank could go on indefinitely circulating the money and each time it went round, the bank could collect fees and interest.

In London there was no shortage of investment banks willing to help to structure and price issues and find buyers for them. The HBOS treasury department became very skilled at securitisation and its variant, covered bonds (similar, but the asset stays on the bank's balance sheet). From the Bank's formation it was routinely securitising £10 billion or more of mortgages a year and selling them on the market, where they were bought (of course) with more borrowed money. By 2007 HBOS had packaged and sold on £82 billion of mortgages in this way. To induce buyers to take on the risk, each issue had to be given a clean bill of health by the ratings agencies like Standard & Poors, Moody's and Fitch. Since the vast majority of HBOS mortgages had been granted on low loan-to-value ratios, the Bank's securitisations were given high ratings and it had no trouble in finding takers.

However sophisticated UK banks thought they might be, they lagged a long way behind the Americans. There the mortgage market boomed in the first years of the new century, fuelled by low interest rates, which brought cheap and abundant credit. Since 'prime' borrowers – people who could afford to meet the repayments on their loans – expected to pay low rates, banks and brokers turned to the 'sub-primes', people who in normal circumstances would have been considered too poor to buy their own homes, or were bad credit risks. In their millions they were induced to take out big mortgages and pay steep fees and high interest for the privilege. Securitisations of sub-prime mortgages were clearly higher risk than primes, so to get around this problem the banks turned to mathematics and portfolio theory: by packaging hundreds of thousands of these high-risk loans with others which were low-risk, it could be demonstrated that some of the risk would be diversified away.

As time went on the issues became more and more complex. They were sliced and diced, mixed and stirred until it was impossible to judge accurately what was inside them and what the real level of risk was. Everyone was involved in the market in one way or another, from small, shady regional banks and brokerages which 'originated' the mortgages (sold them to vulnerable and gullible people) to giant Wall Street investment banks which traded the securities. The market quickly became international, so that European banks would buy securities based on American mortgages and British banks would issue securities in the US. The money wheel might have gone on turning had the Federal Reserve Bank of the United States not decided to cool the overheating housing market by increasing interest rates. Poor people suddenly found their monthly repayments ballooning to levels they could not afford and began to default on their payments. Banks began to repossess their homes, but found that the more they repossessed, the lower house prices fell and the less security they had to back their bonds.

By 2007 the problem was starting to become acute. Some regional US banks went bust, hedge funds which had bought securitised bonds had to write them off as worthless and every bank began to examine its portfolio. HSBC, the international bank headquartered in London, had to swallow big write-downs at its American subsidiary, and French banks disclosed problems, but there was a feeling that it was a US problem and would not cross the Atlantic.

The nineteenth-century Prime Minister Lord Palmerston famously said that only three people had ever known the answer to the Schleswig-Holstein question: one was dead, another was mad, and the third was himself and he had forgotten. A similar situation had happened in the securitisation market. Packages of mortgages had become so complex that no one knew what was inside them – not the banks which had sold them, nor the banks which had bought them, nor the rating agencies which had given them their seal of approval. Since they did not know what they were buying, banks and investors decided not to buy anything at all. The securitisation market froze, so mortgages became harder to obtain, house prices tumbled further and the assets which backed the securities became worth less – and some eventually became worthless. But it went further than that.

Americans, like Brits, had been saving less and spending more, so retail deposits were harder to come by for banks and they had been funding their lending from the wholesale markets, borrowing over years, months, weeks or days to match their obligations. Now this market froze too; if you could not gauge the value of an asset, how could you judge the creditworthiness of the bank which held it?

Banks and other investment institutions began to find it harder and more expensive to obtain the funds they needed, but those rumoured to be nearest to the edge of the precipice found that no one was willing to trust them with money for more than a few days and even then would charge them through the nose for it. Where once they would have laughed scornfully and gone elsewhere, now they had no choice. They had to take what was on offer or declare bankruptcy. The belief that this was an American problem did not last long. Finance was a global industry and US banks traded in European markets just as European banks did in the States.

At the end of August 2007, HBOS delivered a severe shock to its shareholders, which included the two million savers who had taken shares when Halifax demutualised. Many of the Bank's 70,000 staff also took their bonuses in shares or were part of the Bank's share-save scheme. Up until then they had assumed their Bank was not involved in the American mortgage market. Now, through a short statement to the Stock Exchange, they discovered that it was an investor in US home loans on a massive scale. The statement revealed that the Bank had been forced to provide credit for Grampian Funding, a Jersey-registered fund wholly owned by HBOS, which held $36 billion (£18 billion) of assets, $30 billion of which were invested in the US.

Grampian was not a recent invention; it had been formed by the Bank in 2002, but no word of it had ever appeared in the annual reports or statements to shareholders. To find any reference to it you had to obtain a copy of the report of HBOS Treasury Service plc, a subsidiary of the Bank. It was, however, no secret in the international securitisation market, where it had a conservative reputation, despite some lurid press reports. In 2003 the US newsletter *Asset Backed Alert* wrote about it. Under the heading: 'HBOS Arbitrage Vehicle to Gorge on Bonds', it wrote: 'HBOS is laying the groundwork to become an even bigger buyer of asset-backed securities. The Edinburgh, Scotland, lender plans to fund the investment binge via its giant Grampian Funding commercial-paper conduit.'[3]

It was the latest in a line of funding 'conduits' used by the Bank's treasury department, and took over from a fund named Pennine Funding, from which it acquired $11 billion of assets.

Grampian's business was arbitrage – exploiting the difference between the low interest rates it paid by borrowing short-term and the higher rates it could obtain by lending long-term, thus turning on its head the old banker's rule 'borrow long and lend short'. It was prepared to do this because the world had changed since Bank of Scotland experienced its first cash crisis 300 years before and in the twenty-first century the global inter-bank market had made the rule obsolete – or so everyone believed. The range of lenders was so wide – encompassing practically the whole developed world – and the pool of liquidity so deep – trillions of dollars – that there would always be someone, somewhere willing to lend. The worse that could happen to you was that the price would go up.

Grampian raised credit by issuing Asset Backed Commercial Paper, essentially borrowing over a short term, anything from 90 to 270 days. Investors were willing to take them because, although Grampian was a separate legal entity, it was consolidated into the HBOS balance sheet. Most of the time it would act as if it were a separate company, but if there ever came a crisis the Bank would stand behind it. With the money it raised, the conduit bought other securities, mostly packages of American mortgages which paid a good rate of interest. To protect itself Grampian only invested in Triple A-rated paper – the highest and safest rating – and that ruled out sub-prime (although it later revealed that it did have a very small amount, less than 1 per cent of its assets).

A year after its launch Grampian had become the largest conduit in Europe and the third largest in the world. Later it overtook the others to become the biggest player in this market. For five years it performed very well and the HBOS treasury team used its skill at buying and selling debt securities to generate hundreds of millions of pounds in profit for the Bank. But when the scale of the sub-prime scandal became known, the inter-bank market started to seize up. Despite its Triple A portfolio Grampian found the interest rates it was having to pay to borrow shooting up. To meet Grampian's obligations HBOS had to lend it money. This was an embarrassing and costly exercise, but HBOS saw it as a temporary problem which would right itself once the market thawed. Andy Hornby and Mike

Ellis issued reassuring statements saying that the Bank fully expected to get back the money it had advanced to Grampian and that it would have 'no material impact' on the Bank. By October 2007, the worst seemed to be over and the bank was able to issue a press release saying that the conduit was again self-funding.

But it was not quite that easy. Grampian did not hold many sub-prime securities, but it had the next worst thing – Alt-A mortgages. These were loans issued to Americans who on paper at least had the wherewithal to repay, but included categories of borrower increasingly seen in the UK during the house-price boom years. There were borrowers of self-certified mortgages (called 'liar loans' in the US), those with poor credit histories, buy-to-let landlords and those borrowing on high loan-to-value ratios. HBOS tried to play down its exposure to these mortgages, but when its accounts for 2007 were published they showed that it had £7 billion at risk, plus billions more in other debt securities. Although it was not foreseen at the time, most of these investments eventually had to be written off.

Throughout the autumn of 2007 HBOS, along with most other banks, was finding it increasingly difficult and expensive to fund its own lending and pay off the money it had borrowed when loans fell due. 'Spreads', the extra interest payments lenders demanded to compensate for increased risk, increased by five times between June and September. Alongside its activities in Grampian and its securitisation issues, it had been an active issuer of covered bonds, another form of borrowing, but considered safer and more conservative than securitisations. HBOS used the bonds to lengthen the maturity of its borrowing and on occasion had issued 20-year covered bonds. Now that market too was seizing up. In September, HBOS managed to issue a new bond, but at a greatly increased price. In November, the covered bond market was briefly suspended because prices were rising so fast, making it even harder for banks to fund themselves. This was not a problem peculiar to HBOS; all mortgage lenders were suffering and some much more acutely.

Although the sub-prime scandal was a US phenomenon, 125 per cent loans, buy-to-let, self-certified mortgages and high multiples of salary had left many UK homeowners dangerously exposed to a rise in interest rates. Investors began to regard all mortgage banks with suspicion, but attention, inevitably, settled on one of the smallest and most aggressive, Northern Rock. Like HBOS, the Rock had fuelled its rapid expansion with borrowed money, but its situation was more serious. Whereas HBOS could cover around half of its lending from customer deposits, Northern Rock could only manage a quarter. It was dependent on borrowing from other banks in the wholesale market for 75 per cent of its funding, and when the markets froze in August 2007 it found itself with only enough cash to make it through to the end of the month and very little chance of getting any more.

Seeing the writing on the wall, the board of Northern Rock tried to find a bigger company willing to take them over. It opened talks with LloydsTSB, which was prepared to make an offer, but only if the Government would guarantee a £30 billion loan from the Bank of England, which was refused. An approach to the Royal Bank of Scotland also came to nothing.[4] Rumours of the bank's problems were now circulating widely and by September the share price had dived. The Bank of England was at first reluctant to intervene, with its Governor, Mervyn King, believing that the Rock had got itself into this situation by reckless and foolish lending. To bail it out would create a 'moral hazard' by encouraging other banks to believe that they could do anything they liked because the Bank of England would always be there to save them from their own stupidity. The stalemate dragged on for days until, with no private-sector solution in sight, King changed his mind and agreed to pump funds into Northern Rock, with the Bank of England acting as lender of last resort.

A statement was prepared, but before the news could be made public it leaked to the BBC and precipitated a run on the bank. Within three days savers queuing outside the bank's branches, or besieging its call centres and website, had withdrawn £2 billion in deposits. Northern Rock eventually lost £10 billion – a third of its retail deposits. Ironically, HBOS was one of the beneficiaries, opening accounts for former customers of the Rock.

A public run on a bank – the first for a hundred years in the UK and virtually unthinkable in the modern world of close banking supervision and electronic payment systems – is every banker and policymaker's worst nightmare. It is such a visceral image that the television pictures of orderly lines of ordinary people waiting to withdraw their savings flashed around the world, striking fear into the hearts of depositors everywhere who wondered whether their own savings were safe. Alistair Darling, Chancellor of the Exchequer, and Mervyn King were horrified as they watched the drama on screens in

Lisbon where they were attending a meeting of the European Union's economic and financial affairs council. They immediately cut short the meeting and flew back to London.[5]

Inside HBOS the television images sent a chill through the Bank. 'It was a huge blow to us and a real confidence shaker,' remembers one senior manager. Like the Rock, HBOS had been living with the consequences of the freezing of the market for weeks. Securitisations had stopped and other funding, where it could be obtained, was much more expensive. Lending had to be curtailed. It was outside the experience of even the most seasoned bankers. 'Up until then we had always thought that you would always be able to fund a lending book. No one had ever seen a situation where you couldn't. We couldn't just withdraw from the mortgage market because we had deals in progress and in corporate some companies had facilities on which they were able to drawn down money. Also we were trying to secure our good, reliable clients.'

To end the run on Northern Rock, which had continued for four days, Alistair Darling announced that the Government would guarantee all deposits in the bank. The move worked in that the queues disappeared, but there were still questions over the Rock's future. It was forced to borrow from the Bank of England at a punitive rate, which meant sustained losses and sent its share price plummeting. The guarantee only applied to Northern Rock, but there were other mortgage banks – Alliance & Leicester, Bradford & Bingley and HBOS – which were also struggling.

Central banks in the US, Canada and Europe had acted to pump money into the system to try to get the inter-bank market moving again, but with little effect. Those commercial banks which did have surplus cash were hoarding it to fund their own needs. In Britain the Bank of England was still hesitating to take more general action and the tripartite regulatory system – the Bank, the Treasury and the Financial Services Authority (FSA) – was proving ineffective, with each institution waiting for one of the others to take the lead. Senior bankers met the chairman and chief executive of the FSA, with Colin Matthew attending for HBOS, but were told that it was not able to put money into the wholesale market: that power lay with Mervyn King, who was still refusing to act. To the exasperation of the bank chief executives, when they met the Bank of England Governor one evening in mid-September he declined to talk about putting liquidity back into the market and lectured them on the danger of moral hazard instead.

The following morning he had a change of heart. The Bank of England announced that it would lend an initial £10 billion, with possibly more to come, against the security of packages of mortgages. In return, the Bank would charge a 'penalty rate' of interest. Those banks which took the money would make a loss, but they had no choice. The crisis was not over, but at least someone was now trying to do something about it.

HBOS reduced the cash flowing out of the business by closing down as much of its new business activity as it could. 'We effectively pulled out of the SME [Small and Medium-sized Enterprises] market. The Royal Bank of Scotland was circulating internal emails to say that we had stopped lending and this was a good opportunity for them to step in,' remembers one HBOS senior executive. Regular reports were going to Andy Hornby and Mike Ellis, who in turn briefed the board. Everyone knew the situation was serious, but until Northern Rock no one believed it might be terminal. 'The feeling inside was that this was something we had to work through, sooner or later things would get back to normal – but they dragged on and on.'

17

The eye of the storm

By the beginning of 2008 the credit crunch was being seen as a global problem which needed to be fixed by government leaders. Prime Minister Gordon Brown called a meeting of the heads of the G8 largest economies in the world to a summit in London. At a micro level Alistair Darling and a team from the Treasury were still trying to find a solution for Northern Rock, which was being kept on life support by regular transfusions of cash from the Bank of England. In February, with no private company willing to take it on without guarantees, they bowed to the inevitable and nationalised it, the first bank nationalisation since Labour had taken the Bank of England into public ownership in 1945. The crisis was still seen as largely confined to domestic mortgages and government efforts were concentrated on getting this market moving again. House prices were declining, but by a relatively small amount and most people believed this was a reverse which would correct itself within six months or a year, as it had done many times in past cycles.

The residential market was being hit, but the crisis did not yet seem to be serious in commercial property. In February Peter Cummings made a speech at an awards ceremony which would come back to haunt him, being quoted repeatedly in newspaper articles and in the House of Commons: 'Some people look as though they are losing their nerve – beginning to panic, even – in today's testing property environment. Not us.'[1] At the time the speech was received positively; it was only later with hindsight that it was used as evidence of recklessness. Cummings was echoing the traditional Bank of Scotland policy of 'staying at the table', which had been restated by both his chairman and chief executive several times in HBOS annual reports. Losses on the commercial lending book still appeared manageable and Cummings intended to stand by his good customers until the market picked up again.

breached. These were agreements between lender and borrower which specified, among other things, the level and frequency of repayments to be made and the loan-to-value ratio. A generation previously banks would have been able to fudge any breaches of covenants by tucking away problem loans into suspense accounts and trying to help the borrowers work through their difficulties. But new international accounting standards left no hiding place. Banks now had to write down loans and make provisions from their capital against default. Each time they did so their credit ratings suffered and they found it harder to obtain funding.

On 15 April Gordon Brown called bank chief executives to a meeting at 10 Downing Street where, almost unanimously, they demanded that more money be pumped into the inter-bank market. According to Brown most of the men present were suffering 'quiet anxiety', except for Andy Hornby, who sounded very worried.[4] The unthinkable was happening, HBOS was running out of money.

The Government still had not appreciated the threat to the banks and was more worried about the mortgage freeze and the effect it would have on homebuyers, particularly young couples who were being denied a home of their own because they could not get loans. After stepping down from HBOS, Sir James Crosby had become a deputy chairman of the FSA – a poacher turned gamekeeper. Now Brown and Darling asked him to take on an additional role, investigating what measures could be taken to get the mortgage market moving again.

In May HBOS made a tentative return to the securitisation market, offering a package of home loans valued at £500 million. It was a timid toe-in-the-water compared to the £5 billion packages it had been used to issuing, but it was a success – it got its money, in fact it found so many lenders that it was able to up its target and take in £750 million. What shocked investors was the price it was having to pay, which was a huge margin over the interest rates being charged in the inter-bank market and more than the cost of borrowing from the Bank of England, which was supposed to be charging a 'penalty rate'. Some analysts saw the achievement of the issue as proof that the credit crunch was easing, others as evidence of the desperation of HBOS. A move that was seen as a confidence raiser, further sapped morale.

Liquidity – having enough cash – was not the only problem the

Bank faced. It was also running short of capital, its cushion against losses. Since its share issue in 2002 HBOS had been steadily shrinking its capital, spending £2.5 billion of its surplus cash to buy back shares from its investors and cancel them. It had also steadily increased its annual dividend payouts. The effect of both had been to boost its share price and flatter its return on equity, but to reduce its capital. It was not the only bank in this position: the Royal Bank of Scotland and Barclays were also feeling the squeeze.

Since the early 1990s the capital that banks were required to hold against possible losses had been specified by an international agreement called the Basel Accord, after the Swiss city in which the regulators met. The rules were fairly crude and banks quickly found ways around them (moving assets off their balance sheets through securitisation, for example), so a modified system was introduced which became known as Basel II. The amount of capital a bank needed was to be calculated as a proportion of its total lending, but not all loans carried the same risk. Unsecured personal loans, for example, were much riskier than mortgages, where the bank had the security of a house to fall back on if the borrower defaulted. To allow for this, different types of lending were given different risk-weights and then added up to make a total of risk-weighted assets, on which the capital calculation was based.

The new regime made some startling changes. It did end the distinction between on- and off-balance sheet lending, closing one loophole, but it also reduced the risk-weight applied to residential and commercial mortgages from 50 per cent to 35 per cent. There had been strong lobbying from the banks that they were being forced to hold too much capital, which was reducing their profits. Like the old system, Basel II relied heavily on the assessment of risk associated with individual securities made by the ratings agencies. The different weights of risk corresponded to different investment ratings. Two types of asset were given zero risk-weightings (i.e. they were seen as carrying no risk at all). These were lending to governments or central banks, and securities classified by the ratings agencies as AA- up to Triple A, the highest grade.

Banks were given a choice of ways to calculate their risk-weighted assets. They could choose from a menu of risk-weights provided by the Basel committee (using 35 per cent for mortgages, for example). This was known as the 'Foundation' method. Or they could calculate their own risk-weights, known as the 'Advanced Internal Ratings-Based' method, or Advanced IRB for short. To do this banks had to get the consent of their own country regulator (the FSA in Britain) by demonstrating that they had the skills and knowledge to be able to perform the complex calculations necessary. Most British banks opted for the Foundation method, but some, including HBOS and Barclays, applied to be allowed to calculate their own risks. HBOS had a large risk-management department employing over 100 people and headed by Peter Hickman, the Group Risk Director. It also had elaborate procedures for the ways in which it assessed and calculated risk. The explanation of these and a description of the governance process by which risks were sanctioned took up 19 pages of its 2007 annual report. It was confident it could calculate risk accurately and at the beginning of 2008 the FSA announced that HBOS had been granted Advanced IRB status.

Mike Ellis, the finance director, sought to reassure investors that HBOS was taking a very conservative approach. 'Maintaining strong capital ratios is a given at HBOS and we will not compromise in this regard,' he told a conference. 'One of the key tenets of liquidity management is not to take unacceptable credit risks, accepting that you cannot eliminate entirely credit risk, and we are very confident regarding the credit quality of our portfolio.'[5]

It has been argued that HBOS under-calculated the risks it faced, but subsequent analysis has suggested that the bank did take a conservative view and could have reduced its capital requirement by choosing the Foundation method.[6] If HBOS, like the Royal Bank and other banks which failed, had ended up with too little capital, it was a basic problem with the Basel system, rather than the internal calculation.

Faced with sclerosis in the inter-bank lending market and increasing losses on their Triple A-rated mortgage securities, banks in America and Europe were being forced to go back to their shareholders to ask for more cash. In the UK Bradford & Bingley had been first with a call for a modest £400 million, but the issue had turned into a fiasco as the bank was forced to announce a profits warning, a debt downgrade and the retirement through illness of its chief executive before the money could be gathered. The Royal Bank of Scotland came next, seeking to raise a massive £12 billion in new capital and promising to raise £8 billion more by selling off businesses. These were moves which it said would make it one of the safest banks in Europe.

It was a foregone conclusion that HBOS would have to follow suit. It announced that it was asking shareholders to give it £4 billion, but a mark of its concern about its predicament was the price at which it was offering new stock. Its share price, which had once topped £11, had dropped to less than £5 before the announcement. Now it was offering new shares at £2.75 – a 45 per cent discount. It looked like a fire sale and did nothing to bolster the confidence of shareholders.

As a further move to conserve money, the dividend was being cut and half of it would be paid by issuing new shares to shareholders rather than cash. Hornby tried to portray the issue as one of good management, rather than desperation. 'It is a prudent step change in our capital strength and our target ratios. We need to be prepared for all macroeconomic events. Banks that do not have strong capital ratios will find it harder,' he said.[7] But no one was convinced.

In June the Bank published its rights issue prospectus, and again tried to put an optimistic gloss on what were depressing facts for shareholders. Specialist mortgages – buy-to-let and self-certified – accounted for a quarter of the £250 billion mortgage book and over 3 per cent of these were already in arrears – they had missed their mortgage repayments for three months or more. The figure did not include repossessed houses, so the real picture may have been worse. Overall the Bank had £5 billion-worth of souring home loans. In the commercial market HBOS had lent more than £4 billion to house-builders, who were facing a crunch of their own as homes they had completed failed to find buyers. Corporate banking's 'nest egg' equity stakes in this sector had been valued at £200 million, but half of that had now had to be written off.

To make matters worse the ratings agency Standard & Poors reduced the bank's credit watch status from 'stable' to 'negative'.

Investor confidence was severely shaken by the revelations. The share price had fallen since the announcement and had briefly dipped below the rights issue price. If it kept falling the share issue was bound to fail: why would shareholders pay £2.75 for new shares when they could buy existing ones cheaper on the stock market? To guard against this HBOS had spent £160 million on underwriting fees with financial institutions, which would guarantee to buy any shares that were not wanted by HBOS shareholders. 'Our rights issue is fully underwritten, it's on track and we're going to get it completed and get back to normal life,' said Hornby.[8] He probably believed a return to normal was possible, but if so he was in a shrinking minority.

The rights issue in July was the biggest flop since the stock market crash of 1987. Less than 9 per cent of the shares were bought by HBOS shareholders, leaving the underwriters to take over 90 per cent. As the price fell even further they were left with an immediate paper loss. Small shareholders were angry that the Bank had bought back shares between 2005 and 2007 at prices from £8.55 to £10.70, yet now it was trying to sell new ones at £2.75. There were calls for Andy Hornby to resign, but they went unheeded in the boardroom.

The Royal Bank of Scotland and Barclays had fared little better with their rights issues. To Gordon Brown the lesson was clear: 'I interpreted this as meaning that the markets did not believe that HBOS had come clean on its toxic assets and future write-offs. At the same time the RBS share price was at 197.6p, while its rights price was at 200p, and the Qataris had been left with most of the Barclays issue as there was only a 20 per cent take-up. The whole market was simply walking away. They did not believe the banks; neither did I.'[9]

18

Apocalypse now

At the special meeting in Edinburgh to approve the rights issue, chairman Lord Stevenson told shareholders: 'Armageddon may happen, and we should be prepared for it, and we are.' Armageddon came three months later and no one was prepared for it.

The events leading up to the final collapse took place in New York. On 7 September the US Government announced it was taking the Federal National Mortgage Association and the Federal Home Loan Mortgage Corporation, usually known as Fannie Mae and Freddy Mac, into public ownership. This was a huge step for a right-wing Republican administration led by President George W. Bush, which could not bring itself to call it nationalisation, preferring the term 'conservatorship'. The two companies were essentially mortgage wholesalers and had been wrecked by the sub-prime disaster, losing £14 billion in a year. Their bailout would eventually cost the US taxpayer more than $150 billion.

A few days later Lehman Brothers, one of the elite group of Wall Street investment banks, disclosed that it had lost $3.9 billion on mortgage debt in the previous three months alone. There were now severe doubts over the future of even the largest banks and these were reinforced when Bank of America, under strong pressure from the US Government, rescued Merrill Lynch, one of Lehman's competitors, which had lost $20 billion in a year. Through late September the future of Lehman hung in the balance as politicians and regulators on both sides of the Atlantic tried to find a way to save it. Barclays showed interest in acquiring it, but the US Government would not guarantee Lehman's losses and Alistair Darling refused to suspend UK company law to let a deal go through without it first being put to Barclays shareholders. The decision to allow Lehman to go bust destroyed any remaining confidence left in mortgage banks on both sides of the ocean. Five thousand Lehman employees in London lost their jobs.

On 15 September, a day the newspapers called 'Black Monday', 'Meltdown Monday' or 'Panic Monday', the FTSE 100 share index tumbled 200 points and HBOS shares went into freefall. The *Financial Times* described a macabre prediction game in progress: who will be next? The market had already decided: it would be HBOS.

The plight of the Bank had been watched closely by the UK Government throughout the summer. The company's half-year results, revealed at the end of July, showed profits halved after a loss of £1 billion on its investments, a further £2 billion write-off to its reserves and bad debts up again. To save liquidity the dividend was being cut and would be paid by issuing new shares, rather than in cash. Andy Hornby also announced that the Bank was putting some of its best subsidiaries up for sale: BankWest in Australia, the insurance company Clerical Medical and the fund manager Insight Investment. Alistair Darling was sceptical about its future: 'There was a whiff of death surrounding the whole operation. Two once solid institutions, the Halifax Building Society and the Bank of Scotland, were heading for the rocks.'[1] HBOS posed a massive problem for the Government. They had not yet found a permanent solution to Northern Rock's difficulties, but HBOS was much bigger – any collapse would destroy the savings of 20 million people and create havoc in the banking system. The FSA was already searching for options and the Treasury began to work on a contingency plan.

Worries focused on HBOS' capital and liquidity. A further big fall in the value of its reserves following a massive write-off in 2007 suggested that its capital was progressively crumbling away and with it the bank's capacity to absorb losses. It was also running short of cash. Hornby had tried to play down suggestions that HBOS was having problems raising money on the inter-bank market, but to add to its woes the credit rating agency Standard & Poors downgraded HBOS one notch from AA- to A+, increasing the costs it had to pay to borrow.

It was about this time that I attended the dinner where my neighbour gave me the shocking news that he had withdrawn £20 million to put it in a safer place.*

In fact a massive run on the Bank was in full swing, but it was practically unseen by the general public. Unlike Northern Rock a

---

* See Preface.

year earlier, there were no queues outside branches and no television pictures to alarm bankers and politicians, but by electronic transfer, telephoned instructions and face-to-face withdrawals HBOS was haemorrhaging cash as its depositors lost faith. An estimated £30 billion was withdrawn by individuals and companies within a few weeks – a death blow.

On the other side of the balance sheet money was not coming back as quickly as it had done. As the economy turned down, householders could not sell their homes, so they were not moving and paying off their mortgages. Credit card debt was not being paid off as quickly. Companies were taking longer to reduce their borrowings and were unable to refinance deals with other banks. Many of those firms which had over-borrowed in the days of low interest rates and high economic growth were now in trouble. HBOS corporate teams were fighting fires all over the country. McCarthy & Stone, bought by HBOS and Tom Hunter in 2006 for £1.2 billion, was struggling to refinance its £800 million debt. Crest Nicholson was trying to get banks to exchange half of the £1 billion they were owed for shares in the company. Retail chain JJB Sports and property groups Kandahar and Kenmore had breached their lending covenants. The secondary market was also drying up. Recent deals were remaining on the books of HBOS as other British and foreign banks which once would have snapped up portions of HBOS Corporate's loans withdrew from the market, meaning that the whole debt remained with HBOS.

In Bank of Scotland's LIBOR* department staff were trying to complete a routine transaction: 'We were trying to transfer £100 million to another syndicate bank. It was the sort of thing we liked to get done at the start of the morning, but at the end of the day we got a call asking "Where's the money?" We checked everything over and couldn't find anything wrong – the money had left us. The following day it still hadn't arrived – I thought to myself: "Someone in treasury hasn't pressed the right button; they're going to get in trouble for this." But that wasn't the problem; the money never arrived, we just didn't have the funds.'

To keep the bank afloat, Alistair Darling had to authorise the Bank of England to make exceptional loans to HBOS and other troubled

---

* London Inter-bank Offered Rate: the interest rate at which banks trade among themselves.

banks, including the Royal Bank and Bradford & Bingley. In view of the severe fall in the HBOS share price caused by the false rumour six months before, the arrangement had to be kept secret from the market, but in confidence Darling told John McFall MP, chairman of the House of Commons Treasury Select Committee. The full extent of the loans did not become known for a year, when Mervyn King told MPs that, acting in its capacity as lender of last resort, the Bank of England had lent £62 billion to the troubled banks[2]. Over a third went to HBOS, which, with Darling's approval, was also borrowing $18 billion from the US Federal Reserve through Bank of Scotland's American branch.[3]

Darling estimated that HBOS was having to borrow £16 billion overnight, every night, just to keep going.[4] The figure may have been an over-estimate, but the timescale was not. The market had become very short-term. After the collapse of Lehman every bank wanted to conserve as much cash as possible, so lending for 24 hours was as long as they were prepared to let it out of their sight. HBOS had borrowed £278 billion on the wholesale money markets, 60 per cent of this for periods of less than a year. In the next 12 months it would have to refinance £164 billion as its loans fell due and had to be repaid, yet it was living from day to day. The strain on the treasury department was immense, but it remained calm and professional and took each day as it came.

The atmosphere was much more tense in the group's City executive suite. Andy Hornby was feeling the stress of the constant pressure and uncertainty. Until then, in the words of one of his close colleagues, he had led a charmed life. Whatever he had done at school, at Oxford, at Harvard, in his first jobs in Blue Circle, Asda and Halifax, he had excelled. He had been the youngest, the cleverest, the highest achiever. Any setbacks he had encountered had been minor and, with his willingness to listen, learn and work hard, he had won people over and put any difficulties behind him. But this time his problems were of a different order of magnitude. He was having to react hourly to events that he not only could not control, but that he could not understand. His easy likeability was being replaced by irritability, and the lack of sleep and continual worry were showing on his face.

HBOS could not survive on its own. After Northern Rock, Brown and Darling were reluctant to nationalise another bank, so a private-sector solution seemed the neatest answer. Of the possible candidates as acquirer, LloydsTSB was the obvious first choice. It was conservatively run, with a strong balance sheet (dependent on the wholesale markets for only 25 per cent of its funding) and had come through the sub-prime crisis largely unscathed. It also had the most to gain. A takeover of HBOS would give it coverage in the North of England and Scotland, where it was weak, and provide scope to make massive cost reductions by cutting out duplication in back office functions and the branch networks. The HBOS board had often considered a merger between the two banks at strategy planning sessions, but the obstacle in the way had always been the Competition Commission. A combined bank would have a dominant market share in mortgages, personal savings and current accounts that would never be allowed in normal times. But these were not normal times.

Hornby knew the LloydsTSB chairman, Sir Victor Blank, well because they both served on the board of Home Retail Group, the Argos and Homebase retailer. He had also encountered Eric Daniels, Lloyds' chief executive, many times at bank meetings. Daniels, known as the 'Quiet American' in the City because of his unAmerican love of understatement, was a career banker. He had served with Citibank in Latin America and met his wife in Panama, where they still had a house with views from the Atlantic to the Pacific. He spent three years in London in the late 1980s running Citi's private bank during a previous property crash. He joined Lloyds in 2001 as head of retail and moved into the top job two years later. According to *The Guardian*: 'With his slow American drawl, Daniels is the perfect foil to the bank's go-getting chairman, Sir Victor Blank. Although he admits to a love of "over-wrought" Italian opera, Daniels is not a man given to histrionics. He even smokes with an air of quiet contemplation – leading journalists to describe him as the Marlboro man . . . When asked last month [August 2008] whether he would do any more deals he replied: "Don't hold your breath. I don't buy a pair of shoes just because they are cheap." '[5]

Hornby and Daniels had held tentative discussions over the summer, now they began urgent negotiations.

There was a symmetry to the beginning and end of the life of HBOS. On 16 September Hornby, his finance director, Mike Ellis, and main adviser Simon Robey of Morgan Stanley, met Daniels, Tim Tookey, Lloyds' finance director, and their adviser Matthew

Greenburgh from Merrill Lynch, in the HBOS corporate flat in St James's. Seven years before it had been the venue for the meeting between Peter Burt and James Crosby when the merger between Halifax and Bank of Scotland had been hammered out. Then the air had been light with optimism and excitement. Now it was heavy with dejection and resignation.

Daniels knew he had the upper hand and Hornby knew he could not leave the room without a deal. According to the *The Daily Telegraph*: ' "Andy was in a state of panic," one person at the meeting said. There was a lot of aggression between the two teams. You always get that in a bid but this was compressed into a few moments and the stakes were enormous. Obviously, it got heated.'[6] The talks dragged on into the early hours of the following morning before the outline of a deal was agreed. HBOS would be bought by LloydsTSB at 'around' £2.85 a share, a much higher level than the current share price on the Stock Exchange, but less than half of the value at the time the company had started life in 2002. The two sides broke up expecting to meet later that morning, but someone at HBOS leaked the news to Robert Peston at the BBC who wrote on his blog at 9 a.m. that a deal was close at near to £3 a share. Daniels was furious and an hour and a half later Peston blogged: 'Maybe I've slightly over-egged the price that Lloyds TSB will pay for HBOS. Perhaps it will be nearer £2 than £3.'

News of the deal did nothing to steady the HBOS share price and the value of LloydsTSB's shares also dropped as investors worried about what the bank was taking on. All bank shares were tumbling and in a desperate attempt to steady the market the FSA imposed a three-month ban on short selling and the Bank of England announced an extension of its special liquidity scheme, which was keeping several banks afloat.

There was still the competition issue to overcome and later that day Daniels met Darling to ask the Government to suspend competition law to allow a takeover to go ahead. Darling agreed to discuss it with Gordon Brown, but he was still not convinced that Lloyds knew what it was getting into or that a deal was possible at all. He instructed his officials to prepare two alternative statements, one welcoming a takeover by LloydsTSB, the other explaining the nationalisation of HBOS. Victor Blank had already raised the competition issue with the Prime Minister while they were flying back from a trade mission to Israel and Palestine, but had not got a final answer.

The collapse of HBOS, with 30 million customers, was unthinkable, but neither of the alternatives was appealing for the Government either. It had taken nearly six months to decide to take Northern
Rock into public ownership, and apart from the political opposition
and practical problems it was also threatened with legal action by
some shareholders for expropriating their investments. It did not
want to go through that again on a much larger scale with HBOS if
an alternative could be found. But allowing Lloyds to acquire HBOS
had the potential to create a fearsome monopoly. The combination
would give Lloyds market leadership in seven key product areas: in
current accounts and mortgages it would have over 30 per cent of the
market; in savings, credit cards and small businesses it would have
over 20 per cent and it would also lead the personal lending and home
insurance markets too.[7]

The Prime Minister's final consent to suspend competition law was
signalled to Blank during cocktails before a dinner both men were
attending during the week of the final negotiations, but a picture of
the two in deep conversation published in the *Financial Times* on the
day the deal was finally announced gave the impression that it was a
political stitch-up.

Later that day, 17 September, Daniels agreed to an offer at £2.32,
some 20 per cent less than his sighting shot a few hours earlier.
Hornby had little option but to accept. Now began a second sleepless
night as teams from both banks worked through the dark at the City
offices of Linklaters, Lloyds' lawyers, to complete the paperwork.
Tookey left the meeting at 4.15 a.m., only to find that his hotel room
had been given to someone else. He slept for an hour on a colleague's
couch in the Lloyds' City office before meeting Hornby at 7 a.m. in
Daniels' office for the Stock Exchange announcement and the press
calls.

By the time of the press conference on 19 September Hornby had
recovered his composure and Daniels had forgotten his anger. The
two men shook hands, watched over by Sir Victor Blank. Both sides
thought they had got the best from the negotiation. Daniels had
acquired a bank bigger than his own, giving him a commanding
position in the retail market without spending cash and giving his own
shareholders a majority of the equity. He could hardly contain his
enthusiasm: 'We just did an enormously good deal. This is fantastic.
I rarely use superlatives, but this is really a good deal.' Hornby was

congratulated by members of his board for pulling off 'an unbelieve-ably good deal'. The price may have been half what could have been achieved six months before, but it was well above the market price of the shares and he had secured the future of his bank.

Both men were fooling themselves, but neither yet realised it.

For the Government it also looked like a good deal. Brown and Darling had not had to pledge any guarantees in exchange for LloydsTSB taking a problem off their hands and the strength of Lloyds' balance sheet would make it that much more likely that the money lent to HBOS by the Bank of England would be repaid. As an added bonus Lloyds made unsolicited pledges to keep the head-quarters in Edinburgh, to keep printing Bank of Scotland banknotes and to try to safeguard jobs in Scotland. This last pleased the Scottish Labour Party which was fighting a tough by-election in the consti-tuency next to Gordon Brown's, but angered the MP for Halifax, where no such promise had been given.

The deal may have satisfied the two banks' boards, but it changed nothing in the real world. In the following weeks more US banks went bust and the Federal Reserve injected $85 billion into the giant insurance company AIG, which had insured sub-prime securities, to keep it afloat. Icelandic banks, which had expanded massively in the UK, were also collapsing, nearly bringing their country down with them. So were banks in Ireland. On the London Stock Exchange shares in LloydsTSB and HBOS continued to fall, the latter touching 90p at one stage. With each piece of bad news, the capital of banks was being eroded, the economy was getting weaker and their potential losses were climbing.

Gordon Brown realised before the banks that they needed capital as well as liquidity. Some might be able to raise it from their shareholders, but the experience of HBOS in its summer rights issue clearly showed it could not. A plan was hammered out by teams from the Treasury, Downing Street, the FSA and the Bank of England. Darling explained it to the bank chief executives in late night meetings. They did not like it, but they could not reject it. The Royal Bank was in the worst position, but Fred Goodwin remained impassive. HBOS was next, but Hornby was unable to hide his terror and sat with his arms tightly clutched around himself. 'He looked as though he might explode,' said Darling.[8] 'I wouldn't put my money in his bank,' remarked one Treasury official. 'Just look at his body language.'

On 8 October the Government announced its funding package: £50 billion in new capital, £250 billion in guarantees to underpin bank borrowing and £100 billion more for the Bank of England's special liquidity scheme. The Royal Bank of Scotland was the first to agree to take more capital, then HBOS and finally Lloyds. The scheme was portrayed as voluntary, but in fact it was mandatory and there were conditions: remuneration was to be cut, dividends suspended and Hornby and Stevenson were to be fired as soon as the merger was complete.[9] The HBOS chairman took it badly: 'He was absolutely furious,' a Government source told me. 'He didn't see what he had done wrong and why he couldn't stay.'

The takeover was finally agreed in October after the terms had been reduced again. Now HBOS shareholders would get fewer Lloyds shares in exchange for their old ones. The Government would be the largest shareholder, owning 43.5 per cent of the merged company; next came Lloyds shareholders with 36.5 per cent and finally HBOS with 20 per cent – less than half what they would have received with the initial offer. Since the Lloyds' share price was also falling, the cash value of HBOS was dropping by the day.

Inside HBOS staff who were also shareholders were watching their savings evaporate. Employee and trade union rep Margaret Taylor: 'Since the 1990s staff had often taken part of their salary increase in shares or indeed all of it; after all there was a tax incentive to do so. It would not be uncommon for somebody working in the back office who had £3,000 in a bonus to think "I'm going to put some of that into shares." It is not uncommon for somebody working as a teller on £15,000 to £18,000, who's been with the company for 15 years, to have built up £20,000 in shares. Most people thought that anyone who didn't buy into these schemes was crazy because it seemed that you were, you know, why wouldn't you? Based on their own experience the share prices had only gone up for a number of years.

'When the HBOS share price began to go down, nobody believed that it would collapse. It was at £11 and then to go to £9, £8 . . . Staff couldn't believe that had happened but people did still have a feeling that they trusted their employer. Nobody sold their shares because they all thought that it would go back up. The message we got from senior management on a weekly basis was: "This is a strong bank; today we have held a meeting with our most significant investors, and we have told them, we have told the City, this is a strong bank. We have a strong asset base." People really watched in disbelief – and I do mean watched, because the share price was on the intranet and they could watch it daily, live, every 15 minutes – as they began to lose their savings.'[10]

For the HBOS board there was one final humiliation before they were booted out without compensation. They had to face share-holders to recommend the deal.

Daniels, however, put an optimistic gloss on events: if it was a good deal before, it was an even better one now, he claimed.

19

Nemesis strikes

Scotland has been home to many lost causes, and consternation at the loss of the country's oldest bank provoked a rash of hopeless attempts to save it. Sir Peter Burt, Bank of Scotland's last chief executive, called his old adversary Sir George Mathewson, now retired from the chairmanship of the Royal Bank of Scotland, and the two wrote to the HBOS board with a typically radical and outspoken alternative future for the company: Stevenson and Hornby should be kicked out, to be replaced by themselves; the Lloyds deal should be rejected and HBOS should continue as an independent company, bolstered by the injection of government capital and loans.

The move sought to tap into an increasing disquiet among HBOS shareholders that they were being herded into accepting the Lloyds offer without knowing the full facts. 'A properly recapitalised, properly run and independent HBOS appears to be in the interests of the shareholders, its employees, its customers and all stakeholders, avoiding the dangers of an anti-competitive over-mighty leviathan,' said a statement from Burt and Mathewson. 'There has been a complete absence of both transparency and debate on whether or not HBOS shareholders are receiving reasonable terms.'[1] Predictably, the proposal was rejected by the HBOS board and in a circular to shareholders Lord Stevenson raised the spectre of total nationalisation if the Lloyds deal was rejected.

Burt and Mathewson continued for another fortnight before throwing in the towel. They had received 40,000 messages of support from small investors, but the institutions which held the vast majority of HBOS shares were not enthusiastic and neither was the Government. Burt finally admitted defeat: 'The Government's statement has raised several hurdles very high and has made it crystal clear that they do not want and are not prepared to facilitate HBOS remaining independent. The deal had been billed the deal of the century. It is a very good deal for Lloyds. I wish them well through gritted teeth. It's very sad. A lot of people will lose their jobs and families will be devastated by it unnecessarily.' He also criticised the 'apparent apathy' of the HBOS board for failing to explore other options at the time of the Government's bailout.[2]

A separate attempt to provide another choice was made by Jim Spowart, the man who had founded Intelligent Finance, the HBOS telephone and internet bank, but had left in 2003. He tried to interest Bank of China into making a counter-bid, but again met with a blank refusal by the Government to consider alternatives. 'Tens of thousands of extra families will now see their lives blighted by unemployment and its resultant misery,' said Mr Spowart. 'Why? Because politicians put their own egos and political agendas before the welfare of the people they purport to represent.'[3]

In December 2008 a last ditch attempt was made by a group of Edinburgh businessmen who launched a challenge to the Government's agreement to set aside competition policy. A special sitting of the Competition Appeals Tribunal was convened at short notice in London to rule on the appeal before the HBOS shareholders' meeting, but rejected it as having no basis. Trustees of the company pension scheme also threatened action, demanding that Lloyds say how it would make up the £3–£5 billion shortfall in the HBOS pension fund, but that too failed.

The deal had to be agreed by both sets of shareholders. As a concession made at the time of the Lloyds merger with TSB, that company was registered in Scotland, although for all practical purposes based in London. It chose the Scottish Exhibition Centre, a vast, cold, industrial shed on the banks of the Clyde in Glasgow for its meeting. Sir Victor Blank did his emollient best to sell the deal, but small investors were not impressed. 'The [Lloyds] strategy has been very successful . . . why does the board think it is in the interests of shareholders to compromise that success?' asked one. 'I find it profoundly disturbing that this deal was cooked up at a cocktail party with the Prime Minister who set aside competition law. Most of us think this deal stinks,' said another. One investor who travelled from Devon, said the board was 'putting its head in a noose' with the HBOS deal and added: 'It smacks of an ego trip.'[4] Sir Victor, with the proxy votes of institutional shareholders in his pocket, knew the deal was safe and announced its approval by 96 per cent.

For its meeting HBOS kept clear of its Scottish and Yorkshire heartlands, where most of its small shareholders lived, but many journeyed to the equally soulless National Exhibition Centre in Birmingham anyway. They heard Stevenson and Hornby apologise for the state to which the bank had sunk. The chairman told the meeting he had spent £1 million buying HBOS shares during the past year. 'You might ask what kind of chump is that? Andy Hornby has put every single cent of his bonuses into the company's shares – not into yachts and grand houses.' Again, the result was a foregone conclusion, but that did not stop small shareholders from voicing their disgust. One said he was appalled that the board had 'turned a £50 billion company into a basket case in 12 months' and he demanded the board return bonuses they had received in previous years.

Among the attendees was Mike Blackburn, the last chief executive of Halifax before the merger with Bank of Scotland. His remarks echoed the feelings of many Scottish ex-managers: 'I don't think you can put all the blame on what has happened in the US,' he said. 'HSBC, for example, has not had recourse to Government money. There is a benefit to banking being boring. Banking is as much about saying "no" as saying "yes".'[5]

The deal was now cleared to go ahead, but the ground was still shifting and it was apparent no one knew exactly the real state of HBOS, including its own management and board. In November it issued a trading statement for the first nine months of the year, which showed a significant deterioration in its performance. Arrears on mortgages and unsecured personal loans were again up; so were the provisions against bad debts in the corporate banking division, with property-related lending particularly hard hit. The corporate investment portfolio – the nest egg built up by Peter Cummings – was showing a loss of £93 million, compared to a profit of £124 million three months earlier. There were also further write-downs to the American mortgages held in the treasury division and losses from the collapse of Lehman Brothers, US bank Washington Mutual and the Icelandic banks. One piece of good news was the sale of BankWest in Australia, which brought in much needed cash, but also prompted another write-off of goodwill in the balance sheet.[6]

Despite some small good patches, the general message was negative, but there was no hint of the bad news that was to come so soon afterwards. A month later a trading statement showed a much worse position: mortgage bad debts again up, to £700 million, and £1 billion lost on unsecured lending. In corporate, the losses had nearly doubled in a month, from £1.7 billion to £3.3 billion, while the loss on the investment portfolio had gone up by eight times to £800 million. Write-downs in the treasury division now totalled £4.5 billion.[7] What was most shocking was not that these figures were so awful, nor that the pace of losses seemed to be accelerating, but that the management did not appear to know about them just a few weeks previously.

'HBOS is flying blind', said the *Financial Times*. 'That the bank was apparently unaware that October was one of the worst months in its 313-year history when it issued its interim trading statement on November 3 is an alarming indictment of its information management systems. That is why yesterday's profits warning, which was accompanied by the announcement of £3.2 billion of fresh write-downs to duff debts incurred in October and November, knocked a fifth off the value of its shares.'[8]

Given the scale of the problems and the rate at which they were increasing, there now began to be doubts whether Lloyds was strong enough to save HBOS, which was admitting that it would have to write off £8 billion in the full year. That would consume more than half the new capital it had raised from its summer rights issue and from the Government injection. Just two months previously the FSA had 'stress tested' British banks – inventing worst-case scenarios and calculating how much capital they would need to survive them. But the worst cases were not worst enough. If HBOS's losses continued at the same rate, its capital would soon fall below the danger level, meaning that it would have to raise more. But from whom? With its shares still falling and future losses still unquantifiable, the private sector would not provide it. That left the taxpayer and the prospect of Government control.

Lloyds' takeover was finally completed in January 2009. Only two of the HBOS top team were kept on: Harry Baine, the company secretary, and Jo Dawson, head of retail and insurance. In fact the purge of HBOS managers was to reach almost Stalin-esque proportions. Lloyds committed itself to the replacement of all the senior management responsible for the collapse of HBOS. No ex-HBOS executives were to be on the new Lloyds Banking Group board and of the nine senior executives reporting to Daniels, only one was ex-HBOS. Further down the organisation, despite HBOS now making up more than half the enlarged group, ex-HBOS managers accounted for less than a third of the top two layers of management.

In Greek mythology the goddess Nemesis extracted vengeful retribution against those guilty of hubris – arrogance before the gods. Now she visited the HBOS board. Lord Stevenson and all the non-executive directors were fired. Andy Hornby, whose head had been demanded by Gordon Brown as a condition of the Government bailout, had already gone. He had been retained by Lloyds on a £60,000 a month consultancy to help with the integration, but a public outcry forced him to give it up.

Colin Matthew and Peter Cummings were the last survivors from the old Bank of Scotland. Cummings' leaving triggered a wave of vilification in the press that continued for several years. He was described as a reckless gambler, a man who almost single-handedly wrecked the bank. Reporters door-stepped his home in Dumbarton and photographers lurked to snatch grainy pictures of him and his wife shopping at the local supermarket. He was bracketed with the Royal Bank of Scotland chief executive Sir Fred Goodwin as the focus for public anger at the collapse of the two banks and, like Goodwin, his generous pension was seen as an ill-gotten gain. *The Sun* headlined: 'Bungling Fred "The Shred" Goodwin was last night joined in Britain's banking hall of shame – by Pete The Pocket.'[9]

Nemesis, however, did not force them to go empty-handed. Peter Cummings received £702,080 as a redundancy payment, Mike Ellis £670,500, Philip Gore-Randall £568,000 and Colin Matthew £656,405. All had also built up large pension funds: Cummings' £7 million would give him an annual pension of £369,000; Matthew's £9 million a pension of £416,000 and Hornby's £2 million would produce £240,000 on retirement. They had received large salaries and cash incentives, paid as part of a scheme covering 2007 and 2008, but waived their right to the 2008 payments – the year in which the company was effectively bankrupted. Cummings was revealed in the subsequent annual report to have also waived his right to £1.3 million 'earned' in 2007.

The goddess was not entirely done with HBOS. A year later Paul Moore, who had been head of Group Regulatory Risk at HBOS between 2002 and 2005, gave evidence before the House of Commons Treasury Select Committee. He alleged that he had repeatedly warned James Crosby, then chief executive, and other directors that Moore had been fired by Crosby. His allegations were disputed by HBOS directors, but his evidence was enough to force Crosby's resignation from the deputy chairmanship of the FSA.

The demise of HBOS and the clear-out of the board left the way open for attention to be focused on Lloyds. When the final results for HBOS were published it became clear that Lloyds had taken on far greater liabilities than it had realised. The loss was a staggering £10 billion, with corporate banking accounting for two-thirds of that and further losses on the US mortgage portfolios for the rest. It was a final nail in the coffins of the reputations of Hornby, Stevenson and Cummings, but it also cast doubt on the judgement of Daniels and Blank. The deal had been rushed because of the danger that HBOS might collapse before it could be taken over and the Lloyds chief executive admitted that only a third or a fifth of the usual amount of due diligence – the painstaking detailed forensic exam-ination of the books – had been done. It began to look as though the Devon shareholder at the Lloyds meeting had been right: it had been a corporate ego trip. Blinded by the scale of the prize, which would give them unrivalled dominance in the British retail banking market, the Lloyds' board and shareholders had cut too many corners. One analyst commented: 'This looks bad for Lloyds as they may have failed to spot the level of toxicity in HBOS's book. The worry now is that they may have blown up two banks instead of one.'[10]

Lloyds' reputation as a cautious bank which had survived the credit crunch in better shape than its rivals was now shattered. The fear was that the mounting losses would eat up all the extra capital it and HBOS had taken from the Government and that the combined group would be forced to seek more. That could mean the publicly-owned share of the bank rising to above 50 per cent. The ratings agency Moody's took a pessimistic view and downgraded Lloyds' credit status.

Daniels fought against Government control, but he did not have many cards to play. In March Lloyds was forced to take advantage of a government scheme to insure £260 billion of toxic loans, 80 per cent of it made up of HBOS mortgages, commercial property and corporate lending. That lifted the pressure on its capital, but there was a heavy price; the insurance premium would cost several billion pounds. Unless Lloyds could pay that in cash, the Government would up its stake in the company to a level which would give it 60–70 per cent of the shares. To avoid this Lloyds went to its own private shareholders to ask for money in a rights issue. Although a quarter refused to buy more shares, the bank raised enough cash to pay the Government its fee, repay some of its borrowing and avoid nationalisation.

The situation had been saved, but shareholders still wanted someone to pay for the botched takeover. The value of their investment had been reduced by three-quarters by the HBOS acquisition. Pressure mounted on Sir Victor Blank and at the annual meeting in May he announced his intention to 'retire' at the next annual meeting in a year's time. In fact he did not last that long and left early to make way for a new chairman, retired banker Sir Win Bischoff, who began a clear-out of the board members who had voted through the HBOS deal. He replaced them with people with banking experience.

But the misery was not over for Lloyds. In November Eric Daniels had to go back to shareholders again for £13.5 billion in new equity and £7.5 billion in bonds – the biggest capital-raising exercise ever by a UK company. It meant another injection of £5.9 billion in Government money and another massive dilution for Lloyds' and HBOS' shareholders, reducing the value of their investments yet again. There was more pain to come. The British Government may have waived competition law, but the European Commission was not so compliant. It ordered Lloyds to work towards the lower-risk strategy it had followed prior to the HBOS acquisition. This included reducing its loan book by £181 billion. To answer monopolies concerns the bank was also required to sell off 632 of its high-street branches and its TSB and Cheltenham & Gloucester brands. All LloydsTSB branches in Scotland were also to be sold and market share in residential mortgages and current accounts was to be reduced.

Daniels survived repeated calls for his resignation, but was forced to give up a £2.3 million bonus for 2009 when Lloyds had recorded a £6.3 billion loss. Daniels left Lloyds in 2011, six months before his retirement age and dogged until the last by bad news from his HBOS move. Some £500 million had to be spent compensating 300,000 Halifax customers for badly written mortgage contracts, and bad debt provisions on Irish loans cost another £2 billion. He spent his last six months on the Lloyds' payroll sitting at home while his successor, Antonio Horta-Osorio ran the bank, but even in retirement he could not escape the ghost of his acquisition. At the beginning of 2012 a retired Scottish sea captain living in New Orleans raised an action in the US courts against Daniels and Blank claiming that a 'reckless disregard for the truth' during the takeover had cost Lloyds shareholders billions of dollars. The Lloyds board also decided that a share issue worth £840,000 to Daniels for his integration of HBOS should be scrapped.

In 2012 Lloyds estimated that the write-offs from its acquisition of HBOS would total £45–48 billion. Sir Win Bischoff said: 'With the benefit of hindsight now, obviously it has not been as good an idea as people thought at the time, and that includes all the shareholders who voted in favour of it.'[11]

In any big corporate transaction like this, press attention focuses on the high-profile casualties at the top, while those at the bottom are merely mass statistics. Thousands of HBOS employees paid for the debacle with their jobs and savings. At the time the deal was struck Lloyds denied that it would lead to 40,000 jobs being lost, although analysts could not see how the bank could save the £1.5 billion a year in costs it had predicted without this scale of reduction in employment. By the middle of 2011 more than 28,000 jobs had been shed, but it was estimated that a strategy review by Horta-Osorio could result in a further 15,000.[12] Their redundancy payments would be in the thousands rather than the hundreds of thousands and their pensions a fraction of those their former bosses received. Many of those who lost their jobs would also have lost their savings through having been shareholders in the HBOS and Lloyds share-save schemes.

'I estimate that 90 per cent of HBOS staff had shares,' said one Bank of Scotland manager. 'Some had tens of thousands in savings. If any of us had suspected things were that bad we would have sold, but we didn't. Andy Hornby kept telling us it was a safe bank; the message was worded slightly differently, but it was the same every month – and we believed him.'

While this was going on Lloyds also began dismantling the property portfolio and the equity stakes built up by Bank of Scotland Corporate under Peter Cummings. At one stage Lloyds had 1,000 people unwinding the HBOS property book. A number of property companies to which HBOS had lent collapsed into administration or receivership, or the bank was forced to accept equity in exchange for loans which could not be repaid. Others were sold at fractions of the levels at which they had been valued just a few years before, giving the bank some of its money back.

To try to recover some value on the Cummings' 'nest egg' share stakes, Lloyds entered into a joint venture with Coller Capital, a private equity firm, to try to sell the holdings. The new venture, in which Lloyds had a minority share, was headed by Graeme Shankland, formerly head of HBOS's integrated finance unit. An anonymous commentator told the *Financial Times*: 'These guys made some horrendous mistakes, but that doesn't make them incompetent. They know the assets better than anyone else and are best placed to clear up their own mess.'[13]

It was not all fire sales. In 2010 PSN, an oilfield services company which had been a management buyout backed by HBOS and Tom Hunter in 2006, was sold to the Wood Group for £600 million and the following year Mint Hotels (formerly City Inn) was sold to Blackstone for £600 million. In both deals Lloyds recovered debt and equity.

In 2010 Lloyds gave Bank of Scotland branches a makeover. The Halifax name was removed and a new advertising campaign sought to focus on 'traditional banking values'. Television commercials voiced by actor Dougray Scott followed a couple from their meeting, through marriage, having a family and buying a home. Its brand promise: 'With you all the way' echoed the 'Friend for Life' campaign of a quarter of a century before. Media consultant Richard Gold commented: 'In the context of recent crises, the claim and the homely way it is delivered may seem almost ironic – it is as if the past couple of years never happened. Yet viewed within the context of the bank's centuries-old relationship with Scottish people (it was founded in 1695), and at a time when a host of new entrants are trying to establish a high street banking presence to take advantage of public mistrust of the incumbents, it is a bold and sensible approach.

'Bank of Scotland is digging deep into its DNA to recapture and amplify the institution's most appealing brand assets.'[14]

20

Hungry for risk

What went wrong? In the next few chapters I will attempt to find some answers to this question. To say what happened is easier than to say why it happened. In trying to discover the latter I have been hampered by the fact that, although many senior managers and some non-executive board members have been ready to speak to me, the key executives, including Sir James Crosby, first chief executive of HBOS, Andy Hornby, his successor, and Mike Ellis, finance director, have all declined to meet me. I do not criticise them for this: mine is a personal rather than an official inquiry and they did not know how objective or how accurate I would be. But I mention it as a qualification to my conclusions. Their actions are, to a large extent, documented and well known. We can guess at their motivations, but without any certainty because they have refused to speak. Peter Cummings also declined to explain his part, but with a specific justification. At the time of writing he was the only HBOS executive to be notified of possible 'enforcement' actions by the FSA and is understandably talking to no one until the result of that action is known.

I am not the only person seeking answers. The House of Commons Treasury Select Committee conducted extensive hearings and pro-duced two comprehensive reports on the failure of UK banks, including HBOS and the Royal Bank of Scotland. The European Commission touched on the reasons for the HBOS failure in its report on the competition issues raised by the Lloyds takeover. The Independent Commission on Banking has also examined the com-ponents of the collapse and suggested ways in which they would be mitigated in the future. I shall draw on all these, plus numerous press and academic reports. The FSA initially said its report on the collapse of HBOS would be internal only and not made public, but under pressure from MPs and the press it has conceded it will be published.

When is another matter. The FSA will give no guidance. At the time of writing (Spring 2012) it looks as though it will be at least 2013 – four years after the collapse of HBOS – before the financial regulator gives a full account.

What precipitated the crash of HBOS? It can be very simply stated: HBOS broke the basic rules of banking; it ran out of cash and it lent to people who could not repay. From the failure of the City of Glasgow Bank in 1878 to the collapse of the secondary banks a century later, the history of banking is littered with examples of banks that failed for just these reasons. These lessons were not learned. Why not?

There has been criticism of James Crosby, the first chief executive of HBOS, and Andy Hornby, his successor, for their lack of banking qualifications and experience, although Crosby was an actuary with a deep intellectual understanding of risk. For the first few years of HBOS' existence there were several experienced and trained bankers among the executive directors: Peter Burt, George Mitchell, Colin Matthew and Gordon McQueen. At the end there were only Matthew and Cummings. The new promotions to the executive board had financial services backgrounds, but not much banking experience. Was this a critical factor? It is hard to believe that possessing a banking qualification would have altered the behaviour of Hornby. Would things have turned out differently had George Mitchell become the successor to James Crosby rather than Andy Hornby? Perhaps, but that would probably have been as a consequence of his maturity, his temperament and the culture he had imbibed during 30 years at Bank of Scotland rather than the certificate in banking he had earned at the beginning of his career.

The culture at HBOS at its height was very different from that at the old Bank 20 years before. It is tempting to believe that it changed on the day of the merger, but the sales culture had been creeping into most British banks for a decade before 2001 and the Bank was no exception. I remember clearly the day I first noticed that change in the early 1990s when, having discussed a major expansion of my business with my bank manager, he called with an urgent query: could we possibly see our way to draw down the money before the end of the month so that he could meet his target? It was not even a low pressure sell, but it would not have happened even five years before and was the beginning of a process which eventually led to personal account holders being called at home in the evenings to be 'informed' about new products and asked if they wanted to buy. But the change of culture in Bank of Scotland was incremental prior to the merger in 2001. In HBOS it had become revolutionary. One Bank executive making his first visit to the Halifax headquarters shortly after the merger expected to find it like his traditional image of a building society, dusty and conservative. He was shocked to find it like the sales office of a supermarket.

Lord Stevenson and Andy Hornby argued before the select committee that the closure of the wholesale inter-bank market was the sole reason for the collapse of HBOS. They claimed that the Bank had been taking prudent steps to try to reduce this liquidity risk by increasing the length of its borrowings, by trying to increase its retail deposits and so reduce its reliance on wholesale funding and by curtailing the growth of its lending. All this is true, but it was too little, too late. The select committee did not believe them. Its report on the banking crisis was clear where the blame lay: 'Capital and liquidity indiscipline were at the heart of HBOS's downfall, and rather more emphasis was placed in HBOS's evidence to us on the catastrophic global context of recent events than on a genuine recognition that responsibility for the Company's plight lay with the Board and the Board alone.'[1]

By the end of 2008 HBOS was more dependent on short-term funding from the wholesale market than any other major UK bank (Northern Rock having already failed) and its name in the market had been tarnished by doubts over the quality of its assets, exacerbated by the relentless increase in doubtful lending in mortgages, unsecured personal loans and corporate advances. There were also rising provisions against its holdings of US mortgages, the Alt-A securities. Every time it had to restate the level of its 'impaired loans' or written-down assets it lost more credibility. The market was not convinced that the HBOS management knew the depth of the hole into which it had dug itself. Its creditworthiness was undermined and this was reflected in the downgrading of its rating by the credit agencies. This in turn damaged its ability to fund itself.

Hornby and Stevenson also argued that the 'closure' of the wholesale markets was an unforeseen and, in fact, an unforeseeable event. Apart from the short period of dislocation after the Twin Towers attacks in 2001, markets had not suffered a general seize-up since the

Wall Street crash. This was also true, but the market did not cease to operate altogether, although it treated different banks in different ways. Lloyds and HSBC, for example, both much more conservatively run institutions than HBOS and each with much less reliance on the inter-bank market, found it more difficult to raise money in the autumn of 2008 than they had six months earlier, but were able to fund themselves nonetheless. It was possible even for HBOS to borrow, although the terms of its borrowings had shrunk to a day at a time and the price had risen to levels at which it could not operate profitably.

HBOS bore the mark of Cain on its forehead. This had happened to a single bank before, although in a less public way. In 1974 NatWest had got into such trouble by over-extending itself in the property market that other banks were reluctant to lend to it and it faced a liquidity crisis. But the world was different then and the Bank of England could create time to resolve the crisis by keeping the whole issue private. The Bank and NatWest itself told the public a deliberate lie − that NatWest was not in trouble − in order not to shake confidence in the whole banking system. The market was also smaller. Behind closed doors the Bank of England lent heavily on other banks to support NatWest and itself pumped in money to keep it going.

By 2008 regulatory disclosure and a much more active press meant that it was impossible to keep the predicament of HBOS a secret. It was also impossible for the central bank to influence the behaviour of the inter-bank market, which had become global. This time it was the Treasury rather than the Bank of England that took the lead and Lloyds was a willing rather than a reluctant participant in the rescue. But in 1974 NatWest could survive its crisis. This time it was different: HBOS's losses were so heavy and its management had lost so much credibility that it could not continue as an independent bank.

How had it got itself into this position?

To answer that question we need to go back to its beginning. The justification given for the merger in 2001 was to marry Halifax's large, low-risk, but slow growing balance sheet with Bank of Scotland's fast-growing lending book. Analysts were sceptical about the ability of Halifax to expand when it had few skills or experience outside personal financial services. Its dominant market share in its core business, mortgages, would be hard to defend against aggressive competition. Bank of Scotland, on the other hand, had been dogged by concerns over its increasing reliance on wholesale funding, which threatened to curtail its growth. The merger appeared to answer both concerns. By being able to tap into Halifax's market-leading share of retail deposit accounts, the Bank would be able to continue to fund its expansion and the combined group would be able to increase its profitability safely.

That may have been the common perception of how the newly created group would progress, but it was not one held by the management of Halifax. From the beginning James Crosby set startlingly demanding targets – to achieve a 15–20 per cent share of each of the markets in which it operated. That was a huge stretch for corporate and business banking, where the initial market share was in low single figures. In retail banking it meant an aggressive drive to attract new mortgages which inevitably diluted Halifax's safe and solid traditional mortgage book. With a share of existing mortgages of 20 per cent, in some years HBOS also took more than 30 per cent of new mortgages.

How did it do this? The first annual report of HBOS made lofty claims about being on the side of the consumer, but in view of the fines imposed subsequently by the FSA for various lapses in customer service, we can dismiss this as cynical marketing. In common with many other banks, HBOS' most profitable product was payment protection insurance (PPI), one of the most blatant examples of mis-selling by financial services companies. In 2011 Lloyds Banking Group had to set aside £3.2 billion to compensate customers who had been mis-sold PPI, including many from Halifax and Bank of Scotland. The competitive advantage of HBOS was not service or concern for its customers, it was price. It sold products at margins so thin as to be unsustainable; some even though they made a loss. This was market share at any price.

Along with low prices went a willingness to take more risks than its competitors. This led to a rapid increase in unsecured personal loans, credit card lending and 'specialist' mortgages – a euphemism for self-certified, buy-to-let and mortgages with very high loan-to-value ratios, including the notorious 125 per cent loans. Competition in retail financial services was intense and HBOS staff were under constant pressure to keep up with their rivals. Supersalesman Andy Hornby always ended his monthly newsletter to staff with the injunction 'Keep smiling, keep selling' and staff who did sell well were rewarded with cash and other incentives. According to one non-executive director: 'The impression was, "Never mind the quality, feel the bonus".' As Chapter 22 will show, this pattern was repeated in corporate banking.

While the market was booming the policy paid off for everyone. HBOS directors saw the benefits in their salaries and bonuses. Direct comparisons are complicated by changes of role, but in 2001 James Crosby as chief executive received a total of £1,073,000, whereas in 2007 Andy Hornby in the same job received £1,926,000 – an increase of 80 per cent.*

In 2001 George Mitchell as head of corporate banking, received £678,000, but in 2007 Peter Cummings received £2,606,000 – an increase of 284 per cent. Lower down the pecking order rewards were not quite so spectacular, but bank staff did well with average staff salaries growing by 40 per cent over the same time period.

The high-pressure sales culture was not unique to HBOS, but it was not shared by all banks. Among the top five big banks in the UK, HBOS, The Royal Bank of Scotland and Barclays followed aggressive expansion policies, while Lloyds and HSBC were known for being more conservatively run. This can be seen in their results. Between 2001 and 2007 HBOS grew its total lending by nearly 120 per cent, while the increase in Lloyds during the same period was less than 70 per cent. HBOS' profits increased by 90 per cent, whereas Lloyds' rose by only 13 per cent.

It was not only the management which saw big rewards. HBOS investors saw the benefits of the rapid expansion in the share price, which outperformed the FT banking index for most of the period, whereas Lloyds consistently under-performed.

When the market turned, the risks in the policy should have begun to show, yet the pressure on staff to sell continued even after the financial crisis began: 'Despite the recession caused by this financial crisis, the company [did] not reduce staff targets significantly in any area. In some cases the targets [were] increased for retail staff. So if you're in a little branch of HBOS in Auchtermuchty . . . and you were meant to sell five mortgages a week, or three personal loans a

---

* These rises in top pay were not out of line with the rest of the banking sector. Despite Lloyds' less stellar performance over the period, the total remuneration of the chief executive rose from £1,100,000 to £2,884,000.

day, you're still meant to be doing that even though potentially five per cent of your customers are now unemployed or they're probably on salary freezes, you're still meant to be doing that.'²

By then, however, the momentum was hard to arrest. 'The whole mood at the top was that everything had been going so well that anything was possible and nothing could go wrong,' remembers a former director of the bank.

Paul Moore, dismissed as HBOS head of regulatory risk by Crosby in 2005, told the Commons Treasury Committee:

Even non-bankers with no credit risk management expertise, if asked (and I have asked a few myself), would have known that there must have been a very high risk if you lend money to people who have no jobs, no provable income and no assets. If you lend that money to buy an asset which is worth the same or even less than the amount of the loan and secure that loan on the value of that asset purchased and, then, assume that asset will always rise in value, you must be pretty much close to delusional. You simply don't need to be an economic rocket scientist or mathematical financial risk management specialist to know this. You just need common sense. So why didn't the experts know? Or did they but they carried on anyway because they were paid to do so or too frightened to speak up?³

Ordinary staff in the Bank were not rocket scientists, but they had doubts about the sales policy being followed:

Although when the Northern Rock crisis broke in 2008 people saw it as not connected to them, they were stunned by it because they thought 'How could this happen?' They didn't quite see the connection between what a building society in the north of England really had to do with the Bank of Scotland or HBOS. Not that long afterwards there was an end to the property boom and that had a massive impact on HBOS because it meant they didn't have enough money. HBOS had the highest percentage of mortgages on its books in Britain, and lending practices had potentially not been as resilient as they could have been, with people lent much larger amounts than they previously would have been under a more conservative traditional banking model.

Staff were doing what they were told and were following the rules given to them under the risk strategy that applied. But that exposed the company to quite a lot of potentially bad lending in housing, and that was a bit of an open secret.[4]

How much risk a bank is prepared to take is no longer a subjective process. Where once bank executives would have examined a lending proposal and rejected it on the grounds that 'it did not feel right', now banks measured deals against their 'risk appetite'. This is a complex formula, which includes among other things the probability of default and the exposure – how much money the company is prepared to risk at any one time. It also takes in more general concerns such as earnings volatility, capital requirements, reputation, credit ratings and the requirements of the regulatory regime under which the bank operates. The way HBOS went about calculating, allocating and reviewing risk I will examine in the next chapter, but here I want to look at the size of its appetite for risk compared to less adventurous banks.

There is a direct relationship between risk and reward. Compared to its competitors, HBOS was hungry for growth and profit and therefore willing to take more risks. A stark illustration of that came in 2009 when Tim Tookey, finance director of Lloyds, which by then had acquired HBOS and was belatedly going through its books in close detail, gave a presentation to a New York conference. He examined HBOS' lending and compared it with Lloyds' more conservative 'risk appetite'. Of the £255 billion lent by HBOS retail, £65 billion, or a quarter, would not have been lent by Lloyds because it was outside their 'risk appetite'. In corporate banking £80 billion of the £116 billion was outside Lloyds' appetite – more than two-thirds. In international the figures were £20 billion of the total £61 billion lent by HBOS would not have been lent by Lloyds, nearly a third. In total Lloyds would not have lent £165 billion of the total £432 billion – 38 per cent.[5]

Admittedly this is comparing one of the most aggressive banks with one of the most conservative, but it does illustrate the extent to which the management culture at HBOS encouraged it to take higher risks in order to gain larger rewards. That is not to say that Lloyds would not have done any of the deals; indeed it was the second-largest taker of secondary debt from HBOS corporate – that is, it took a propor-tion of the lending which HBOS sold down to reduce its own exposure. In these cases Lloyds was willing to accept the same probability of default as HBOS, but not to risk the same amount of money: it made the same bets, but its stakes were smaller.

It was not only liquidity which sank HBOS. It was also bad lending. That in turn led to a third factor: lack of capital. Again, I will explore the way in which capital is calculated and the regulatory regime operated later, but here I want to make a simple point. By the middle of 2008 mounting bad debts had consumed so much of HBOS's capital that it was forced to go to its shareholders for more. The failure of its 2008 rights issue showed how far investor confidence had fallen, with less than 10 per cent of its shareholders prepared to buy more shares, even at a substantial discount to the then market price. Further revelations of bad debts through the following months effectively ended any opportunity to raise more capital from private sources, leaving only the Government as the investor of last resort.

All three factors which contributed to the collapse of HBOS – lack of liquidity, bad lending and lack of capital – were connected. During the boom years the fact that all banks, but especially mortgage banks like HBOS, Northern Rock, Bradford & Bingley and Abbey National, could borrow in seemingly unlimited amounts at cheap rates from the wholesale money market, enabled them to flood the property market with cash. This was a major factor in pushing up property prices and land values, which in turn were the security used for more lending. When the money tap was turned off banks ran out of money, falling prices eroded the collateral which underpinned their lending and the resulting bad debts destroyed their capital.

Banks had ignored another of the fundamental rules of banking: look at the borrower, not the asset.

21

Why didn't they realise?

In his foreword to the 2007 annual report, HBOS chairman Lord Stevenson wrote: 'If ever the boards of banks, regulators or rating agencies needed a reminder of the importance of strong liquidity and strong capital, the second half of 2007 served as a wake-up call. Seemingly overnight, we moved from a scenario where the economic cycle looked set to play out in a relatively benign way, to one where a credit crunch in the USA rapidly deteriorated into what is, as I write this, a worldwide liquidity dislocation.' So far so good, few would dispute his analysis. He went on: 'In the eye of the storm, nemesis followed hubris, with traditional market solutions seemingly impossible. Banks now know, as in truth they always did, that first and foremost, it is the duty of the board to ensure that the group has financial stability and the wherewithal to continue in business profitably. Gradually this current market liquidity dislocation will pass.'

Few would disagree with that sentiment either. It was his conclusion which now looks extraordinary:

> For 2008 we will continue to pay careful attention to the importance of both strong capital and strong liquidity and to size our balance sheet to the certainty of both. We are, I believe, rightly proud as a board that we have been altering the risk profile of our liquidity requirements over the last four years, long before the current so-called liquidity crunch and without any external pressures from regulators or other shareholders but purely as part of being good custodians of your business. You may be quite sure that we will continue to bring to bear the same standards of rigour and financial conservatism as the business moves forward.

We now know that it was complete nonsense. HBOS did not have strong capital, and within ten months of those words being published would have to forfeit its independence and accept government cash to avoid bankruptcy. The self-congratulation over the liquidity management of HBOS was unjustified: the dependence of the bank on the wholesale funding market made it acutely vulnerable. Rigour and financial conservatism were the last adjectives you would have used to describe the quest for profit that the Bank had been and was still pursuing, regardless of risk. The HBOS board turned out to be anything but good custodians of the business.

Dennis Stevenson is not a cynic. When he wrote those words I am sure he believed them and so did all, or at least most, of his board. The fact that Stevenson, Hornby, Cummings and other directors piled into the shares at a time when others were selling shows how much they believed in the business. They subsequently lost most of their money. Were they naïve? Were they misled? Were they incompetent? Did they rely on checks and balances which looked sound on paper, but were so flawed as to be useless?

Two things can be said with certainty about the corporate governance of HBOS. First, it was very elaborate. The Bank took expert advice from some of the leading consultants in the field on the design of its structure, which involved numerous committees monitoring all aspects of risk. These groups included executive and non-executive members and were supported by a large department of risk and governance specialists, who produced huge volumes of reports. Able men and women spent substantial amounts of their time reading and discussing these thick documents. There was a clear upward line of reporting, which ended with the bank board.

Second, it did not work.

A devastating critique of corporate governance and risk management in HBOS was published by the FSA in 2012. It showed a system undermined by a culture that put revenue before risk, management information which failed to show the real dangers the group was running, ineffective control and monitoring and a bias towards optimism, particularly when deciding how big provisions against bad debts should be.[1]

Corporate governance had developed dramatically since the 1980s; in fact, then the term would not have been used or understood. Boards, even of the largest companies, were chosen by the chairman, who sometimes was also the chief executive. A former Governor of Bank of Scotland described the process to me: 'When there was a vacancy coming up, I asked around and when I thought I had a likely candidate I might have discussed his name with the deputy Governors, but then I just called him up.' Criteria for choosing board candidates would not have been explicit, even to the person making the appointment, but included experience, connections and personal preference – 'Will he fit in?' Again, I say 'he' because women on boards were still very rare. The Bank board of the 1970s and 1980s would not have looked very different from any other major company board of the period: white, middle-aged, middle-class and male.

Some high-profile financial scandals in the early 1990s, largely seen as the result of loose systems of corporate governance, which allowed crooked individuals to manipulate companies, triggered a revolution. The Cadbury report recommended a much more systematic approach to appointing directors and to their rights and responsibilities, especially over the financial oversight of the company. This was followed a few years later by the Greenbury report, which suggested further refinements, particularly over the way in which executive pay was determined. These two reports were merged into a combined Code of Corporate Governance which was modified by a series of later inquiries and given semi-legislative status by being incorporated into the Stock Exchange listing rules and policed by regulators. At the same time there was a general acceptance that boards should be more diverse, include more women, younger people, more ethnic minorities, more people with disabilities.

The assessment and control of risk in financial companies was also undergoing a reappraisal. National and international regulation, globalisation and the fear of 'contagion' – the fall of one institution bringing down others – led to a formalising of the systems for monitoring and controlling risk. New international accounting standards were introduced, which changed the way in which assets and liabilities were to be treated and demanded more detailed reporting. 'Gut feel' was to be replaced by a much more systematic, formulaic and mathematical approach. Part of the drive was intended to make companies themselves think more seriously about the risks they were running and partly it aimed at a more public process so that shareholders, regulators and counterparties (the companies and individuals with whom banks and financial institutions do business) would be able to gauge the level of risk more accurately.

'Gut feel' had severe limitations, but in the best institutions it was never just an instinctive feeling. It had been shorthand for an experience-based approach. In the Bank, lending and other major financial decisions were subjected to several levels of scrutiny: credit committees, area boards, general managers and the Chief Executive, and often the main board of the Bank. When executives said a deal 'did not feel right' they were not expressing a vague dislike, but drawing on years or decades of experience. In the 1990s this was supplemented by more sophisticated analysis, but underlying it was the fact that the 'ownership' of the risk was always with the manager making the loan, who was likely to be in post for a long period. It was his or her responsibility to know the customer, assess the creditworthiness and see the loan repaid – with the implicit sanction that too many bad debts would damage career chances.

The Bank's area boards also brought in outsiders, businessmen with knowledge of local industries and individual companies. This was obviously fraught with potential for conflicts of interest: how did you know whether an area board member was expressing a genuine concern over the creditworthiness of an applicant, or trying to damage a business rival? But for the Bank, it seemed to work. The whole system was driven by an ingrained culture which valued ethics and trusteeship – the acknowledgement that the money being handled did not belong to the Bank, but to its depositors and its shareholders, which the Bank called 'proprietors' – owners.

Halifax, in its years as a building society, would have had a very similar ethos, derived from its roots in the savings and self-help movements of the nineteenth century. Those arrangements were breaking down, even before the HBOS merger, to be replaced by a much more formal and transparent system. Professionalism had to replace amateurism. Written codes had to replace unspoken culture. Risk departments supplanted individual responsibility.

The new system also broke the direct relationship of the lending officer to the risk. At the same time the sales culture, which was reaching all parts of banks, emphasised sales performance as the principal measure of achievement. In the old days managers who wanted to get on had to prove they could bring in the business, but also knew that too many bad debts would blight their careers. In the new system risk could seem like someone else's responsibility. For ambitious managers, sales were what mattered.

'It seems some of them envisaged they could further their careers by creating the biggest possible loan portfolio and if the risk department turned some down they would find other loans to take their place,' comments one retired senior bank executive. 'Lack of continuity in career structures also meant they would probably not be around when the loan was due to be repaid. In my day the senior team also had continuing access to the composition and spread of the total portfolio of loans and how this changed over time. I considered that one of my prime responsibilities was to understand the risks we were taking on and whether the balance was acceptable. This was my/our job – not that of a risk department inside the bank or an external regulator.'

Business grandees, like Cadbury and Greenbury, and regulators like the FSA may have seen the new corporate governance and risk disciplines in terms of principle and ethics, but to professional services companies they were a new business opportunity. The major accountancy firms and international consultancies set up corporate governance and risk departments, which would help companies design their systems to be 'compliant' and 'state of the art'. HBOS took expensive advice – indeed it would have been open to criticism had it not done so. Systems had not only to be comprehensive and sophisticated, but they had to be seen to be so.

In the 2007 HBOS annual report and accounts, 40 pages are given over to corporate governance, describing in detail the structure of the board and its committees, the way they are expected to work and the individuals who serve on them. A further 19 pages describe the risk management procedures followed by the Bank. Search the report for the word 'risk' and you come up with more than 500 references. You could get the impression that the Bank was obsessed by risk. Yet many of the thousands of words contained in these pages are bland statements of the obvious, clearly included as part of some box-ticking exercise. Under the heading: 'Key risks and uncertainties facing the group' for example, are the unsurprising assertions that earnings could be affected by an economic downturn and that 'future earnings growth and shareholder value creation depend on the group's strategic decisions'.

There follows a diagram of the 'Three lines of defence' against risk: first the divisional chief executives supported by the divisional risk committees, second, the whole executive structure, from the chief executive and his senior management committee, through the Group Finance Director and the Group Risk Director to eight divisional risk committees. The final defence line includes the audit committee, the divisional risk control committees and the group internal audit function. Over the whole army sits the general staff – the group board.

In an investigation of HBOS corporate banking between 2006 and 2008, the FSA uncovered significant failings in all three lines of defence.[2] The picture painted of the corporate division is explored in more detail in the next chapter, but the report also exposed gaps in the general risk management framework. Corporate banking's internal controls should have provided the first line of defence, but the FSA found that the low credit quality of the deals it was doing meant that there was a relatively high risk of default. Effective monitoring of individual transactions and the portfolio as a whole should have been important, but credit skills and processes were inadequate and key controls were ineffective – weaknesses that were pointed out in repeated control reports.

Throughout the period the corporate division was being pushed to handle greater and greater numbers of new transactions, which were increasingly complex. There were 'continuing, significant and widespread' weaknesses in the effectiveness of the management of the relationship managers, who initiated the deals, and the key sanctioning committees which were supposed to check and authorise these deals had less time to scrutinise each one. Rather than concentrating on reducing risk, the FSA found that the pressure to increase growth and the time taken up by a wide range of change management projects meant that less attention was paid to risk management. As a consequence the control framework failed.

The second line of defence should have been provided by the Group Risk department but the FSA found that this failed too. The picture here is of a department lacking in resources and expertise which could not exert adequate controls. It realised that the difficult economic situation and strong competition posed threats and that its own procedures were not up to the challenge, yet it periodically assured the firm that the credit risk framework was sound and fit for purpose.

There was no group-wide framework for credit risk management. Although Group Risk recognised the need for a clear statement of the 'risk appetite' the company was prepared to accept, which would provide a consistent view across the Group of the maximum tolerable risk in all types of lending, what was produced was no more than a regurgitation of divisional profit targets and forecasts of the provisions which might be needed to cover dubious debts. This statement took little account of the challenges in the market where competitive pressures were leading to increased levels of risk and did not factor in the risk of an economic downturn. The FSA found that the Group Risk department failed to provide effective challenge to the corporate division, either in setting risk limits or responding when it broke these limits.

The third line of defence should have been provided by the Group Internal Audit department, which had the responsibility of checking other controls and providing assurance to the board that they were functioning properly in measuring and managing risk. But here too the FSA found a lack of business expertise and resource. The department focused on major regulatory and change projects rather than business as usual, and it was uncertain where the responsibility of the internal audit department ended and the Group Risk department began. The result was, according to the FSA 'an underlap' between the two departments – a gap which meant that some risks were not adequately monitored or assessed.

The FSA judged that HBOS was guilty of very serious misconduct, in that the corporate department, trading under the Bank of Scotland name, failed to comply with one of the FSA's 11 Principles for Businesses: 'A firm must take reasonable care to organise and control its affairs responsibly and effectively, with adequate risk management systems.' Between January 2006 and March 2008, the FSA found that HBOS failed to take reasonable care to organise and control its affairs responsibly and effectively, with adequate risk management systems to cope with the aggressive growth, high-risk business and lending strategy it was pursuing.

Overseeing all three lines of defence and ultimately responsible legally and morally, was the board of the bank, made up of full-time executive directors including the chief executive, finance director and the divisional heads; as well as non-executive directors who were supposed to add extra skills, experience and, above all, independence. The key responsibility of a non-executive director is to challenge the executive – to rock the boat – yet in HBOS there seems to have been a serious lack of challenge.

At its beginning the HBOS board inherited some directors from both sides of the merger who were prepared to hold the executives to account, men nearing the ends of their careers who had nothing left to prove and were not afraid to contradict the chief executive or the chairman. These included Sir Bob Reid, from the Bank of Scotland board, and Louis Sherwood, who had been on the Halifax board. 'The executive and Dennis [Stevenson] didn't like Louis,' one of his non-executive colleagues remembers. 'He was continually asking blunt questions and if he didn't get an answer he would ask it again, and again, and again. It didn't make him popular, but every board needs a Louis Sherwood and every audit committee needs a Louis Sherwood.' As these men retired they were replaced with younger faces. 'They were very talented and competent business people and they were conscientious, but they did not have the experience or the confidence of the older board members and they did not ask as many questions.'

Although part-time, the job of a non-executive on the HBOS board could be very demanding. There were ten board meetings a year and numerous committee meetings. The audit committee met seven times. For each meeting there would be hours of preparation, going through mountains of complex documentation. On paper, board members also bore a heavy responsibility: they were liable under the Companies Acts for the conduct of the business and held accountable by the FSA. So far these have been theoretical rather than practical sanctions. No non-executive has been criticised by either the Department of Business, or the FSA. The posts were well rewarded. Ordinary non-executives earned £100,000–£200,000 in 2008, with Sir Ron Garrick, the senior independent director being paid £258,000 and Tony Hobson, chair of the audit committee, £230,000. Lord Stevenson, the chairman, received £815,000 and, unusually among non-executives, also received shares under a long-term incentive plan.

It is a matter of debate whether payments at this level to non-executive directors ensure that companies get high-calibre people who are properly rewarded for the large amount of work they are expected to do, or whether such large payments prejudice their independence by making them less likely to challenge the chief executive or chair. There is also a question mark over how much scrutiny non-executives are able to perform at a practical level if they are not party to individual lending decisions and do not have banking experience.

The overriding culture of HBOS was that of a retail company and many of its later non-executive board recruits were skilled and experienced retailers or marketeers. It lacked banking expertise among its non-executives until late in its life when it recruited John E. Mack, who had been Corporate Treasurer of Bank of America and Chief Financial Officer of Shinsei Bank of Japan, who joined in May 2007. Despite the resources it apparently devoted to governance and risk management, they ultimately failed to protect it and it is difficult to escape the conclusion that, despite their efforts, non-executive board members did not know what the bank was doing, even less the implications.

Yet the implications could not have been more serious and the warning signs should have been there for the board to see. According to the FSA report:

> From April 2008, as it became apparent that high value transactions were demonstrating signs of stress, it should have been apparent to Bank of Scotland that a more prudent approach was needed to mitigate risk, yet it was slow to move such transactions to its High Risk area within its Corporate Division. There was a significant risk that this would have an impact on the firm's capital requirements. It also meant the full extent of the stress within the corporate portfolio was not visible to the group's board or auditors. In addition, while the firm's auditors agreed that the overall level of the firm's provisioning was acceptable, in relation to the corporate division provisions were consistently made at the optimistic rather than prudent end of the acceptable range, despite warnings from the divisional risk function and Bank of Scotland's auditors.[3]

Tracey McDermott, FSA acting director of enforcement at the time, commented: 'Banks and other firms have to manage their business by ensuring that their systems and controls are appropriate for the risks that they are running. The conduct of the Bank of Scotland illustrates how a failure to meet regulatory requirements can end not just in massive costs to a firm, but losses to shareholders, taxpayers and the economy.'

This was a severe censure; however, coming nearly four years after the event, it was far too late to influence any change in HBOS. Public criticism of the institution was also as far as the regulator was prepared to go. No individuals were named, nor were any sanctions imposed. The FSA suggested that had a fine been imposed it would have set a record, surpassing even the £17.5 million imposed on Goldman Sachs for breaches of rules. Since the horse had not only bolted, but sent to the knacker's yard and slaughtered, there was hardly any point in making the owner pay for a new stable door.

'The severity of Bank of Scotland's failings during this time would, under normal circumstances, be likely to warrant a very substantial financial penalty. However, because public funds have already been called on to address the consequences of Bank of Scotland's mis-conduct, levying a penalty on the enlarged Group means the taxpayer would effectively pay twice for the same actions committed by the firm. Therefore, to reflect these exceptional circumstances, the FSA has not levied a fine against Bank of Scotland but has issued a public censure to ensure details of the firm's misconduct can be viewed by all and act as a lesson in risk management failings.'

Will anything be done to reform the corporate governance of banks? The signs are not hopeful. In 2009 a review led by Sir David Walker,[4] a former Treasury and Bank of England official, conducted a consultation and published a report which saw very little wrong with the system which had failed to stop the collapse of HBOS, The Royal Bank of Scotland and Northern Rock. Its five recommendations amounted only to tweaking a system which was clearly inadequate. The existing code for bank boards, it concluded, combined with tougher capital and liquidity requirements and a tougher regulatory stance on the part of the FSA, provided 'the surest route to better corporate governance practice'. It did concede some failings in bank boards, but said these related much more to patterns of behaviour than to organisation. 'The sequence in board discussion on major issues should be: presentation by the executive, a disciplined process of challenge, decision on the policy or strategy to be adopted and then full empowerment of the executive to implement. The essential "challenge" step in the sequence appears to have been missed in many board situations and needs to be unequivocally clearly recog-nised and embedded for the future.' How boards were to be made more assertive and challenging it did not say.

Walker's report also called for more board involvement in 'risk oversight' with particular attention to the monitoring of risk and discussion leading to decisions on the bank's risk appetite and tolerance, but how this was to be achieved by non-executives having to grapple with the scale of complexity of modern banking it again did not specify. It did make a plea for a greater involvement by institutional shareholders. On remuneration, it looked only at executive pay and did not comment on the objectivity of non-executives.

HBOS clearly exhibited a breakdown in corporate governance, which despite many thousands of words of lip service paid to it, failed to control the group. But do not expect change – at least not in the near future.

22

The drive for profit at any price

It is not often that the veil which shields the inner workings of a massive corporation is lifted to let us see the machinations hidden behind it, but the 2012 FSA report into HBOS corporate banking[1] gave some astonishing insights. Here was a division that had delivered phenomenal growth, being constantly pressed to go further – whatever the consequences.

The regulator looked specifically at the corporate department, yet it also threw a strong light on the group management of HBOS, which had a seemingly insatiable demand for more profit regardless of the economic or competitive situation. It was an executive which did not address the inadequacies in its monitoring, control and management of risk and deluded itself on the chances it was taking. Its internal business plans spoke of 'measured lending growth', 'sound credit quality' and 'a conservative approach to credit risk management', when all the time it was pushing more and more lending, reducing the quality of the deals it was doing and running higher and higher risks.

The FSA looked in detail at the period from 2006, when the economic boom was reaching its peak, to 2008 when HBOS had to be rescued by Lloyds. During this time HBOS made repeated statements in its internal plans that the business was adopting a selective and cautious approach to lending, sentiments it repeated in its annual reports to shareholders. The truth, however, was very different. Succeeding plans set ever-increasing and highly challenging targets for profit growth from the corporate banking division, which was being forced to make up the shortfall in the profits from the retail division. This could only be achieved by rapid increases in the amount of lending it was doing, with consequent effects on the quality of the commitments it was taking on and the risks it was running.

At the end of 2005 HBOS realised that the market was becoming more difficult. The boom was topping out, strong competition for leveraged debt deals were cutting margins and increasing risks and internally the corporate banking division still had management issues it had not resolved. In its business plan, corporate proposed increasing its lending by 6 per cent during 2006 and generating 9 per cent more in profit. This was not considered good enough: HBOS ordered the division to double its profit target. In fact it nearly achieved that higher level, turning in 17 per cent more profit on lending up 8 per cent. But there was a cost; much of the lending was in property and higher-risk transactions.

By the start of 2007 it was clear the economy was deteriorating and that risks were increasing, particularly in leveraged finance. Corporate banking budgeted for a profit growth of 10–12 per cent for the year, but was again directed by the HBOS group management to up the target. A new plan was written showing profit growth of 22 per cent on lending up 9 per cent. Even this was not good enough. The FSA found that the HBOS group management increasingly looked to the corporate division to make up for the underperformance of residential mortgages and personal lending. In April 2007 the profit growth target was increased to 30 per cent. In June 2007 the targets for the year were increased again to 35 per cent. By the end of July 2007, corporate banking had generated 85 per cent of the profits it made in the whole of 2006 and was 21 per cent ahead of plan. Lending grew by 5 per cent in this period.

This astonishing performance was achieved by doing bigger, riskier deals and committing more money to property. Credit standards were already low, but the quality fell below even the levels set in the division's plan.

By the autumn of 2007 the credit crunch was beginning to bite. In the US two hedge funds had collapsed, French bank BNP Paribas had difficulties and Northern Rock was teetering on the edge of bankruptcy. The property market was looking bad and the syndication market for loans, an important part of HBOS's strategy to spread risk, had practically dried up. Despite all this, corporate kept lending. 'This strategy involved supporting existing customers (which in turn further increased the business's exposure to significant large borrowers) and actively seeking to increase market share. Significant volumes of new business continued to be sanctioned by the corporate division in this period,' the FSA said.

The corporate division's business model depended on being able to unload risk by selling part of any transaction to other banks. It would typically take 100 per cent of the exposure of any deal it made onto its own loan book and subsequently try to sell part of this to other banks until it reached a targeted 'hold position'. Its preference to find and structure deals itself meant that it earned more fees, but it also ran more risk than if it did them on a club basis with other banks, with the risk and the fees shared from the start. As 2007 went on it was becoming increasingly difficult to sell down, but still the deal-making went on. A number of large deals were done against the advice of the corporate banking division's loans distribution unit and without any proper assessment of the increased risks from not being able to sell down. Deals awaiting syndication piled up so that by 30 April 2008 the value of the corporate division's loans waiting to be sold down was £9.7 billion.

Despite the difficult economic environment in the last five months of 2007, corporate had achieved impressive growth for the year. Profits were up 32 per cent – 7.5 per cent above the original plan target and just £60 million short of an ambitious target of £2.4 billion set at the end of June. Lending grew by 22 per cent; but again there was a price. Property lending had been increased by 15 per cent, just as the market was turning down, the equity portfolio was being built up and there were large increases in higher-risk structured and leveraged deals. The division continued to lend and buy equity stakes in ventures into 2008, doing bigger and riskier deals. In the first three months of the year it did 46 deals of £75 million or more, with a total value of £11.6 billion. At the top end, 11 transactions were worth £250 million or more each, adding up to a total value of £7.1 billion. Again, credit quality was lower than planned.

The report showed a division running fast just to stand still. The high turnover rate on the corporate loan book meant that approximately 30 per cent more deals had to be done each year just to ensure that the size of the book did not reduce. But corporate banking was still being urged to do more. It was given challenging growth targets – which were often met and exceeded.

There was only one way to satisfy these demands: take bigger risks. The corporate division was the riskiest part of HBOS and it took more risks than other major UK banking groups. The corporate banking loan book was already high-risk and low quality, considered sub-investment grade by the ratings agencies. But in achieving its lending and profit targets, the corporate division went lower than even its own plan demanded. A substantial proportion of the profit growth was coming from higher-risk areas of the business, in particular Joint Ventures and ISAF (Integrated, Structured and Acquisition Finance, the bank's debt-to-equity one-stop shop) which originated the majority of corporate's risk capital deals. Overall the average credit quality of new and renewal business remained low, but deals originated by these two departments turned out to be even lower in quality.

A high proportion of lending was in property, which meant that the bank was heavily exposed to a downturn. At the start of 2006, 52 per cent (or £44.4 billion) of the money corporate had lent was to the commercial property market. By the end of 2008, this proportion had risen to 56 per cent (or £68.1 billion). Another factor was that it was unduly exposed to large 'single name' borrowers. At the start of 2006, its top 30 borrowers accounted for 15 per cent of the value of the corporate portfolio (£19.2 billion). By the end of March 2008, this had increased to 23 per cent (£34.1 billion). To compound the problem in many transactions, corporate's exposure to a large single-name borrower also involved commercial property and/or risk capital and/ or were highly leveraged, further deepening the level of concentration and risk. The size of these exposures meant that any default would have a high impact on the loan book.

Peter Cummings' policy of buying shareholdings in companies and of providing equity finance alongside debt also came in for scrutiny and the old danger of a conflict of interest between the lender which wants to get its money back and the shareholder trying to protect its investment began to surface.

The corporate division operated a 'one-stop-shop' model for integrated finance, which meant that the risk in individual transactions received less scrutiny than if debt and equity had been required to be approved and managed separately. This was the highest-risk area of the corporate book. Compared to lending 'senior debt' where the borrowing was secured against the assets of the company, buying shares was much more risky. There was no collateral to back the risk capital (shares) and shareholders had less control over the assets of a company compared to lenders, who could insist on covenants. These risks were compounded by conflicts of interest, which would become particularly acute if the transaction became 'stressed' as the interests of senior debt holders would differ from those of risk capital holders. Despite this, the division's exposure to risk capital grew rapidly. At the start of 2006, the reported value of corporate's debt securities and equity shares was £2.3 billion. By the end of August 2008, this had increased by 139 per cent to £5.5 billion. To meet the challenging targets it had been set by the group executive, corporate generated significant profits by selling investments. But these were one-off gains and in order to keep the profit stream going, new deals had to be found.

If the risks were going up, so were the stakes. Deals which involved lending over £75 million, or making a substantial equity investment, had to be sanctioned by the Executive Credit Committee. There was a significant increase in the volume and complexity of deals that this committee approved during 2006 and 2007. In 2006 199 deals of more than £75 million were approved, which represented total lending of £56 billion. The following year this went up to 361 approvals, with a total value of £96.2 billion. At the higher end of the lending scale there were 56 approvals of lending over £250 million in 2006 (total lending: £36.2 billion), which nearly doubled to 110 approvals in 2007 (total lending: £64 billion). The size of these transactions meant that any default would have a high impact on the book.

To achieve the levels of profit it wanted, HBOS concentrated on low-grade/high-risk opportunities which would command higher interest rates and fees. Yet it never made this explicit to its share-holders. In the annual report for 2007, for example, the comments of chief executive Andy Hornby were all about return and played down the higher risk that inevitably went with bigger returns. Low-grade investments were euphemistically called 'alternative asset classes' and a concentration on a few high-risk areas was described as 'value-enhancing specialisation'. There was a comforting allusion to redu-cing risk by sell-down, even though by the time the report was written the syndication market was effectively shut.

Hornby wrote:

In our corporate business we continue to concentrate on markets where we have real expertise and can generate superior returns. Through a focus on the individual risk:reward characteristics of alternative asset classes, we aim to bring a clear value-enhancing specialisation to our customer relationships. Assets are originated on the basis that they will be held on the balance sheet in their entirety, even if subsequently a proportion of debt or equity positions are sold down to other market participants. This discipline ensures there is no disconnect between a decision to lend and the potential availability of higher returns through sell-down activity when market conditions are supportive.

In the corporate banking section of the 2007 annual report, Peter Cummings commented: 'Controlled credit risk: Selective specialisation and strong client partnerships are all designed to manage the balance between risk and return.' In fact the corporate division had a specific focus on sub-investment grade lending. It had a target portfolio rating of 5.2 (BB), which was considered sub-investment grade by the ratings agencies, but it failed to meet even that and consistently did deals which had a lower credit rating than the target. A proportion of the portfolio in particular risk capital transactions was not rated at all, which made it the highest-risk part of the book.

Throughout this period there was strong competition for deals among banks, and to hold on to customers the corporate division often had to increase its exposure on transactions that were already lowly rated. It did this by resorting to aggressive deal structures – for example high leverage multiples, low interest margins, weak covenants and/or riskier subordinated debt tranches such as PIK notes ('Payment in Kind', where the bank does not receive any interest until the loan is paid off). These aggressive structures increased risk as they made it more difficult for the corporate division to 'sell down' its exposure to other banks, which were much less willing to take them on.

The low credit quality of deals meant that there was a relatively high risk of default. Effective monitoring of individual transactions and the portfolio as a whole was therefore important. For example, the monitoring of deals to see whether a borrower was likely to break a lending covenant was vital because a breach was a trigger to consider whether to put a deal on the watch list or make a provision against possible default. HBOS relied on its relationship managers to do this, but the FSA found that there were continuing and significant weaknesses in credit skills and processes at all stages, from the origination of the loan to the final repayment. There were also repeated failings across all areas of the business of key controls, which were crucial to the effective sanctioning and monitoring of individual transactions.

The reason all this was allowed to happen was that HBOS' corporate division operated in a culture that valued and encouraged sales above all else. Risk management was regarded as a constraint on the business rather than an integral part of it. Managers were incentivised to focus on revenue rather than risk, which increased their willingness to meet customers' demands, increase lending and take on greater risk. Managers concentrated on one deal at a time, with insufficient regard to the portfolio as a whole and the business was resistant to change.

Achieving sell-down to the target hold position was a vital element of the corporate business model as a means of reducing its exposure to large leveraged transactions. But there were significant problems. The division's loans distribution capability was limited in comparison to other banks and there were issues with the effectiveness and authority of the loans distribution unit. Deal teams resisted selling down parts of their deals because part of the fees earned had to be passed on to the buying banks and this directly affected their results and incentives. They priced transactions primarily in order to secure the business rather than in order to facilitate sell-down. The aggressive deal structures used by HBOS also made selling down loans harder, but deal teams continued to structure deals aggressively in order to secure the business.

In a number of large transactions, the corporate loans distribution unit expressed concerns about their ability to sell down particular transactions given the proposed pricing and/or structuring of the transaction. Those concerns were overridden and the transactions were sanctioned. In a number of these transactions, the target level of sell-down was not achieved and HBOS remained exposed to the whole risk.

Throughout the corporate division there was a 'culture of optimism' which made managers reluctant to admit how bad things really were. This meant that, even when potential or actual default had been identified, managers were slower than they should have been in referring the transaction to the specialist High Risk team, which meant that the risk of defaults was under-estimated. The FSA commented: 'There was a significant risk that this would have an impact on HBOS's capital requirements. It also meant that the full extent of stress in the corporate portfolio was not visible to the group executive, auditors and regulators.' It added: 'This optimism was unwarranted, without foundation and at the expense of prudence.'

HBOS adopted an optimistic approach to levels of provisioning against problem loans despite repeated warnings from its auditors and the corporate division's risk specialists. The optimism bias was not challenged by the Group Risk department. The FSA listed the deteriorating situation as illustrated by HBOS' repeated restatements of the level of 'impaired assets' within the corporate division's portfolio and the level of provisions which had been made:

> On 19 June 2008, HBOS issued a prospectus in relation to its rights issue. Corporate's year-to-date impairment losses were not quantified or commented on in the prospectus, but management information indicated that, as at 31 May 2008, it had year-to-date impairment losses of £369.9 million. However at the end of July, HBOS published its interim results which stated that, as at 30 June 2008, there were year-to-date impairment losses of £469 million – a rise of £100 million in a month.
>
> On 18 November 2008 in its prospectus for the placing of shares to the Government, HBOS said that, as at 30 September 2008, there were year-to-date impairment losses of £1.7 billion – a rise of £1.2 billion in three months. One month later – HBOS published a trading update which stated that, as at 30 November 2008, there were year-to-date impairment losses of £3.3 billion – a rise of over £2 billion in two months.
>
> Throughout this period, HBOS' auditors KPMG agreed that the overall level of the firm's provisioning was acceptable. However, in relation to corporate, they consistently suggested that a more prudent approach would be to increase the level of provision by a significant amount. The firm consistently chose to provision at what KPMG identified as being the optimistic end of the acceptable range for corporate. KPMG's view of what constituted the acceptable range was informed by management's assessment of the degree of credit risk in particular transactions,

the FSA said.

The corporate division's risk department also consistently suggested that a more prudent approach would be to increase provisions significantly, but HBOS consistently rejected this advice. 'For example, in December 2008, the Corporate Risk function identified a range of between £4.5 billion and £6.4 billion for provisioning to the year-end. The Corporate Risk function specifically warned against provisioning at the lower end of this £2 billion range, given the likely impact of deteriorating economic conditions on the transactions they had assessed and the anticipated migration from the good book of other transactions, and recommended that provisions should be taken at a higher level. However the firm rejected this recommendation and set the provision at the lowest end of this range,' said the FSA.

The December 2008 management accounts issued by HBOS had assessed corporate's year-to-date impairment losses as at 31 December 2008 as £4.7 billion. On 16 January 2009, Lloyds completed its takeover of HBOS and a month later issued a trading update, which noted that impairment losses for the corporate division as at 31 December 2008 were now assessed at approximately £7 billion. On 27 February 2009, Lloyds issued HBOS' preliminary results for 2008. This confirmed the impairment losses in corporate as £6.7 billion including £1.6 billion against property lending, £1.3 billion against deals done by HBOS' Joint Ventures team and £900 million on deals done by ISAF.

These impairment amounts were approximately £2 billion higher than the equivalent amounts accounted for by HBOS. This difference was attributable to the level of corporate's exposure to property, where pronounced falls in property values and other investments had also resulted in substantial losses from the investment portfolio, primarily in Joint Ventures and ISAF. The shape of the corporate book and in particular its exposure to house builders, risk capital and large single credit exposures, also exacerbated the impact of the economic downturn. Property-related sectors accounted for around 60 per cent of the individual impairment provisions.

The FSA concluded that the corporate division's credit risk management had been unable to react quickly enough to contain the severe economic deterioration in the second half of 2008. This was made more difficult by the concentration in property-related sectors and had resulted in a dramatic increase in impairment losses. The substantial increase was partly the result of economic conditions, but it also reflected the imposition of more prudent and robust risk management and impairment policies and methodology by Lloyds. Ironically, HBOS' own corporate risk department had recommended an increase in the level of provision of up to approximately £6.4 billion in December 2008, but had been ignored.

23

Why didn't the regulators stop HBOS?

Banking regulation is a fearfully complicated subject and I am not an expert, so what follows is subjective and simplified. Compared to the cut and thrust of banking, it can also be boring and you could argue that the role of a successful regulator is to make banking, if not boring, then certainly less exciting. The last 30 years have seen successive governments wrestle with the problem of the extent to which banks should be confined and restricted. The instincts of the right have been towards less regulation and allowing enterprise and competition to guide the market and protect consumers. The left distrusts the motives of bankers and believes they must be controlled. You cannot easily allocate these opposing views to the Conservative and Labour parties. In government at some point each has swung from one side to the other.

Where to start? In the context of Bank of Scotland and HBOS the changes made by the Conservative government of Margaret Thatcher are certainly relevant. The removal of exchange controls, while they had no immediate effect, opened the way for Britain to join the globalisation of banking. The exposure of HBOS to overseas markets, particularly the US, was limited in comparison with the investment banks and its rival the Royal Bank of Scotland, but had exchange controls still been in place it would not have been able to hold as high a proportion of its assets in US mortgage securities as it did. I am not arguing for exchange controls – their abolition undoubtedly enabled a big expansion in trade – but it was a factor.

So too was the removal of restrictions on building societies. It is possible to argue that this too led to substantial social and economic benefits, such as enabling a big expansion of home ownership. But it is worth remarking that none of the building societies which took advantage of the freedom to demutualise and turn themselves into banks now survive as independent companies. Some, like the Woolwich and Cheltenham & Gloucester, were taken over while they were viable. Others like Northern Rock, Halifax (HBOS), Bradford & Bingley and Abbey had to be rescued. There was a precedent for this in the deregulation in the 1980s of the Savings & Loans, or 'Thrifts', the US equivalent of building societies. Freed of restrictions, nearly a quarter of the 3,200 institutions went bust.

In 1986 the Thatcher Government also ushered in 'Big Bang', an ending of restrictive practices in the London Stock Exchange, which was also the signal for the start of an era of massive expansion in financial services, with little regulatory constraint. 'Self-regulation' was the fashion. For the first time banks were allowed to buy stockbroking firms, market makers, insurance companies and investment managers. The lines between banking and other services blurred and business models were developed which depended not on service to customers, but on cross-selling 'products'.

In the United States the Glass-Steagall Act, the banking reforms which had followed the Wall Street Crash and the Great Depression, was abolished, allowing banks unfettered freedom to enter the securities industry.

Up until 1997, the banking regulator in Britain was the Bank of England which operated through a series of rules, some written, some not, to police the banking system. It was not perfect and under its supervision periodic banking crises occurred, such as the near bankruptcy of NatWest in the secondary banking collapse, of Lloyds in the Latin American debt crisis and the failure of Barings Bank in the Nick Leeson scandal. The Bank also had economic duties and powers, particularly over monetary policy and in 1997, as one of its first acts, the Labour Government with Gordon Brown as Chancellor, took banking supervision away from the Bank of England and gave it to a new 'super-regulator' the Financial Services Authority (FSA), which also had responsibility for overseeing the rest of the financial services industry.

FSA policy towards the banks was partly shaped by domestic considerations and partly by international regulation. Since the early 1970s international banking standards have been determined by a committee of regulators from the major economic nations meeting in Basel, home of the Bank for International Settlements. The first Basel rules were introduced in response to the failure of a German and an American bank, events that seem trivial compared to the spectacular crashes of the credit crunch, but were enough to alert governments to the fact that banking crises could spread across borders and needed co-ordinated action. At the beginning of the 1990s the Basel committee introduced a system of international regulation (now known as Basel I) which sought to standardise the amount of capital banks should be required to keep.

I touched on the need for banks to keep capital in chapter 5 and on the Basel accords in chapter 17. To recap briefly, banks are required to keep capital (their shareholders' equity, plus any profits retained in the business and some specified other securities which could be easily sold for cash in an emergency) to protect their depositors. Any losses from defaulting loans should be met from the capital, not deposits. Basel I set a minimum capital – 8 per cent of risk-weighted assets (loans). Risk weighting was supposed to compensate for the fact that some borrowers were more unreliable than others. Lending to Western governments was assumed to have no risk, and therefore carried a risk weighting of zero, meaning that you could do as much of it as you liked and it would not affect your capital requirement. (This was long before Greece's default.) On the other hand, lending to large businesses carried a risk weight of 100 per cent, meaning that for every loan you made, a sum equal to 8 per cent of it had to be maintained in capital.

Banks try to minimise their capital requirement because it is very nearly dead money – investing in risk-free assets earns very little return. The problem with Basel I was that it left too many loopholes. The risk weights specified were fairly arbitrary: lending to a blue-chip FTSE 100 company carried the same risk weight as lending the same amount in unsecured personal loans. For the same total of lending both needed the same amount of capital to be set aside, but you could charge the personal customers a lot higher interest and make more profit from them. The consequence was that within the same band of risk, banks moved their lending towards the more profitable categories. They also found other ways around the rules. Securitisation was one, parcelling up bundles of loans and moving them off the balance sheet. This enabled banks to grow without increasing their capital, indeed between 2004 and 2008 HBOS expanded its balance sheet very rapidly through securitisation among other means, but at the same time reduced its capital by buying back £2.5 billion of shares.

Basel II, which was introduced after five years of consultation, was intended to be a much more comprehensive attempt at regulation and more sophisticated in its approach. It refined the risk weights and allowed banks to calculate their own weights if they could persuade their own national regulator that they had the ability to do it properly. In addition it laid down guidelines for individual country regulators and forced the banks to disclose more information about how they calculated risk and the amount of capital they set aside against it. HBOS adopted the Basel II approach at the beginning of 2008 and was given permission by the FSA to calculate its own risk weights under the 'Advanced IRB' system.

The new accord was thought by the banks to be more advantageous to them than the old one (HBOS expected to be able to make a higher return on equity), but this did not stop them lobbying for even more relaxation. The submission by Bob Brooks, the HBOS head of balance sheet risk, to the Basel committee arguing against further regulation on grounds of cost and complexity, looks ironic given the date on which it was sent, 3 October 2008, by which time HBOS was hurtling towards bankruptcy. 'The events of the last 12 months have demonstrated that the level of VaR [Value at Risk] based capital has proved inadequate to withstand the impact of unprecedented market stress and, with hindsight, should have been somewhat higher particularly for credit instruments,' he concedes. 'However, going forward, there would seem to be equal systemic dangers associated now with erring too much in the other direction and constructing a regime that is overly calibrated to abnormal conditions.'

The Basel accords clearly failed to prevent banks getting into trouble and may have exacerbated things by giving a spurious sense of comfort in apparently being able to calculate risk and set aside adequate capital to absorb expected defaults. The level of capital required had been set against historical norms in an environment where bank managements and governments were in league in lobbying against too stringent regulation. No one had realised that globalisation and the prolonged economic boom ushered in by an era of cheap money had changed the game. Banks were taking much bigger risks and the longer they got away with them, the more they felt justified in taking on more risk.

HBOS does not appear to have been any guiltier of using the

system to its own advantage than many other banks. To a certain extent banks were aided and abetted by their own governments in trying to make the rules as least burdensome as possible. 'Light touch regulation' was a bi-partisan policy in the UK, the US and much of Europe for the first decade of the twenty-first century. Governments had a vested interest in seeing their financial institutions make as much profit as possible, because profit meant wealth creation and tax revenue. On becoming Chancellor, Alistair Darling was surprised to find how dependent the UK was on receipts from the financial sector, which made up 25 per cent of corporate taxes.

The FSA when it was set up in 1997 had a gigantic task. Not only was it responsible for supervising the banking system, which was itself growing and becoming more international by the day, but also the rest of the financial services sector – investment, insurance and everything else. At one end of the scale it was meant to be controlling the risk in complex international derivative trading, at the other seeing that consumers were not misled in buying basic financial products. Nevertheless it monitored HBOS closely and investigated a number of concerns.

The first full risk assessment of HBOS (known as an Arrow assessment) came in late 2002 soon after the formation of the group. This was the standard regulatory examination of a bank's risk and control systems and usually results in dozens of small points, which require attention and changes. However, the FSA found a larger systemic issue which it felt needed further work and commissioned a 'Section 166' report from the accountancy firm PwC, which recommended management changes. Divisions within the group had different methods of assessing and managing risk and there was no consistency. It was also concerned that departments dealing with credit risk, operational risk and regulatory risk all reported to the group head of risk, who then reported to the finance director. There was clearly a concern that the head of risk did not have the authority to challenge the dominant sales culture in the group and the FSA recommended that risk should have a higher profile.

In December 2004, after a further full assessment, the FSA concluded that the risk profile of the group had improved and that it had made good progress in addressing the risks highlighted in the earlier investigation, but that the group risk functions still did not carry enough weight. This was seen as a key weakness. HBOS' response was to appoint Jo Dawson to the board as Group Risk Director. This surprised some of the non-executives on the HBOS board, who questioned her lack of previous experience in risk management, but her appointment was confirmed. This provoked a complaint to the FSA by Paul Moore, who had been sacked as head of regulatory risk. 'In his view,' said the FSA, 'the new group risk director was not "fit and proper" to be approved by the FSA to hold that post, by reason of lack of integrity, lack of experience in risk management, and of general attitude and approach; he also made other allegations about HBOS' overall risk framework.'

To answer these criticisms, with the approval of the FSA, HBOS commissioned an external review from its auditors KPMG. The accountants spent 80 hours in interviews and meetings with 28 individuals including the chief executive, finance director and then head of retail, as well as with Paul Moore. KPMG's report said it 'did not believe that the evidence reviewed suggested that the candidate was not fit and proper' and added 'the process for the identification and assessment of candidates for the group risk director position appeared appropriate' and 'the structure and reporting lines of Group Regulatory Risk are appropriate'.

As a sanction the FSA had required HBOS at the beginning of 2004 to increase the level of capital it held by half a percentage point. This would have impacted on its profitability and acted as a spur to management to put things right. By the end of the same year the FSA was satisfied and reduced the capital requirement again.

However, the regulator was still concerned about the risk manage-ment framework in HBOS and in 2006 made another Arrow risk assessment. It found that whilst the group had made progress, there were still control issues. In particular the growth strategy 'posed risks to the whole group and . . . these risks must be managed and mitigated'.[1] The FSA told the group it would closely track progress in putting these deficiencies right.

The Arrow process was meant to be comprehensive and covered an examination of the group's strategy and business, principal activities, capital and liquidity positions and the nature of its funding. Clearly the FSA had concerns because it did not allow HBOS the 'regulatory dividend' it granted to firms it considered were 'doing the right thing' – extending the period between regulatory assessments from the normal 24 months to 36 months. Ironically, it granted this concession to Northern Rock, a company which shared with HBOS many of the risk factors later identified – high revenue and profit growth targets (15–20 per cent), low interest margin, low cost/income ratio and relatively high reliance on wholesale funding and securitisation.[2]

With the benefit of hindsight we can see that the assessment of HBOS in 2006 was completely inadequate. The very thorough investigation six years later by the FSA's enforcement division of the failings of HBOS corporate banking found numerous flaws in risk monitoring, management and reporting and followed them right up to group level. These went back at least to the beginning of 2006, the year in which the Arrow assessment had been carried out. At the very least this suggests that the Arrow assessment was no better than superficial.

The FSA has at the time of writing (Spring 2012) yet to produce a comprehensive report on the collapse of HBOS, but in its reports on the Royal Bank of Scotland and Northern Rock it admitted to failings both in the international system of regulation and of its own supervision. Lord Turner, chairman of the FSA, admitted that the regulator was too focused on conduct regulation at the time (that RBS got into difficulties) and its prudential supervision of major banks was inadequate. 'The FSA operated a flawed supervisory approach which failed adequately to challenge the judgement and risk assessments of the management of RBS. This approach reflected widely held, but mistaken assumptions about the stability of financial systems and existed against a backdrop of political pressures for a "light touch" regulatory regime.'[3]

It was not only politicians who were trying to rein in the regulator, there were also frequent complaints from banks and other financial firms about the level of the contributions they made to the FSA's funding though levies. Under pressure to cut costs, the regulator actually reduced its staff in its Major Retail Groups Division by 20 people between 2004–8 at a time when it was taking new responsibilities such as supervision of the introduction of Basel II. In its report on lessons to be learned from the Northern Rock collapse, the FSA also found that where its staff had doubts about the management of banks they were not always raised with senior management at the regulator or with the bank itself.[4]

The FSA admitted many of its failings and is to be abolished and replaced with a new regulator and a new supervisory system. In the report on the Royal Bank of Scotland, Turner describes

an overall approach to the regulation and supervision of banks which made it more likely that poor decisions by individual bank executives and boards could lead to failure. In retrospect, it is clear that:

The key prudential regulations being applied by the FSA, and by other regulatory authorities across the world, were dangerously in-adequate; this increased the likelihood that a global financial crisis would occur at some time.

In addition, the FSA had developed a philosophy and approach to the supervision of high impact firms and in particular major banks, which resulted in insufficient challenge to RBS' poor decisions. The supervisory approach entailed inadequate focus on the core pruden-tial issues of capital, liquidity and asset quality, and insufficient willingness to challenge management judgements and risk assess-ments. Reflecting the overall philosophy, supervisory resources de-voted to major banks and specialist skills in place were insufficient to support a more intensive and challenging approach.[5]

For 'RBS' in the previous paragraphs we could reasonably sub-stitute 'HBOS'.

In his evidence to the Treasury select committee Lord Turner also drew attention to the failures of both the Basel I and Basel II international regulatory regimes. 'The global capital standards ap-plied before the crisis were severely deficient and liquidity regulation was totally inadequate. Banks across the world were operating on levels of capital and liquidity that were far too low. These prudential regulations have been changed radically since the crisis, with the internationally agreed Basel III standards.' His conclusion on the Royal Bank was: 'Had Basel III been in place at the time, not only would RBS have been unable to launch the bid for ABN AMRO, but it would have been prevented from paying dividends at any time during the Review Period, i.e. from at least 2005 onwards.' In the case of HBOS we could surmise that its pace of growth would have severely slowed had it been required to retain more capital.

It could be argued that every society gets the regulators it deserves. The last decade was a period when we were all not only permitting bank executives and boards to pursue reckless growth policies, but encouraging them to do so by favouring the shares of fast-growing companies over the more cautious ones and enjoying high dividends, high interest on current accounts and easy low-cost mortgages. Successive governments, encouraged by the banks themselves, urged 'light touch' regulation and turned a blind eye to excessive executive salaries and bonuses. The reward was high tax revenue which paid for high public spending. The press was mostly uncritical, fawning over 'successful' chief executives. At the height of the boom, very few journalists were calling for tougher regulation and the cost in time and money of supervision was seen as unnecessary and expensive 'red tape'.

In an environment like that we can no more expect a financial regulator to stop all bank collapses than we can expect the police to stop all crime. If we want things to change, the remedy is in our own hands.

24

The end of history

In the summer of 1981 during a period of austerity imposed by Mrs Thatcher's government, English cities erupted in sustained and violent rioting. Afterwards Environment Secretary Michael Heseltine led a party of business leaders to look at the devastation in Liverpool, a city which had been deprived of investment. 'Where are the financial services companies,' he demanded? Bruce Pattullo, then Treasurer of Bank of Scotland, replied that once every English region – including the North-west – had had their own local banks, responding to local needs and supporting local industry and jobs. The Bank of Liverpool, founded in 1831, took over Martins Bank and grew to 700 branches before being absorbed by Barclays in 1969. By the 1980s only Scotland and Yorkshire still had financial institutions with any autonomy. Now those too have succumbed to consolidation.

This is not just a regional loss, it is part of the cause of the national disaster of the banking crash of 2008. A banking system loses its resilience if it is reduced to a handful of national institutions which are too big to fail. A sustainable ecosystem has big and small, specialist and generalist, regional and national. Local banks used to attract managers who were able and talented, but knew the limits of their ambition. I remember in the early 1980s attending the annual results press conference of Yorkshire Bank in Leeds. The chief executive wilfully misheard a question on the bank's exposure to sovereign debt in Mexico and started talking about what it was doing in Mexborough, a town in the south of the county. His intention was to show that the bank did not take big risks by investing outside its area of competence, but it did know and care about what was happening in its own locality. Mexborough was not without its problems, but it did not have the potential to bring down major financial institutions, which is what nearly happened to much bigger banks that bet too heavily on Mexico.

That was in a different age. Then the *Financial Times* could, with approval, call Bank of Scotland 'the most boring bank in Britain' for its failure to do any of the spectacular things which regularly hobbled its larger, London-based competitors. When John Smith was elected leader of the Labour Party, newspapers were able to describe him as being like a Scottish bank manager. It was a simile everyone recognised: a bank manager was sober-suited, calm, competent, reliable and possibly also a little boring – but who wanted to deal with an exciting bank manager? Banks were trusted by their customers and regarded by investors as safe and consistent, not 'growth stocks' expected to double in size every few years. A fund manager, who was also a director of Bank of Scotland, told me he put all his widow and orphan clients into the Bank's shares. 'Money in the bank' was an everyday phrase which meant 'secure'.

The change did not come suddenly, but by the *fin de siècle* banks were regarded as either predator or prey: being efficient, dependable but unexciting was not an option. This coincided with a progressive deskilling of banking, partly as a result of technology but also through the rise of the profession of 'manager' as a generic skill. The MBA replaced the banking diploma as the passport to the top.*

The professional manager did not need to know every aspect of the business because he could rely on other professionals – risk specialists, consultants, auditors, ratings agencies. Risk was no longer a matter of experience and judgement and you did not have to be cautious because the market would prevent you from going too far. You could take any risk as long as you priced it correctly. If the price went too high, no one would buy and you would not run the risk. The correct price could be determined by mathematics and calculated on a computer. Amazingly this belief persisted after the collapse of Long Term Capital Management in the US in 1998, a company that had two Nobel Prize-winning mathematicians on its board. As we have seen, professional managers turned out to be incompetent, mathematical models were inadequate and some risks were not worth taking no matter what the return.

Another ingredient in the sour mix was the change from regarding lending as a service to be provided to account holders, to being a product to be sold to customers. If a bank offered products, then why

---

* I confess to having an MBA, but I have never been a banker.

would it not employ the same techniques as a retailer? No one stopped to think of the difference. Years after selling a customer a tin of beans, a supermarket does not ask for it back in perfect condition. But a bank does expect the money it lends to be returned. A better analogy would be with a car hire company, except that the car hire firm owns its cars, a bank does not own the money it lends – that belongs to its depositors.

Losing sight of that fact was fundamental to the collapse of HBOS. Depositors' money is finite, whereas the money borrowed from the wholesale market was infinite. Although the savings of millions of ordinary people were nice to have, they were not essential because you could go on borrowing and lending eternally from the global market. There was no limit to the growth of the bank. The Philosopher's Stone had been discovered – except, of course, that the interbank market was not everlasting, at least not for banks like Northern Rock and HBOS. In 2008 it came to a halt. Base metal could be converted, but only into fool's gold.

The banking crisis destroyed public trust in banks and bank managers. They regularly now feature in lists of the top ten hates. Senior bank executives – like the other titans of the corporate elite – are seen as greedy. It was not always like this. Thirty years ago Lord Kearton was a highly successful chief executive of the textile company Courtaulds, who went on to chair the British National Oil Company for the Government of the day. When he retired it was revealed that he had never taken a salary from BNOC. I asked him why. 'I had enough money already,' he replied. Now men and women who are already millionaires many times over, demand more millions for running banks – and we give it to them. I am not sure why. Does running a bank take more skill than, say, being a brain surgeon? Do bank chief executives work longer hours than the Prime Minister? Are they more knowledgeable than the President of the Royal Society? Banking is complicated because the men who run banks have made it so, yet the most successful banks are the simplest.

Even after the crash, banks have hardly changed their ways. Public trust no longer seems important to them. Go into a bank and attempt to deposit a reasonable sum of money and you will be urged to speak to an 'investment adviser', who is, of course, nothing of the sort: his or her primary aim is not to give you dispassionate investment advice, it is to sell you a product which will make money for the bank. It is so transparent. No wonder people are cynical. Is it ever possible that we could get back to a situation where banks are trusted, where banks realise that their success depends on the long-term well-being of their customers, not on selling them products which produce a profit for the bank, but may actually do the buyer financial harm? Will we ever see again banks which know and care about the communities in which they operate, above a superficial level required to fill the pages of 'corporate responsibility' reports? The enforced sale of branches from Lloyds gives that possibility, but doesn't guarantee it.

The character of Bank of Scotland took 300 years to evolve. It is tempting to think it changed overnight when the Bank merged with Halifax, but in truth it had been gradually shifting for years, if not decades. The sales culture had been creeping in, dependence on wholesale funding had been increasing and most pernicious of all, the growth imperative had become ingrained. The Bank believed that if it stopped growing it would lose its independence. So it made a Faustian bargain, it gave up its independence in order to keep growing.

It is fruitless to speculate on what might have been if the HBOS merger had not taken place. It did and Bank of Scotland was destroyed in seven years by men who were intelligent, hard-working and meant well, but focused only on growth. Everything else was subordinated, with the result that they lost sight of the simple rules of banking, which had not changed since 1695.

Notes & references

CHAPTER 1: BANKER TO THE STARS
1 *The Sunday Telegraph*, 15 May 2005
2 *The Daily Telegraph*, 19 November 2010

CHAPTER 2: BASE METAL INTO GOLD
1 T.M. Devine, *The Scottish Nation 1700–2000*, Allen Lane, 1999, xxii
2 S.G. Checkland, *Scottish Banking, a history 1695–1973*, Collins 1975, 6
3 Ibid., 7
4 Ibid., 11
5 Andrew Forrester, *The man who saw the future*, Thomson Texere, 2004. 1–9
6 David Armitage, 'Paterson, William (1658–1719)', *Oxford Dictionary of National Biography*, Oxford University Press, 2004; online edn, Sept 2010 [http://www.oxforddnb.com/view/article/21538]
7 Douglas Watt, *The Price of Scotland; Darien, Union and the Wealth of Nations*, Luath Press, Edinburgh 2007, 1
8 Ibid., 17
9 Forrester, 62–3
10 Checkland, 15
11 Alan Cameron, 'Holland, John (1658–1721)', *Oxford Dictionary of National Biography*, Oxford University Press, 2004; online edn, Jan 2008 [http://www.oxforddnb.com/view/article/13531]
12 Forrester, 140
13 Alan Cameron, *Bank of Scotland 1695–1995: a very singular institution*, Mainstream 1995, 21
14 Checkland, 29–30
15 Watt, 63
16 Checkland, 33
17 Ibid., 36
18 In the event only the Scottish commissioners got all the money promised them, leading them to be dubbed 'a parcel of rogues bought with English gold.' Cameron, 32
19 Cameron, 36
20 *Queen Anne*, David Green, Collins, 1970, 335
21 Checkland, 60

CHAPTER 3: A COSY WORLD
1 There are two histories of Bank of Scotland's first 300 years. See bibliography
2 Now the Chartered Institute of Bankers in Scotland
3 Cameron, *Bank of Scotland*, 225
4 Quoted in 'Banks, bailouts and bonuses: a personal account of working in Halifax Bank of Scotland during the financial crisis', Vaughan Ellis and Margaret Taylor, *Work, Employment & Society, December 2010; vol. 24, 4:* 803–812. N.B. 'Margaret Taylor' is a pseudonym
5 *Financial Times*, 30 October 1999
6 Richard Saville, *Bank of Scotland: a history, 1695-1995*, Edinburgh University Press, 1996, 700
7 Ibid., 718
8 Cameron, 230
9 Saville, 783

CHAPTER 4: COMETH THE HOUR, COMETH THE MAN
1 Saville, 792
2 *The Glasgow Herald*, 3 May 1984
3 Saville, 796

CHAPTER 5: THE CULTURAL REVOLUTION
1 By assets. Saville, 809
2 *The Times*, 26 September 1985
3 *Financial Times*, 27 April 1989
4 *Financial Times*, 26 April 1990
5 *The Times*, 23 April 1985
6 M. Oram and R. Wellins, *Re-engineering's Missing Ingredient: The Human Factor*, IPD, 1995

CHAPTER 6: THE MOST BORING BANK IN BRITAIN
1 *Management Today*, 1 October 2001
2 *Financial Times*, 27 April 1997
3 Saville, 815
4 *Financial Times*, 25 April 1996
5 Saville, 800
6 *Financial Times*, 14 May 1996
7 *Bank of Scotland annual report and accounts*, 1998

CHAPTER 7: A DARK LAND – WE NEED TO PRAY FOR THEM
1 *Financial Times*, 26 April 1997
2 *Financial Times*, 2 March 1999
3 *The Scotsman*, 3 March 1999
4 *The Scotsman*, 5 March 1999
5 *Financial Times*, 6 March 1999
6 BBC News, 3 June 1999

7 *Financial Times*, 3 June 1999
8 *Financial Times*, 10 June 1999

CHAPTER 8: NO TURNING BACK AT DERBY
1 *Financial Times*, 2 October 1999

CHAPTER 9: MORITURI TE SALUTANT
1 Reuters, 24 September 1999
2 *The Economist*, 30 September 1999
3 Sandler was later to lead Northern Rock after its nationalisation
4 *The Economist*, 2 December 1999

CHAPTER 10: 'THE NEXT THING HE DOES HAS GOT TO WORK, OTHERWISE HE'S TOAST'
1 *Financial Times*, 18 February 2000
2 *Financial Times*, 28 September 2000

CHAPTER 11: PETER'S LAST SUPPER
1 *The Daily Telegraph*, 5 May 2001
2 HBOS annual report and accounts 2001

CHAPTER 12: A CLASH OF CULTURES
1 http://www.george-fieldman.co.uk/executive_coaching/exec_coa-ching_5.htm
2 http://news.bbc.co.uk/1/hi/programmes/moneybox/transcripts/jan02_-july02/1866378.stm
3 *The Daily Telegraph*, 4 May 2001; *Financial Times*, 7 May 2001
4 *The Sun*, 27 February 2002

CHAPTER 13: ROOM AT THE TOP
1 *The Observer*, 3 March 2002
2 *Daily Mirror*, 28 February 2002
3 *The Daily Telegraph*, 29 March 2003
4 *Financial Times*, 26 February 2004
5 *Financial Times*, 15 December 2004
6 *Financial Times*, 6 January 2006
7 *Financial Times*, 6 January 2006

CHAPTER 14: GIVE ME ENOUGH DEBT AND I'LL MOVE THE WORLD
1 *Who Runs Britain?* Robert Peston, Hodder & Stoughton 2008, 93
2 Ibid., 95
3 *The Daily Telegraph*, 13 October 2003
4 *Financial Times*, 22 October 2004
5 Peston, 135
6 *The Daily Telegraph*, 13 October 2003
7 *Financial Times*, 24 November 2003

8 *Financial Times*, 9 October 2006
9 *The Daily Telegraph*, 4 April 2010
10 *Financial Times*, 9 October 2006

CHAPTER 15: AS SAFE AS HOUSES
1 *Daily Mail*, 1 November 2006
2 BBC, 2 February 2004, http://news.bbc.co.uk/1/hi/business/3478635.stm
3 *The Daily Telegraph*, 28 June 2008
4 *Financial Times*, 2 March 2006
5 *The Independent*, 3 October 2007
6 HBOS Report & Accounts, 2007
7 Quoted at http://www.ianfraser.org/a-brief-history-of-halifax-bank-of-scot-
   land/

CHAPTER 16: ZIGGY'S STARDUST
1 Bowie Bonds did not fare well. The singer's later albums were not as popular
   as his earlier ones and the bonds, never very highly rated, were marked down
   to 'junk' status.
2 Saville, 796
3 *Asset Backed Alert*, Harrison Scott Publications Inc., 21 November 2003
4 *The Credit Crunch*, Alex Brummer, Random House Business, 2008, 78
5 *Back from the Brink*, Alistair Darling, Atlantic Books, 2011. Kindle edition
   location, 281

CHAPTER 17: THE EYE OF THE STORM
1 *The Times*, 13 December 2008
2 *Financial Times*, 27 February 2008
3 *The Times*, 13 March 2008
4 *Beyond the Crash*, Gordon Brown, Simon & Schuster, 31
5 *Sunday Herald*, 8 March 2009
6 See http://www.breakingviews.com/europes-great-bank-balance-sheet-fid-
   dle/1615635.article where it is argued that Lloyds reduced HBOS risk-
   weighted assets by £34 billion by switching from the IRB to the Foundation
   method
7 *Birmingham Post*, 30 April 2008
8 *The Times*, 20 June 2008
9 Brown, *Beyond the Crash*,35

CHAPTER 18: APOCALYPSE NOW
1 Darling, *Back from the Brink*, location 1876
2 http://news.bbc.co.uk/1/hi/8375969.stm
3 http://www.bloomberg.com/data-visualization/federal-reserve-emergency-
   lending/#/HBOS_PLC/?total=true&mcp=true&mc=true&taf=fal-
   se&cpff=false&pdcf=false&tslf=false&stomo=false&amlf=false&dw=false/

4 Darling, location 2291
5 *The Guardian*, 17 September 2008
6 *The Daily Telegraph*, 16 September 2009
7 Presentation by Tim Tookey to UBS Global Financial Services Conference, New York 12 May 2009
8 Darling, location 2581
9 Brown, *Beyond the Crash*, 65
10 Ellis & Taylor, Banks, bailouts and bonuses, 806

CHAPTER 19: NEMESIS STRIKES
1 *Financial Times*, 13 November 2008
2 *Financial Times*, 22 November 2008
3 *The Daily Telegraph*, 17 November 2008
4 *Financial Times*, 20 November 2008
5 *Financial Times*, 13 December 2008
6 HBOS Interim Management Statement, November 2008
7 HBOS Trading Statement, November 2008
8 *Financial Times*, 13 December 2008
9 *The Sun*, 12 Jan 2011
10 *Financial Times*, 14 February 2009
11 *The Times*, 25 February 2012
12 *The Daily Telegraph*, 13 June 2011
13 *Financial Times*, 7 June 2010
14 *Financial Times*, 9 February 2010

CHAPTER 20: HUNGRY FOR RISK
1 *Banking Crisis: dealing with the failure of the UK banks*, House of Commons Treasury Committee, HC 416, 1 May 2009, 8
2 Ellis & Taylor, Banks, bailouts and bonuses, 807
3 *Banking Crisis: Vol. II Written Evidence*, House of Commons Treasury Committee, HC 144, 1 April 2009, 440 para 2.8
4 Ellis & Taylor, 807
5 Tim Tookey to UBS Global Financial Services Conference, New York, 12 May 2009

CHAPTER 21: WHY DIDN'T THEY REALISE?
1 Financial Services Authority FSA/PN/024/2012 9 March 2012
2 Ibid.
3 Ibid.
4 *A review of corporate governance in UK banks and other financial industry entities*, final recommendations, 26 November 2009

CHAPTER 22: THE DRIVE FOR PROFIT AT ANY PRICE
1 Financial Services Authority FSA/PN/024/2012, 9 March 2012

Chapter 23: Why didn't the regulators stop HBOS?

1 FSA statement on HBOS, 11 February 2009
2 *The Supervision of Northern Rock; Lessons Learned Review*, FSA, March 2008, para. 15–16
3 *The Failure of the Royal Bank of Scotland*, FSA, December 2011
4 *The Supervision of Northern Rock*, para. 32
5 *The Failure of the Royal Bank of Scotland*, 10

Bibliography

BOOKS

Armitage, David, 'Paterson, William (1658–1719)', *Oxford Dictionary of National Biography* (Oxford University Press, 2004), online edn, Sept 2010, [http://www.oxforddnb.com/view/article/21538]

Brown, Gordon, *Beyond the Crash* (Simon & Schuster, 2010)

Brummer, Alex, *The Credit Crunch* (Random House Business, 2008)

Cameron, Alan, 'Holland, John (1658–1721)', *Oxford Dictionary of National Biography*, (Oxford University Press, 2004), online edn, Jan 2008, [http://www.oxforddnb.com/view/article/13531]

Cameron, Alan, *Bank of Scotland 1695–1995 a very singular institution* (Mainstream 1995)

Checkland, S.G., *Scottish Banking, a history 1695–1973* (Collins, 1975)

Darling, Alistair, *Back from the Brink* (Atlantic Books, 2011), Kindle edition

Devine, T.M., *The Scottish Nation 1700–2000* (Allen Lane, 1999)

Forrester, Andrew, *The man who saw the future* (Thomson Texere, 2004)

Green, David, *Queen Anne* (Collins, 1970)

Peston, Robert, *Who runs Britain?* (Hodder & Stoughton, 2008)

Saville, Richard, *Bank of Scotland: a history, 1695-1995* (Edinburgh University Press, 1996)

Watt, Douglas, *The Price of Scotland; Darien, Union and the Wealth of Nations* (Luath Press, Edinburgh, 2007)

ANNUAL REPORTS & ACCOUNTS

HBOS, 2001–2010
Bank of Scotland, 1980–2000
Lloyds Banking Group, 2008–10

RESEARCH PAPERS

'Banks, bailouts and bonuses: a personal account of working in Halifax Bank of Scotland during the financial crisis', Vaughan Ellis and Margaret Taylor, *Work, Employment & Society, December 2010, vol. 24*

M. Oram and R. Wellins, *Re-engineering's Missing Ingredient: The Human Factor*, IPD, 1995.

Official reports
House of Commons Treasury Committee
Banking Crisis: dealing with the failure of the UK banks, HC 416, 1 May 2009
Banking Crisis: Vol.I, HC 261-I, 29 March 2010.
Banking Crisis: Vol.II Written Evidence, HC 144, 1 April 2009

Financial Services Authority
Bank of Scotland, Final Notice Ref: 169628 9, March 2012
Statement on HBOS, 11 February 2009
The Supervision of Northern Rock; Lessons Learned Review, March 2008
The Failure of the Royal Bank of Scotland, December 2011

Other
State aid No. N 428/2009 – United Kingdom: Restructuring of Lloyds Banking Group, European Commission, Brussels, 18 November 2009
A review of corporate governance in UK banks and other financial industry entities, Final recommendations, 26 November 2009. HM Treasury, 26 November 2009
Final Report Independent Commission on Banking, 12 September 2011

Index